W9-AOD-731

Jean Rhys's Historical Imagination

Jean Rhys's
Historical Imagination

Reading and Writing the Creole

Veronica Marie Gregg

The University of North Carolina Press *Chapel Hill & London*

Library of Congress Cataloging-in-Publication Data

Gregg, Veronica Marie.

Jean Rhys's historical imagination : reading and writing the creole /
by Veronica Marie Gregg.

p.   cm.

Includes bibliographical references (p.) and index.

ISBN 0-8078-2196-9 (cloth : alk. paper). —

ISBN 0-8078-4504-3 (pbk. : alk. paper)

1. Rhys, Jean. Wide Sargasso Sea.   2. Women and literature—West
Indies—History—20th century.   3. Historical fiction, English—History and
criticism.   4. Identity (Psychology) in literature.   5. West Indies—In
literature.   6. Creoles in literature.   7. Self in literature.   I. Title.

PR6035.H96W535   1995

823'.912—dc20   94-32011

CIP

99 98 97 96 95   5 4 3 2 1

TO MY PARENTS

Gwendolyn & Stanley Gregg

Contents

Preface

Some of the key terms that are used in this book have somewhat different connotations in United States, as opposed to British or Caribbean English usage. I wish to briefly clarify these. The term *Creole*, to refer to a person, is a descendant of European settlers born or living for an extended period in the West Indies or Central or South America. *Metropolitan, metropole, metropolis*, in the specific context of colonialism, refer to the colonizing European powers, the "mother countries" as distinct from the colonies or the so-called periphery. The racial typology "black" as used by Jean Rhys herself and many pre-twentieth-century writers on the West Indies refers to people of predominantly or exclusively African ancestry. People of mixed race (black and white) are sometimes referred to as "coloureds" or "mulattoes." This distinction is crucial.

The list of people who deserve my gratitude is a long one. I should like to acknowledge in particular the support extended to me, especially during some difficult periods, by my thesis supervisor at the University of Kent at Canterbury, England, C. L. Innes. My senior colleagues at the University of Michigan also offered invaluable assistance and support. Early versions of some chapters were read and commented on by Ross Chambers, the Marvin Felheim Distinguished University Professor of French and Comparative Literature, and by Simon Gikandi of the English Department. My former chair, Robert Weisbuch, gave me tremendous support. My Caribbean women colleagues, Natasha Barnes, Cecelia Green, and Verene Shepherd, shared with unbounded generosity the fruits of their own research, for which I am deeply grateful.

I also wish to thank the editor-in-chief of the University of North Carolina Press, Barbara Hanrahan, for her kindness, patience, and support.

I follow in the footsteps of many West Indian scholars, writers, and professors whose pioneering endeavors encouraged and created a space for my own. Among these I must single out the work of Sylvia Wynter. The moral and intellectual example of her body of work has been a major influence on my own. I owe her an incalculable debt. The late Michael Cooke of Yale University, with characteristic grace and kindness, gave me much.

In the execution of this project, I received support in the form of grants and fellowships from the National Endowment for the Humanities (1989) and the Ford Foundation (1990). I also received from the University of Michigan a Postdoctoral Teaching Fellowship, a Minority Faculty Development Fellowship, and a grant from the Office of the Vice President for Research. These grants and awards allowed me to pursue my research at the British Library, the McFarlin Library at the University of Tulsa, the libraries of the University of the West Indies in Jamaica and Trinidad, and the public library in Roseau, Dominica. I specifically wish to acknowledge the generous help I received, over an extended period of time, from the staff of the McFarlin Library.

I am particularly indebted to Francis Wyndham, the literary executor of the Jean Rhys estate, for his permission to quote from unpublished material and archival sources in the Jean Rhys Collection and in the British Library.

Some of the material and early versions of individual sections of this book appeared in my essays, which I have cited in the bibliography. The arguments in those essays have been significantly recast or expanded in this study.

ABBREVIATIONS USED

FOR JEAN RHYS'S WORK

ALMM   *After Leaving Mr. Mackenzie*
CS   *The Collected Short Stories*
Letters   *The Letters of Jean Rhys*
Voyage   *Voyage in the Dark*
WSS   *Wide Sargasso Sea*

Jean Rhys's Historical Imagination

Introduction
The Creole: "I Am Not . . . English"

I . . . was tired of learning and reciting poems in praise of
daffodils, and my relations with the few "real" English boys and girls
I had met were awkward. I had discovered that if I called myself English
they would snub me haughtily: "You're not English; you're a horrid colonial."
"Well, I don't much want to be English." . . . Then I was too killingly funny,
quite ridiculous. Not only a horrid colonial, but also ridiculous.
Heads I win, tails you lose — that was the English.
("The Day They Burned the Books")

"Do you consider yourself a West Indian?"
She shrugged. "It was such a long time ago when I left."
"So you don't think of yourself as a West Indian writer?"
Again, she shrugged, but said nothing.
"What about English? Do you consider yourself an English writer?"
"No! I'm not, I'm not! I'm not even English."
"What about a French writer?" I asked.
Again she shrugged and said nothing.
"You have no desire to go back to Dominica?"
"Sometimes," she said. (Plante, "A Remembrance," 275–76)

As the above exchange indicates, the answers to questions about Jean Rhys's nationality and her writing will not be supplied unproblematically by the writer's words on the subjects. Rhys's responses—the silences, hesitations, and strong assertions—may suggest a resistance to attempts to fix her complex "identity." They may also, as I hope to demonstrate, emblematize her attempts to challenge the politics and histories through which "identity" is constructed. In this project I do not intend to retrieve "Jean Rhys" from historical or biographical ambiguity. I shall attempt to explore the determinants that give rise to the questions of "identity," nationality, and authorship as these are figured within her writing. In order to do so, I shall focus on questions of history, reading, writing, "race," and the self.

Rhys's attitude to questions about her nationality is shifting, ambiguous, even contradictory. She says different things at different times. In a letter to Selma Vaz Dias on 15 December 1959 she says, "I've found some photographs of my island [Dominica]. . . . Perhaps you will understand why I can't 'forget Jerusalem' though my right hand has seemed so slow. *Why I am homesick*" (Rhys, *Letters*, 178–79). She also says, in a letter to Diana Athill in 1964, "I have never liked England or most English people much — or let's say I am terrified of them" (280). In an interview with Ned Thomas, she observes: "I don't belong to anywhere but I get very worked up about the West Indies. I still care. I read [Derek] Walcott, [V. S.] Naipaul, [Alfred] Mendes; and . . . I want to write about my childhood there" ("Meeting Jean Rhys," 31). She tells Peter Burton in an interview in *Transatlantic Review*: "I was brought up in Dominica . . . and was able to get a good deal of material out of it" (108). After reading a critique of *Wide Sargasso Sea* by John Hearne, a West Indian writer and critic, Rhys complains to Oliver Stoner (E. Morchard Bishop) in an unpublished letter dated 29 August 1974: "Again I am in danger of really becoming a recruit. . . . Well, it's a point of view of course. . . . I think *being* born in the West Indies is an influence very strong perhaps but . . ." (Jean Rhys Collection).

On the question of "place" and "influence," Rhys observes, "I can only write for love as it were. . . . When I say write for love I mean that there are two places for me. Paris (or what it was to me) and Dominica . . . where I was born. . . . Both these places or the thought of them make me want to write. . . . [T]he West Indies started knocking at my heart. So — 'Voyage in the Dark.' That (the knocking) has never stopped" (*Letters*, 171). She also says, "For years, I escaped from an exclusively Anglo Saxon influence and have never returned to it" (281).

In answer to the question "Which writers would you say have influenced you most?" Rhys responds, "There was a time when I read nothing but the Russians and a time when I read nothing but the French. . . . Something in the air at that time [Paris of the 1920s] influenced you, if you see what I mean." Likened to Colette, Rhys says she admires her. But Colette "uses different subjects. . . . She was brought up in the country whereas my life has been mostly lived in towns" ("Interviewed by Peter Burton," 109).

How important are questions of nationality, "identity," and "place" in Jean Rhys's writing? I believe they are crucial, for, as Jean D'Costa has so nicely summed it up, "Rhys presents problems of classification which disguise problems of interpretation and acceptance" ("Jean Rhys," 390). The problems of placing Jean Rhys subtend problems of reading her writing. There seems to be a wide range of interpretive options for an analysis of Jean Rhys's writing: West Indian, Third World, British, Euro-American, European, feminist, postcolonial. Regardless of the theoretical models used, many of these critiques take for granted, or as a point of departure, a psychobiography of the writer herself: her birth in the West Indies, her peripatetic life, her being a British or colonial woman writer, or a writer who does not seem to fit anywhere.

In 1950 Francis Wyndham put forward the theory of the composite heroine, observing that "essentially the novels deal with the same woman at . . . different stages of her career" ("Inconvenient," 16). This has been the single most influential approach to the Rhys texts. The notion of a composite heroine, referred to as the Jean Rhys woman, has often led to a conflation of "heroine" and author, a process sometimes astonishing in its cruelty. Employing this approach, other commentators, though not Wyndham himself, have suggested that Jean Rhys engaged in prostitution, labeled her paranoid, and claimed she was negligent in the death of her infant son, along with other negative "personal" characteristics.[1]

It is equally important to note that many of the commentators of the 1920s and 1930s, like some contemporary (post-1960s) commentators, do not base their analyses of Rhys's texts on biographical criticism. Several of these have offered effective critiques of the biographical reading of Rhys's fiction. Todd Bender's assertion, in his brief review of Thomas Staley's *Jean Rhys: A Critical Study* (1979), is particularly apt:

> Staley tends to think that "her art developed out of an intensely private world—a world whose sources of inspiration were neither literary nor intellectual" (p. 36). If this is true of her early work, then how do we account for the late masterpiece, mushrooming out of a literary source? We would like hard answers to concrete questions: What did

Rhys read? Did she read voraciously for the twenty [-seven] years from 1939–1966? . . . Rhys . . . herself is an example of a woman whose force of intellect and sense of style has won her a place in the inner circle of great modernist writers. . . . There is a subtle drift . . . toward seeing Rhys as a simple, childlike figure, a writer who innocently stumbled onto insights into European society and literature that would have been hidden from a more mature, conventionally educated person. An argument so damaging to Rhys needs to be carefully documented. ("Jean Rhys," 251–52)[2]

The movement of Rhys's biographical life seems straightforward enough. She was born and raised in the West Indies and was sent to school in England at age sixteen. She moved to Europe for a period of about twelve years, returned to England, and lived there until she died. There are other West Indian writers who left the region at an early age or who spent long periods or most of their lives away from their place of birth. What makes Jean Rhys "different?" Questions of place, identity, difference, and Jean Rhys can be most fruitfully posed within an analysis of her writing; its historical and cultural framework, its theoretical postulates. Such an examination discloses that her hesitations and adoption of various identities strategically redefine her relationship to writing and history.

1 : History, Reading, Writing, and the Creole Woman

History and the Creole Writer

From the beginning of her career, some of the most influential critiques have focused on Rhys as colonial and West Indian. In what follows I shall discuss some of the salient features of this critical literature, as it provides the pretext for my analysis of Jean Rhys as Creole reader and writer.

The preface to Rhys's first collection, *The Left Bank and Other Stories* (1927), was written by Ford Madox Ford, Rhys's mentor and editor. His long introduction serves effectively to contextualize the cultural and political framework, of which Ford himself is a part and in which Rhys writes and is being read. His first comment on Rhys significantly identifies her as an oppositional critic of the world he so carefully details in his introduction: "What . . . is the lot of the opposition who must wait till their Thought is the accepted Thought of tomorrow? . . . To some extent the answer will be found in . . . Rhys's book" (23). His reading of *The Left Bank* identifies Jean Rhys as a writer and thinker whose ideas are out of step with contemporary ideologies, ahead of their time:

> And coming from the Antilles, with a terrifying insight and a terrific—an almost lurid!—passion for stating the case of the underdog, she has let her pen loose on the Left Banks of the Old World—on its gaols, its studios, its salons, its cafés, its criminals, its midinettes—with a bias of admiration for its midinettes and of sympathy for its lawbreakers. It is a note, a sympathy of which we do not have too much in Occidental literature with its perennial bias towards satisfaction with things as they are. But it is a note that needs sounding . . . since the real

activities of the world are seldom carried much forward by the accepted, or even by the Haute Bourgeoisies! (24)

Ford suggests that Rhys's position as a colonial contributes to her ability to represent the case of the "underdog" and makes her acutely critical of divisions inherent in European social structures. He places her writing outside of Western literature, which, in his view, conforms with more often than it questions or undermines dominant social systems. "Let[ting] loose her pen" suggests combativeness and intense criticism of a social and historical order. The attributes identified by Ford signal the major impetus of Rhys's writing: Europe and the West Indies and a focus on what she calls "the other side."

As her mentor and editor, Ford observes that he tried hard to induce her to introduce topography, in the way Flaubert, Conrad, or Maupassant did, but she eliminated with "cold deliberation" all traces of descriptive matter. Ford concludes that Rhys's business was with passion, hardship, emotions: "The locality in which these things are endured is immaterial. So she hands you the Antilles with its sea and sky . . . the effect of landscape on the emotions and passions of a child being so penetrative, but lets Montparnasse, or London, or Vienna go" (26). For Ford, the Antilles is not a place (to be written) in the same sense as London, Montparnasse, Vienna, but landscape, or as Edward Said terms it, "imaginative geography." The West Indies, then, is seen as "nothing" but/and landscape. Edouard de Nève, like Ford, points to the ways in which the West Indies—as beautiful-landscape-and-immense-blue-sea—shaped Rhys and made it impossible for her to become acclimatized to Europe ("Jean Rhys," 8). That Ford and his contemporaries lacked the conceptual tools and the critical vocabulary to read the West Indies as anything other than "nothing" or landscape is a function of the imperial history to which Rhys's texts obsessively call attention.

In the 1940s travel writer Alec Waugh observed:

In England I was to meet Jean Rhys. Her novels have not reached a large public, but they have a personal flavor. Jean Rhys in her writing is herself and no one else. There are no echoes. The central character in her best known novel is a composed and assured person, unable to fit herself into organized society, who recognizes this idiosyncrasy in herself and is undisturbed by it. She told me she had been born in Dominica. Rereading *After Leaving Mackenzie*, I could see how many flashbacks to Dominica — imperceptible to the unacquainted reader — occurred in it. I could see how Dominica had colored her temperament and outlook. It was a clue to her, just as she was a clue to it. People who could not fit into life elsewhere found what they were looking for in Dominica. Jean Rhys, who had been born there, chose as her character one who could not adjust herself to life outside. (*Sugar Islands*, 95–96)

This circular argument connects Jean Rhys and the West Indies and mystifies both.

In the introduction to his edition of *The Letters of Jean Rhys* (1984), Francis Wyndham provides a reading of the writer's psychological disabilities and her West Indian origins:

Ever since the end of her first love affair she had . . . been cursed by a kind of spiritual sickness — a feeling of belonging nowhere, of being ill at ease and out of place in her surroundings wherever these happened to be, a stranger in an indifferent, even hostile, world. *She may have wanted to think* that this crippling sense of alienation was merely that of a native West Indian exiled in a cold foreign land, *but in fact* she believed that the whole earth had become inhospitable to her after the shock of that humdrum betrayal. *All that had happened was* that a kind, rather fatherly businessman, who had picked up a pretty chorus girl . . . decided after a year or so to pension her off. (10–11; emphasis added)

Diana Athill, the editor of *Wide Sargasso Sea* and later works, observes: "She had lived in the Caribbean until she was sixteen; in England (which disappointed and frightened her) until she was twenty-nine. . . . She . . . escaped from the cold-eyed English and her sense of herself as despised by them for being an ignorant 'colonial.' . . . Jean Rhys's *truth* was that of a woman who was no good at managing life . . . and who suffered from a tendency to be paranoid" (Introduction, vii–viii; emphasis added).

Jean Rhys's constitutive otherness, this critical reading suggests, derives (in part) from her West Indian birth, her colonial status. The historical Jean Rhys and the West Indies become the fixed, passive objects of study, understood and defined by others. Meaning and subjectivity are assigned within a politics of representation that constructs "Jean Rhys" as the subaltern of metropolitan systems of knowledge. The West Indies is simultaneously written by these commentators as a projection of Europe's imaginary and the unspoken Other of Europe. Hence, the problems in and of her writing are displaced onto Rhys's "pathological" personhood and naturalized as a function of her individual, spiritual, and emotional defects. In the case of Francis Wyndham, his personal generosity toward and staunch support of Rhys and her writing is unquestioned, beyond reproach. It is the ideological position, which prescribes the reception of "Jean Rhys" and "the West Indies," that is of particular concern to this study.

I agree with the premise, which underlies much of the critical literature I have cited, that it is only through an examination of Jean Rhys's Creole identity as subjectivity and location (and the ways in which her gender identity is dependent on this) that the structures of Rhys's fiction can be adequately deciphered. I believe that there must be an examination of the history which underwrites and drives her work and without which she could not have produced the kind of fiction she did. But, as Hayden White teaches us, "we are indentured to a *choice* among contending interpretative strategies in any effort to reflect on history-in-general" (*Metahistory*, xii).

The lifespan of the historical Jean Rhys, 1890–1979, traverses crucial periods of European and West Indian history, marked by imperialism, colonialism, anticolonial struggles, two world wars, and the constitutional independence of formerly colonized countries. But it is the immediate postslavery period, the 1830s and 1840s, a watershed in British and Caribbean colonial history, which marks the obsessive beginning in Rhys's writing on the West Indies. This period is one of the most ideologically contested moments in Caribbean history—then and now. The ideological struggle to construct the narrative of this definitive moment in the history of the region remains today in the ongoing debates among professional historians of and from the Caribbean as they analyze "push/pull" factors that shaped postslavery labor and social relations. (Simply stated, "push" refers to the factors that forced the freedpersons away from the plantations, "pull" to the factors that seemed to offer better alternatives.)

The historical narratives that I shall focus on begin in this postslavery period. The second significant historiographical break begins almost a century later, from the 1930s to the 1960s, the decades of Caribbean-wide social revolts, the Second World War, and the independence movements in colonized countries. The third period covers the 1960s and 1970s. An analysis of these historical moments can help to contextualize not only the structures of Jean Rhys's writing but may shed some light on the conditions of its production and reception. In the section that follows, I shall summarize some of the main strands of the arguments that comprise the "history of the West Indies." These debates reveal how events accrue historical significance according to successive and even contending interpretations. In order to fully understand the Creole perspective from which Rhys writes and the ways in which she seeks legitimacy for this position, these contending interpretations must be taken into account. There are important differences in the ordering of and emphases on events among European/imperial, settler/Creole, and later cultural nationalist histories of the West Indies.

Some Versions of the Imperial History: The "Nigger Question"

In "The Postslavery Labour Problem Revisited," Woodville Marshall observes:

> [The] "pull" interpretation is as old as the slavery abolition question itself, [it] is therefore the staple of the historiographical tradition. Briefly, this interpretation suggests that a mix of psycho-cultural and objective factors were critical: ex-slaves, because of the experience of slavery, possessed a long-standing antipathy to the plantation and all its works *and* a "natural" desire to exploit the abundant land outside the plantation for a "simple" peasant-type existence. This was the view propounded by officials in the Colonial Office, by some abolitionists and naturally by the slave-owners as soon as slavery abolition became a practical possibility. All accepted that the lure of the available land would destroy the blacks' "inclinations to industry" and therefore remove all possibility of the plantation retaining an adequate labour force. These fears and suppositions received theoretical formulation in 1841 when Herman Merivale, an Oxford Professor (and later Permanent Under-Secretary of State for the Colonies) published his . . . *Lectures on Colonization and Colonies.* (3)

The writing of such nineteenth-century figures as Thomas Carlyle, John Stuart Mill, Karl Marx, and William Sewell also helped to shape the ideological grounds of the debate about the recently freed people in the Caribbean and their relationship to labor and to the plantocracy. It is

Thomas Carlyle, arguably the leading ideologue of his class and of imperialism during this period, who offers some of the most valuable insights. Klaus E. Knorr, in an interestingly worded observation in *British Colonial Theories 1570–1850*, notes that

> Carlyle has been called a founder ... of modern English expansionist imperialism. That is an exaggeration. ... He was not interested in the subject of colonies *per se*. ... If he had an imperialist theory, he did not state it. Whatever influence he had—and he had more on the imperialism of his posterity than on that of his contemporaries—was through *the propagation of a particular philosophy and the diffusion of an intellectual temper conducive to the development and acceptance of some components of later British expansionist imperialism. But even in this respect he has a claim to the noteworthiness of the propagator, not to that of the originator.* (104; emphasis added)

Carlyle's importance as "propagator," as amply recognized in the work of historians and literary critics, is what concerns me here.[1]

In terms of Caribbean history, Carlyle's "Occasional Discourse on the Nigger Question" understands and articulates the business of empire and colonialism as a *relation*. Metropolitan politics and imperial policy, the construction of the domestic subjectivity and that of the colonized Other, are inseparable. The "Negro Question ... lying at the bottom" forms part of the foundation on which the edifice of imperial might is built: "Taking ... an extensive survey of social affairs, which we find all in a state of the frightfulest embroilment ... the Council has decided ... that *the Negro Question, as lying at the bottom, was to be the first handled, and if possible the first settled*" (August, ed., *Carlyle and Mill*, 2; emphasis added).

Carlyle also expounds the view that the postslavery period in the West Indies was one of prosperity, leisure, and the "good life" for the freedpersons at the expense of the suffering Creoles and metropolitan whites:

> West-Indian affairs ... are in a rather troublous condition this good while. ... [H]owever ... the Negroes are all very happy and doing well. ... West Indian Whites ... are far enough from happy; West Indian Colonies not unlike sinking wholly into ruin: at home too, the British Whites are rather badly off. ... But, thank Heaven, our interesting Black population ... are all doing remarkably well. ...
>
> The West Indies ... are short of labour; as indeed is very conceivable

in those circumstances. Where a Black man, by working about half-an-hour a-day (such is the calculation), can supply himself, by aid of sun and soil, with as much pumpkin as will suffice, he is likely to be a little stiff to raise into hard work! . . . The fortunate Black man, very swiftly does he settle *his* account with supply and demand:—not so swiftly the less fortunate White man of those tropical localities. A bad case, his, just now. He himself cannot work; and his black neighbour, rich in pumpkin, is in no haste to help him. Sunk to the ear in pumpkin . . . he can listen to the less fortunate white man's "demand," and take his own time in supplying it. (3–7)

As Eric Williams aphoristically puts it, the fact that Carlyle never visited the West Indies "allowed him to speak with the greatest authority" about the region (qtd. Lamming, *Pleasures*, 93). An important reminder that the invention of the Caribbean as a European enterprise required little knowledge of the region and, in fact, depended upon a willed ignorance, an always already constructed narrative of the Other within and by metropolitan discourses. The trope of the "lazy black" whose refusal to work poses a threat to civilization is reproduced in Anthony Trollope's *The West Indies and the Spanish Main* (1860). He actually visits the Caribbean briefly and changes Carlyle's "pumpkins" to mangoes, breadfruit, and coconuts while "discovering" the same lazy, self-indulgent blacks of Carlyle's discourse:

If I have means to lie in the sun and meditate idly, why, O my worthy taskmaster! should you expect me to pull out at thy behest long reels of cotton. . . . Why indeed? Not having means so to lie, I do pull out the reels, taking such wages as I can get, and am thankful. But my friend and brother over there, my skin-polished, shining, oil-fat negro, is a richer man than I. He lies under his mango-tree, and eats the luscious fruit in the sun; he sends his black urchin up for a breadfruit, and behold the family table is spread. He pierces a cocoa-nut, and, lo! there is his beverage. He lies on the grass surrounded by oranges, bananas, and pineapples. Oh, my hard taskmaster of the sugar-mill, is he not better off than thou? why should he work at thy order. . . . It will be quite as bad in the long run for the negro as for the white man—worse, indeed; for the white man will by degrees wash his hands of the whole concern. . . . The question stands thus: cannot [the black man] be made to [work]? Can it not be contrived that he shall be free, free as is the Englishman,

History, Reading, Writing : 11

and yet compelled, as is the Englishman, to eat his bread in the sweat of his brow? (111)

James Anthony Froude, an Oxford history professor of preeminent stature and Carlyle's biographer, would produce *The English in the West Indies: The Bow of Ulysses* in 1888. He too predictably "discovers" "black people" to be prelapsarian Adams, blissfully occupying the tropical garden of Eden: "They live surrounded by most of the fruits which grew in Adam's paradise—oranges and plantains, bread-fruit, and cocoa-nuts, though not apples. Their yams and cassava grow without effort, for the soil is easily worked and inexhaustibly fertile. The curse is taken off from nature, and like Adam again they are under covenant of innocence. Morals in the technical sense they have none, but they cannot be said to sin, because they have no knowledge of a law, and therefore they can commit no breach of the law. They are naked and not ashamed" (49). Like Carlyle, Trollope, and others, Froude notes the extreme state of satisfaction and luxury in which the "black people" reside, due not only to abundant nature but also to the largesse and moral ascendancy of the English: "In no part of the globe is there any peasantry whose every want is so completely satisfied as her Majesty's black subjects in these West Indian islands. They have no aspirations to make them restless. . . . They have food for the picking up. Clothes they need not, and lodging in such a climate need not be elaborate. They have perfect liberty, and are safe from dangers, to which if left to themselves they would be exposed, for the English rule prevents the strong from oppressing the weak. In their own country they would have remained slaves to more warlike races" (50).

In "The Creolization of Caribbean History: The Emancipation Era and a Critique of Dialectical Analysis," William Green, like Carlyle, Trollope, and Froude before him, calls attention to the early postslavery period as "a kind of golden age for Caribbean working people—to the extent, that is, that Caribbean working people have ever enjoyed a golden age. Employment was abundant; wages were relatively high; and collective actions calculated to preserve pay levels and enhance the terms of work generally succeeded" (32). As a corollary, he too "discovers" a tendency in some contemporary Caribbean historians to misrepresent the planter class of the postslavery era: "The old image of the slothful, hide-bound and technologically backward West Indian planter dies hard, but it is, nevertheless, a regrettable stereotype that sorely misrepresents the prodigious efforts of many energetic, modernizing agriculturalists in the emancipation era" (31).[2]

There have also been contending interpretations from other metropolitan critics. Karl Marx offers another important contribution to the debate:

> *The Times* of November 1857 contains an utterly delightful cry of the outrage on the part of a West-Indian plantation owner. This advocate analyses with great moral indignation—as a plea for the re-introduction of Negro slavery—how the *Quashees* (the free blacks of Jamaica) content themselves with producing only what is strictly necessary for their own consumption, and, alongside this "use value," regarding loafing (indulgence and idleness) as the real luxury good; how they do not care a damn for the sugar, and the fixed capital invested in the plantation, but rather observe the planters' impending bankruptcy with an ironic grin of malicious pleasure, and even exploit their acquired Christianity as an embellishment for this mood of malicious glee and indolence. They have ceased to be slaves, but not in order to become wage labourers, but, instead, self-sustaining peasants working for their own consumption. As far as they are concerned, capital does not exist as capital, because autonomous wealth as such can exist only either on the basis of *direct* forced labour, slavery, or *indirect* forced labour, *wage labour*. Wealth confronts direct forced labour not as capital, but rather as *relation of domination*; thus, the relation of domination is the only thing which is reproduced on this basis, for which wealth itself has value only as gratification, not as wealth itself, and which can therefore never create general industriousness. (*Grundrisse*, 325–26)

In *The Ordeal of Free Labor in the British West Indies* (1861), William Sewell, who visited the West Indies, describes the West Indian planter class as "extravagant in all that pertained to their own ease and luxury; penurious when the improvement, moral, social, or political, of the people was in question; tenacious of their aristocratic privileges, opposed to reform and behind the age in political, agricultural, and mechanical science" (38). Sewell also observes: "I am sick of the statement so constantly and thoughtlessly repeated that the African won't work. This . . . is said of . . . islands where land is plentiful and labor scarce. Won't work? Why should they work for the planter, and bind themselves to a new tyranny? Where is the moral obligation that chains them forever to the serfdom of estate labor? Why should they work for a master when they can work more profitably for themselves, and enjoy at the same time a perfect independence?" (47)

If Sewell attacks the West Indian planter class, he shares Carlyle's assessment of the "character of the untutored negro. His degradation I do not doubt; his moral and intellectual deficiencies can not possibly excite surprise" (44). Carlyle's "Occasional Discourse" understands, too, that the process of racial identification, according to hierarchically arranged binary oppositions, is by its very nature parasitic. Carlyle's own emphasis on the prefixes of negation underlines his awareness of the inseparability of the categories "black" and "white":

> What are the true relations between Negro and White, their mutual duties under the sight of the Maker of them both; what human laws will assist both to comply more and more with these? The solution, only to be gained by honest endeavour, and sincere reading of experience, such as have never yet been bestowed on it, is not yet here; the solution is perhaps still distant. But some approximation to it, various real approximations, could be made, and must be made:—this of declaring that Negro and White are *un*related, loose from one another, on a footing of perfect equality, and subject to no law but that of supply-and-demand according to the Dismal Science; this, which contradicts the palpablest facts, is clearly no solution, but a cutting of the knot asunder; and every hour we persist in this is leading us towards *dis*solution instead of solution! (33–34)

It is important to note too that, less than twenty years after the publication of his essay, Carlyle would chair the Eyre Defence Committee in support of John Eyre, governor of Jamaica in 1865 following the Morant Bay uprising in that country. Eyre's suppression of the revolt is often cited as one of the most violent acts of British imperial aggression.[3] As Eric Williams indicates, graphic samples remain of the evidence presented to the Royal Commission charged to investigate the conflict: "Hole is doing splendid service . . . shooting every black man who cannot give an account of himself. . . . This is a picture of martial law. The soldiers enjoy it" (qtd. *British Historians*, 118–19). Eyre defended his actions by noting, "It was necessary to [strike] terror. . . . [The] negroes from a low state of civilization and being under the influence of superstitious feelings, could not properly be dealt with in the same manner as might the peasantry of a European country." Eyre further noted that "the steps taken were, under God's good providence, the means of averting from Jamaica the horrors of a general rebellion, and that they saved the lives and properties of Her Majesty's subjects confided to my care. [It] is not my opinion only, but the opinion of the large majority of the intelligent and reflecting portion of the [British] community" (122–23).

In England the Eyre Defence Committee comprised Carlyle as well as some of the literary and intellectual giants of nineteenth-century England: John Ruskin, Charles Dickens, Alfred Tennyson, Matthew Arnold, and Charles Kingsley. Carlyle observes: "The clamour raised against Governor Eyre appears to me to be disgraceful to the good sense of England. . . . I . . . consider it of evil omen to the country, and to its highest interests, in these times. For my own share, all the light that has yet reached me on Mr Eyre and his history in the world goes steadily to establish the conclusion that he is a just, humane, and valiant man, faithful to his trusts everywhere, and with no ordinary faculty of executing them; that his late services in Jamaica were of great, perhaps of incalculable value" (129).

Carlyle's writing and his actions in support of Governor Eyre effectively dramatize how the domain of language and representation intersects with other violent forces within the framework of colonialism to produce the (history of the) West Indies for Europe. It demonstrates that colonialist discourse is not mere representation but an event that helps to create "History" and shape materially the lives of people in the metropolis *and* the periphery.

John Stuart Mill issued a sharp response to Carlyle's essay, observing that his doctrine was "not new. It is ancient as tyranny or any of the bad passions that have desolated the earth. . . . The dogma that some men have a right divine to compel others to work by any means that will serve the purpose, is no part of [the] Gospel. It is a heresy truly Satanic and detestable" (August, ed., *Carlyle and Mill*, 53). Mill also chaired the committee against Governor Eyre, known as the Jamaica Committee, which included Herbert Spencer and Thomas Huxley and was supported by Charles Darwin and Leslie Stephen.[4]

Within the field of literary criticism, readers of Jean Rhys's writing in post-1960s United States and England articulate the "history of the West Indies" in ways that are strikingly similar to that of Carlyle and his heirs. Any claim that Carlyle's position is unrepresentative, anachronistic, or extreme is readily disarmed by a reading of the post-1960s critical literature.[5] Benita Parry's incisive formulation of some of the features of metropolitan writing on formerly colonized societies remains relevant:

> Affiliated to the hegemonic explanatory order and written with the same ideological code as the discourse of colonialism, this . . . discussion [endorsed] the affirmations and prohibitions authorized by the culture pursuing and implementing colonial power. . . . Mimeticism was the name of its interpretative mode; establishing the historical accuracy, psychological truthfulness and humanist perceptions of the fictions, its game. The verisimilitude was checked out against other fabrications— the books, reports, surveys, treatises and ruminations written by western scholars, colonial civil servants, army officers, missionaries, journalists, explorers and travellers; the ethics were judged by the effort to understand the incomprehensible ways of the native. . . . Because the critics shared the cultural assumptions and commitments of the fictions they were discussing, they were unable . . . to distance themselves from inscriptions of the colonial worlds as deviant; and by colluding in displacing a conflictual political relation with a metaphysical and moral contest, their exegesis constituted itself as yet another discourse of colonialism. ("Problems," 33)

Some Cultural Nationalist Perspectives

Within the metropolitan centers, the claims constituting the assumptions about the Caribbean and "Jean Rhys" are produced by and within an essentially colonialist/colonizing discourse, which also reproduces what is considered to be the "history" of the region. But the legacy of Carlyle's words and actions has another important dimension that is of crucial significance to the present study. The novel most often cited as a symbol of the era of burgeoning nationalism in the twentieth-century Anglophone Caribbean is Vic Reid's *A New Day* (1949), which rewrites the history of the Morant Bay uprising from the point of view of Caribbean people, focusing on the heroism of the Jamaicans Paul Bogle and George William Gordon. Reid himself, in an interview with Daryl Dance in the 1980s, observes that the other side needed to be told: "[Caribbean] history was never written. What was written were some works done by the English telling the

English side of [Caribbean] history. . . . I used to read old council minutes written in script. . . . And you could pick between the lines, see how frequently the events were distorted to show the conqueror's point of view —the Englishman's point of view. I am not blaming him at all . . . but somebody has to show another point of view. . . . [T]he history books treated us very scantily, and very frequently quite ungraciously" (Dance, *New World*, 209, 216).

Sylvia Wynter, in "Novel and History, Plot and Plantation" (1971), makes a similar observation of *A New Day*: "Reid . . . caught up in . . . the growth of national feeling, wrote his novel to restore the written past to a people who had only the oral past; and to the middle class who thought . . . there was no history" (102). Edward Baugh, on the occasion of Reid's death in 1987, also returns to this crucial point: "He wrote to give his people a nurturing sense of their own history, to set over against those distortions of history by which others had sought to shackle their minds" ("Tribute," 2). The white Jamaican writer H. G. DeLisser also produced a fictional account of the Morant Bay uprising, *Revenge* (1918), from a Creole perspective. Writing as rewriting and a struggle for representation is a fundamental feature of West Indian literature even to the present day, as Derek Walcott's *Omeros* (1990) emblematizes.

Contemporary professional historians, too, continue to intervene in the dominative system of knowledge, questioning and displacing the "English side" of history imposed on the Caribbean region. O. Nigel Bolland argues that

> With few exceptions . . . most histories of the British West Indies view emancipation in a less critical light than did the former slaves themselves, and uncritically conceptualize the post-1838 colonies as "free" societies in contrast to the slave societies that preceded them. A clear distinction is rarely made between emancipation as an event and emancipation as a human, social condition. . . . The . . . study of the interrelatedness of the control of land and labor as key aspects of a structure of domination suggests the need for a more critical examination of the real meaning of the terms "emancipation" and "freedom" for the postslavery period. . . . If historians are to be anything other than representatives of the Colonial Office and the planter class, self-

confessed or otherwise, we should commence a critical reevaluation of these concepts in relation to the changes which occurred in the mid-nineteenth century. ("Systems of Domination," 107)

One of the earliest historical analyses that sought to include the perspectives of the freedpersons during the postslavery period is Douglas Hall's pathbreaking essay "The Flight from the Estates Reconsidered: The British West Indies, 1838–1842." It examines "the reasons why after their emancipation many of the ex-slaves in the British Caribbean removed themselves from the estates and established households elsewhere. A related concern is the extent to which withdrawal of residence reflected an intention to withdraw their labour from the plantation economy" (55).

Hall, although pointing to the scarcity of information from the ex-slaves themselves, draws on rare documents provided by them in the form of two letters articulating their grievances and desire for redress. The first is addressed to the local stipendiary magistrate in British Guiana, dated 3 January 1842:

> It appears that within the pale of this week certain resolutions has passed, debiliting the wages of us labourers. We do now wishful of ascertaining the case from you in its minute order. Wheather we are bound by our Queen to act in accordance with these resolutions, or wheather we are to submit to what offer the managers choose to give. We leave it to you to give us your opinion on this most momentous subject. It is offered three bitts to one guilder per day for our labour per day. We are told we must pay for our provision ground, doctor fees, finding ourselves with all necessarys, etc. What will be remaining for us in case of sickness? We feel this case too hard upon us, and we hope that your worship will not consider that we have spoken hard, but it is a fraud that is wishful of placing on us, and unless other measures are adopted, we will be obliged to send to Her Most Gracious Majesty to justify us. (57)

A second letter from workers on another estate makes the point even more forcefully:

> Sir! We free labourers of Plantation Walton Hall are already to work our liberty hours in putting hands and heart providing in we getting what is right. As to say for taking one guilder per day, we can not take it

at all. Sir, you will be pleased to understand us to what we say (those few years since we got free), and so soon brought on a reducing price, which is now offered to we labourers. We certainly thinks it to be very hard. If you take it in consideration, when calling on us. We shall be proud to know from, if such laws came from the Queen, or any of her Majesties Justice of Peace. During our slavery we was clothed, ration and seported in all manner of respects. Now we are free men (free indeed), we are to work for nothing. Then we might actually say, we becomes slaves again. We will be glad to know from the proprietors of the estates, if they are to take from us our rights all together. . . . [W]e cannot work for a smaller price. You will be please to take the law in consideration in set-tling this matter. (57)

In addition to citing the position of the workers and that of the planters, Hall also quotes extensively from interviews and observations made by English visitors to the Caribbean. The historian concludes that the "movement of the ex-slaves from the estates in the immediate post-emancipation years was not a flight from the horrors of slavery. It was a protest against the inequities of early 'freedom' " (62).

Other historians have argued with Hall's analysis and conclusion. Of particular relevance is Michel-Rolph Trouillot's "Labour and Emancipa-tion in Dominica: Contribution to a Debate." He notes that "the ten-dency . . . to analyze the whole Caribbean in terms of two or three 'more important' territories . . . or in terms of a few large estates is extremely dangerous when the argument advanced seeks to integrate the conscious-ness and the volition of historical actors" (76). Basing his analyses on stipendiary magistrates' reports comprising four lists of more than fifty estates, he concludes, inter alia, that "in the first four months following the Emancipation of 1st August, 1838, Dominican estates lost a substantial proportion . . . of their labour force. [T]he decrease was . . . originally due to the ex-slaves' impulse to leave the plantations . . . an impulse later cir-cumscribed by the existential and structural constraints that reduced both the statistical availability of alternatives and the former apprentices' per-ception of their options" (82).

Russell E. Chace Jr. observes that one of the most important "distur-bances" of the postslavery period was the "Guerre Negre" of Dominica, which occurred in June 1844. "An examination of this protest," he asserts, "provides important insights into the complex tensions which characterized post-emancipation plantation societies, the contrasting attitudes and expectations of the dominant elements of society and the freedpersons, and the unequivocal commitment of the ex-slaves to the most important 'right' of all, freedom itself." Citing parliamentary papers and newspaper reports, Chace provides a detailed analysis of the events as recorded and the contexts in which they occurred. He observes there was "an image of orderly and respectful behaviour on the part of the freed persons. . . . Dominant elements of the society, therefore, reacted with shock and anger when, during the taking of the census on Monday, June 3, 1844, reports began to filter into Roseau of armed freedmen resisting the 'taking of names' and attacking enumerators and commissioners of population" ("Protest," 118–21).

One of the major sites of the dispute was the Geneva/Genever plantation, belonging to Jean Rhys's maternal grandfather, Mr. Lockhart:

> In the Grand Bay region . . . the opening assault on the census-takers became organized attacks on estate property and management personnel. One witness testified that on the night of June 3 he was advised "to get his breakfast boiled early, and come down to the Bay to meet Buckra, as Mr. Lockhart had gone to town to look for white man." On the morning of June 4 labourers from the Grand Bay estates assembled on the beach of Geneva estate. . . . Laurent [leader of one group] organized two gangs to loot the stores and houses at Geneva and Bericoa. . . . Though the demonstrators threatened the lives of most of the management personnel in the area, in every case except [one], labourers from the estates intervened to prevent any action more drastic than the beatings administered. (122–23)

One week after the beginning of the protest, it was declared smashed by Governor Fitzroy. Three of the 1,200 to 1,500 freedpersons were killed by the militia, 5 were wounded, and 300 were imprisoned. The protesters wounded between 10 and 12 militiamen, enumerators, and managers. Claims for loss of property totaled £1,375 sterling (124).

Chace concludes that "almost every affidavit and piece of testimony taken after the protest . . . points to the same conclusion, that the freedpersons firmly believed that they were to be re-enslaved and that many of them were prepared to resist to the point of death" (129). He also quotes from a letter by a freedperson:

> I think that our freedom can be taken away from us, because it was once done in another country near to us; it was the French who gave their people free, and afterwards made them slaves again; my parents told me so when I was quite a child, and I have remembered it ever since; what is done once can be done again, and we all know that liberty is good; I don't know but what the English will do like the French one of these days; it is only for the Queen to send a Gazette, and say "make them slaves again," and they will be all made slaves; if a man pays money, and does not get a receipt, he can be made to pay the money again; so it is with freedom; if we have been made free and have no paper to show for it, we can be made slaves again. (129–30)

The Creole Perspective and the "Mulatto Ascendancy"

I shall undertake a detailed analysis of Rhys's own version of history, as written in *Smile Please*, later in this chapter; but it may be useful at this point to compare Chace's historical account of the "Guerre Negre" with Rhys's brief, elliptical articulation of the same "event" as part of her family history. In a chapter of *Smile Please* entitled "Geneva," the narrator says:

> My mother was a Miss Lockhart, a granddaughter of the James Gibson Lockhart who had arrived from Scotland at the end of the eighteenth century. He died before the Emancipation Act was passed, and as he was a slave owner the Lockharts, even in my day, were never very popular. That's putting it mildly.
>
> It was during my grandfather's life, sometime in the 1830s, that the first estate house was burnt down by the freed negroes after the Emancipation Act was passed. He was, apparently, a mild man who didn't like the situation at all and he died fairly young but not before a new estate house had been built, the one I knew. (33)

In Rhys's account, no explanation is given for the burning of the house. There is an emphasis on the innocence of her grandfather and a suggestion of the unreasoning violence of the black people who destroyed his property even after the passage of the Emancipation Act. Later in the same chapter, the narrator recalls going back to Dominica "long afterwards" and observes: "Where the house had been was an empty space, the Geneva house was burnt down two, or was it three, times. I stared at it trying to remember. . . . But there was nothing, nothing. Nothing to look at. Nothing to say" (37–38).

English critic Louis James offers a similar account: "In 1844 there was a census on the island. Rumours spread that it was the preliminary to a return to slavery. The black population rioted. At Genever, on Jane Maxwell's deposition, 'the estate was broken into by a body of labouring people and every article therein . . . either stolen or destroyed.' The house was burned down, and Jane barely escaped with her life. It was a night the like of which Jean Rhys was to recreate in *Wide Sargasso Sea*. [A]nother [house] was made. . . . Then in 1932 the blacks burnt down the new house" (*Jean Rhys*, 47).

Historical records indicate that emancipation in the West Indies meant the payment of twenty million pound sterling to the West Indian plantocracy as a form of compensation for their loss of property and a period of apprenticeship for the former slaves. Under the apprenticeship system, "all registered slaves over the age of six years were initially to become 'apprenticed labourers' who would be compelled to work without pay for forty-five hours each week for the same masters as they had prior to abolition. The original intention was to apprentice field workers for six years and others four, but eventually all were freed in 1838" (Bolland, "Systems of Domination," 108). Like the metropolitan commentators, the Creoles blamed the postslavery labor problems on the "laziness" or intransigence of the black people — the solution to which should be importation of a new labor force. A planter, writing in the Dominican newspaper *Colonist* in 1842, suggested that "immigration and immigration alone . . . is the only way in which you can meet this growing evil, and save the colony from eventual ruin" (qtd. Honychurch, *Dominica*, 95).[6]

Not only did the Creoles face the crumbling of the plantation system as they had known it, but in Dominica, Rhys's birthplace, they faced challenge from what has been called the Mulatto Ascendancy. Joseph Borome, citing documents from the Public Records Office, notes that the passage of the "Brown Privilege Bill" in Dominica in 1831 granted full political and social rights to free nonwhites. The election of 1832 brought three colored men to the Assembly, and by 1838 they formed a majority. But the white attorneys, merchants, and traders, allied with the numerous absentee owners, constantly threw up legislative roadblocks in the Assembly and Council alike. Two political parties developed rapidly, supported by two news-papers, the *Colonist* (white) and the *Dominican* (colored). Charles Gordon Falconer, described as the "sharp-tongued and sharp-minded editor of *The Dominican*," was one of the major political figures of the period. Under his leadership the Mulatto Ascendancy operated as a bloc. Unable to defeat the passage of liberal measures, the whites formed the Dominican Association for the Reform of Abuses in the Administration of Public Affairs. Lieutenant Governor Thomas Price dissolved the House of Assembly and called new elections, which returned several members of the Mulatto Ascendancy to power, including Falconer, who described the occupant of the Government House as "despotic" ("Crown Colony," 120–23).

If the mulatto Falconer was against the white politicians, he was also strongly opposed to the African people's struggle for civil rights. Falconer saw the "Guerre Negre" of 1844 as a "shameful rebellion against lawful authority." He further argued that it represented

a determination to impoverish the Proprietors of the Estates by a wanton destruction of property, and in some cases of dishonestly converting it to their own use reckless of consequences. . . . We must believe that the rebels consider themselves to have been first wronged. It is a fact that many have always regarded their freedom to be only a *part* of the restitution due to them for their former bondage and that between their Queen and their former Owners some thing more ought to have been given them—and that *something* many have not scrupled in times past to say—should have been "a small piece of land!!!" (Chace, 124–25)

The historical perspectives that I have briefly cited are particularly relevant to the contexts in which Rhys's writing is located and also to the internal structures of the fiction itself. This is especially true of *Wide Sargasso Sea*, whose structure and emplotment are based on precise and strategic interventions in these historical records and narratives. "Again the Antilles" (1927), *Voyage in the Dark* (1934), and "Fishy Waters" (1976) also deal very specifically with the same historical materials that I have highlighted: the "black people's" "refusal to work," the question of immigration and Asian indentured labor, the postslavery compensation for the plantocracy, "black violence" against the Creoles, the Mulatto Ascendancy, and the mulatto politician Falconer.

It is important that Jean Rhys's fiction use as a point of departure this crucial postslavery period in the Caribbean. She grasps that her own locational identity as a Creole woman is a function of, and can be made intelligible only in terms of, this period, which was both a beginning and an end. It is this time and space that she elucidates with unswerving persistence in her work. This postslavery era in Rhys's writing is, to borrow Sylvia Molloy's observation, "a scene of crisis necessary to the rhetoric of self-figuration, a critical space, fraught with the anxiety of origins and representation, with which the self stages its presence" ("Unquiet Self," 29). The "subject," in all senses of the term, of Rhys's writing, as she well understood, cannot be contained by the dates or the experiences that framed her personal "life" or by her "psychological deficiencies," however these are defined and labeled. The *historical and discursive processes* through which the Creole subjectivity is construed forms one of the most significant aspects of her writing.

The Creole account of West Indian history that Rhys's writing articulates has an interesting relationship with the European production of the "History of the West Indies," on the one hand, and that of present-day professional historians of and from the Caribbean, on the other, who sometimes combine analyses of Caribbean folk, oral, and Creole cultures, with study or revision of European documents and archival sources. And the interpretative and narrative dimensions of history make for interesting interaction among the practitioners of Caribbean history and Caribbean literature. For example, historian Trouillot criticizes Rhys's idiosyncratic use of dates and events in *Wide Sargasso Sea*, attributing it to her departure from the West Indies at an early age. He counters Rhys's apparent inaccuracy through a reliance on techniques based on uncovering "facts": "Jean Rhys . . . pushes the legend of heavy banana consumption as far back as the days of slavery. Yet when forced to uncover systematically the factual past within their present, most men and women over fifty refer to a diet in which bananas were once much more of a fruit than a cooked staple" (*Peasants*, 131). Trouillot's reading of a particular scene (the Tia-Antoinette relationship) in *Wide Sargasso Sea* places it in the period of slavery, when the period covered is the postslavery era. In addition, with respect to the leading protagonist of the Mulatto Ascendancy in Dominica, different historians refer to the same person by different names: Charles Gordon Falconer (Borome, "Crown Colony," 121) and George Charles Falconer (Chace, "Protest," 121). The estate belonging to Rhys's grandfather is referred to as

"Geneva" by historian Chace, who meticulously cites archival documents, and "Genever" by Louis James, a literary critic who also meticulously cites archival material from the Dominica National Archives (*Jean Rhys*, 45, 63). These relatively minor but telling points call attention to the discursive dimension of "history" and "facts" and to the fugitive nature of "Truth." The extent and manner in which Jean Rhys's own artistic imagination and writing, from the perspective of a West Indian Creole, participate in the contending representations of the West Indies is the central problematic that this book seeks to investigate.

The ongoing and rigorous debates among historians and writers from within and outside of the Caribbean serve to confirm the obvious point that there is no place outside of history and historical discourse from which to referee these debates and vouch for authenticity or correctness. All the interests are vested. The "history of the West Indies" that guides my own work incorporates the accounts of the region, which take for granted and as their starting point an uncompromising acceptance of the *humanity* and agency of African Caribbean people; which recognize them not as cultural objects about whom statements are made but as actors, along with others, in the construction of the societies in which they live(d).

"A New Day" and the Silent Years: 1930s to 1960s

The Caribbean-wide social revolts of the 1930s would set into motion the process of decolonization and the movement toward constitutional independence in the 1960s. As many historians have noted, this was not an isolated moment in Caribbean history but a part of the continuous struggle on the part of the working people dating back to the eighteenth century and beyond. Woodville Marshall summarizes the meaning of this important period:

> If slave emancipation can be regarded as a social revolution, the events of the decades, 1930–1960, about a century later, must surely rank as at least our second social revolution. This period of intense political ferment altered forever the features of the political landscape, producing party political and trade union organization, mass political participation and constitutional de-colonization. Above all else, it was a period of excitement, enthusiasm and activity on a number of levels: the character of the political succession allowed new social and economic pos-

sibilities to be brought within reach, social change was clearly accelerated, and various strains of nationalism flourished, then withered or mutated. . . . [F]or most, the various developments represented, in Vic Reid's words, "a new day." (Preface, i)

The ideologies that informed the strikes and demonstrations were shaped in large part by Marcus Garvey's black nationalist movement, the Universal Negro Improvement Association. Tony Martin notes that "by 1919 the UNIA in the West Indies was firmly entrenched enough to figure prominently in the labour riots and racial unrest that swept the area. The British colonialists blamed the [association's] *Negro World* for the upsurge of race consciousness which formed a backdrop to the disturbances. . . . After 1919 the UNIA maintained its links with the budding West Indian labour movement. . . . Garvey's impact . . . both within and without the labour movement, can be said to have been substantial" ("Marcus Garvey," 360).

Several other important historical events coalesced to trigger the social revolts: the social and economic problems of unemployment, appalling working conditions, and a low standard of living were the immediate causes that catalyzed the working people's revolts. The low price of sugar, tied to the depression of the 1930s in industrialized countries, was another contributing factor. Some of the best-known records of the upheavals are *Labour Conditions in the West Indies* (1939) and *West India Royal Commission Report* (June 1945), commonly known as the Moyne Report. The work that I have found most useful is that of Arthur Lewis, *Labour in the West Indies: The Birth of a Workers' Movement* (1938).

Lewis was one of the first to note that if the social upheavals dramatized the economic and social injustices of the colonial system, they were also clear indicators of a growing desire for political and constitutional changes:

What has emerged from these years of working class upheaval, with their tale of strike and riot, death and victimisation? Two things: the rise of trade unions, and the entry of the working classes into West Indian politics. . . . Important as have been the results on the trade union front, on the political front nothing short of a revolution has occurred. . . . The real significance of the revolution of 1935–38 is that . . . [t]he major issues discussed today no longer revolve round the aspirations of the middle classes, but are set by working class demands. . . . The Labour Movement knows that measures of the kind which it proposes can only be enacted if there is strong mass pressure on the Legislature. That is why constitutional reform is in the foreground of the programme. . . . Until the franchise is extended as widely as possible . . . it is unlikely that there will be any substantial improvement in the standard of living, and useless to dismiss the inevitable disturbances as "political agitation." (38–51)

Although the first generation of Anglophone Caribbean writers actually emerged before the social and political eruptions, these events acted as a catalyst to the cultural imperatives out of which West Indian literature blossomed. In "Talking about the Thirties," an interview with Alfred Mendes, one of the founding fathers of West Indian literature, Clifford Sealy points to a notable feature of the emergence of this body of writing: "There doesn't seem to be any kind of lineal descent from a previous movement." Mendes observes: "No. We were indeed the first of the indigenous writers . . . in the sense that we took the material that we found in our backyards, so to speak, and used that material for fiction. There had been writers before using the *locale* of . . . the Caribbean, but they were foreign writers. . . . They were travelling tourists and things of that sort. . . . They . . . wrote tropical novels; but they were not genuine . . . Caribbean works" (4).

In acknowledging the prior metropolitan discourse as a pretext for West Indian writing, Mendes emphasizes the entanglement of writing in a complex of historical, social, and political practices:

We were probably urged into doing something that would smell of our own island[s], using the techniques that we borrowed from these people. But I think that it goes a little more deeply . . . in the sense that . . . the motivating forces that drove us . . . into writing at all, stemmed from two world-shattering events. The first was, of course, the first world war . . . and . . . the second . . . was the Russian Revolution. . . .

[T]hough . . . we consciously forged the stuff that we happened to be engaged upon at any particular moment, the power behind the urge to write, and write about what concerned us most . . . [was inspired by] these particular events. (5–6)

Alfred Mendes coedited with C. L. R. James the literary magazine *Trinidad*, which appeared briefly in 1929 and survived for only two issues. These two and Albert Gomes were part of what came to be known as the Beacon Group, intellectuals who coedited the *Beacon*, a literary and cultural journal founded by Mendes in 1931. In the October 1931 edition the journal called attention to the "ubiquitous tragedy of squalor and starvation [which] is no unusual spectacle" in the Caribbean (21). A few years later the eruption of the social revolts would call attention to this "tragedy" in a different way. The journal was also explicit in its nationalist orientation: "It is important . . . that we break away as far as possible from the English tradition; and the fact that some of us are still slaves to Scott and Dickens is merely because we lack the necessary artistic individuality and sensibility in order to see how incongruous that tradition is with the West Indian scene and spirit. . . . [T]he fact remains that the sooner we throw off the veneer of culture that our colonization has brought us the better for our artistic aims" (April 1933, 3).

This short-lived though very influential journal, published between 1931 and 1933 and reappearing briefly in 1939, is an important part of the sociocultural and political ferment of the 1930s. Brinsley Samaroo notes that its end came because it had dared to challenge the status quo. Advertisements ceased, and the fear of police action intimidated potential writers and contributors (Introduction, xiii). Before its demise, however, the *Beacon* saw the appearance of the *Outlook* (1932) and the *Forum Quarterly* (1932) in Barbados. Their appearance leads Albert Gomes to observe: "Recent publications in the West Indies suffice to explode the myth of isolation which travel writers are always so eager to apply to these islands. Good landscape, sugar and cocoa are not our only products" ("Periodicals," 24).

In Jamaica Una Marson founded and edited the *Cosmopolitan* (1929–32) and published two volumes of poetry before leaving for England. There she became secretary to the League of Coloured People in London and later private secretary to the emperor of Ethiopia, who was then exiled in Britain. She returned to Jamaica in 1936 and was influential in the founding of *Public Opinion*, one of the most significant publications of this and later periods and also the *Jamaica Standard*. The first anthology of Jamaican poetry, *Voices from Summerland*, was compiled and edited by J. C. Clare McFarlane in 1930. C. L. R. James, who had left Trinidad in 1932, was articulating in London "The Case for West Indian Self-Government" (1933), published by Hogarth Press, owned by Leonard and Virginia Woolf. In the 17 June 1933 issue of the *Port of Spain Gazette* he published "A Century of Freedom." His "British Barbarism in Jamaica! Support the Negro Workers' Struggle" appeared in *Fight* in June 1938. *Minty Alley* appeared in 1936, and the classic *Black Jacobins* in 1938. In New York Jaime O'Meally also published "Why We Demand Self-Government" (1938).

Prior to the appearance of the first generation of Anglophone Caribbean writing within the region, there was the development in the Francophone Caribbean (specifically Haiti) of a cultural and literary ethos that celebrated the African heritage of most of its people. The U.S. military occupation of Haiti between 1915 and 1934 provided one vital impetus for a cultural reassessment. J. Michael Dash, in *Literature and Ideology in Haiti, 1915–1961*, observes that "the continued American presence and the colonial nature of this presence . . . created a real *crise de conscience* among Haitian writers and intellectuals." In 1927 the literary journal *La Revue Indigène* was founded. Its editors sought to maintain a strictly literary focus, with its overtly political counterpart, *Le Petit Impartial* (1927–31), articulating an "uncompromising nationalism" (Dash, 67–78). Some of the literary figures of the period include Carl Brouard ("Nostalgie," 1927); Jean Price-Mars (*Ainsi parla l'Oncle*, 1928), who shared with Marcus Garvey a commitment to recuperating an African civilization; Léon Laleau (*Le choc*, 1932); and Léon Damas (*Pigments*, 1937). In some senses these Haitian writers were the forerunners of the Negritude movement, which began in Paris in the 1930s. The Negritude group, comprising African and West Indian writers and intellectuals, was also drawing support from the Harlem Renaissance, which included the Jamaican Claude McKay.

The journals, newspapers, and little magazines that appeared in the Anglophone Caribbean in the following decade, the 1940s, would provide the "cradle" for the work of a second generation of West Indian writers who developed as writers during and after the anticolonial movements. (These are the best-known West Indian writers today.) Among these publications are *Bim* (1942), *Focus* (1943), and *Kyk-over-al* (1945). George Lamming, one of the outstanding practitioners of this group, notes that the social revolts and the literary and cultural journals played seminal roles in the evolution of the regional literature. He states that he and his contemporaries "lived" the 1930s social revolts: "I still remember that one day when I was on the way to school there were people fleeing in the opposite direction. . . . We were told they were rioting in town, that was 1937–38" (Sander and Munro, *Kas-kas*, 7). Lamming's *In the Castle of My Skin* (1953) is among the most celebrated fictional representations of this historical period. With respect to *Bim*, he points out that although it started in Barbados in 1945 as a publication for a small racial elite, Frank Collymore, its editor, took the journal out of the club and out of Barbados and made it into a regional institution. Other writers whose early work appeared in *Bim* include Samuel Selvon, Edgar Mittelholzer, V. S. Naipaul, and Clifford Sealy.

In Guyana during the same period there developed "a community of the imagination," including such writers as Jan Carew, Edgar Mittelholzer, Martin Carter, Ivan Van Sertima, Wilson Harris, and others associated with *Kyk-over-al*, under the editorship of A. J. Seymour. As Wilson Harris notes, "It is clearly a magazine of great interest, because it reflects many issues which would have sprung out of the historical situation within which the magazine appears" (Sander and Munro, *Kas-kas*, 49).

The founder of *Focus* and one of Jamaica's leading sculptors, Edna Manley, observed in 1945, "Great and irrevocable changes have swept this land of ours in the last few years, and out of these changes a new art is springing" (qtd. Oakley, "Patriotism," 19). One important writer of this period was the poet George Campbell, who in 1946 published *First Poems*— a book "that was hailed in some quarters as embodying the first representation in verse of the nationalist spirit. . . . With Trade Unionism and party politics, with Universal Suffrage came the songs of this . . . rhetorician in an idiom that owed very little to external influences" (McFarlane, "Jamaican Poetry," 209). The novelist and journalist Roger Mais paid a very high price for his writing. In the article "Now We Know" (*Public Opinion*, 14 July 1944), he attacked the injustices and hypocrisies of colonialism. This led to a police raid on the newspaper's offices and Mais's imprisonment for six months on charges of seditious libel. There was also in this period an upsurge of "protest" songs and poetry in the popular culture, which "had its generic roots in such oral forms as protest songs and work songs which not only formed an integral part of West Indian plantation culture but also survived through the post-emancipation period" (Asein, " 'Protest' Tradition," 40). Gordon Rohlehr notes that in Trinidad "calypso emerged during this period [into] a flexible medium capable of accommodating narrative, social and political protest, scatological humour and celebration" (*Strangled City*, 4).

The social revolts of the 1930s in the Anglophone Caribbean catalyzed the movement toward nationalism and engendered major new cultural imperatives, out of which the work of contemporary (post-1940s) novelists, poets, critics, journalists, and songwriters emerged. Concomitantly, the critico-aesthetic forms developed during this period helped to shape the epistemological and ethical possibilities of the emergent nationalism. Comments by writer George Lamming and critic Gordon Rohlehr illustrate the dialectical relationship between the social and discursive realms. In the 1950s Lamming wrote:

> The West Indian novel, by which I mean the novel written by the West Indian about the West Indian reality[,] is hardly twenty years old. . . . The education of all these writers is more or less middle-class Western culture, and particularly English culture. But the substance of their books, the general motives and directions, are peasant. . . .
>
> Unlike the previous governments and departments of educators, unlike the businessman importing commodities, the West Indian novelist did not look out across the sea to another source. He looked in and down at what had traditionally been ignored. For the first time the West Indian peasant became other than a cheap source of labour. . . . It is the West Indian novel that has restored the West Indian peasant to his true and original status of personality. (*Pleasures*, 38–39)

Gordon Rohlehr qualifies Lamming's position, pointing out that human agency and a history of struggle had been important features of the Caribbean peasantry for centuries:

> It is . . . possible to see the West Indian peasantry as less passive, inert and invisible than Lamming seems to believe they were before the advent of the West Indian novelist. . . . Long before the novelist had even acknowledged his existence the peasant had been working steadily and against tremendous odds, towards an essential independence. The presence and "living existence" of the peasant found its earliest incarnation not in literature, as Lamming claims, but in what the peasant . . . had, without benefit of middle class intellect, been able to build for himself. . . . [It is] the efforts of the West Indian people as a whole which provided a dynamic powerful enough to charge the writers of the fifties. The writers expressed an awareness which had been there for

some time, and on various levels; *reflecting* rather than *restoring* whatever finer quality had been immemorially there in the creative struggle, rebellion and movement of the West Indian people. (*Strangled City,* 54–55)

If the "shock and revelation" of the labor and social revolts in the West Indies brought an awareness of the need for political changes, World War II also played a decisive role in the movement toward constitutional decolonization. Caribbean political scientist Trevor Munroe notes that though "cracks in the British colonial system were clearly visible" in September 1939, the war

> was decisive in opening these fractures beyond the point of mending. Pressure on the colonial system became irresistible. . . . The war effort against fascism in Europe, the struggle for freedom and equality in Europe was in a sense identical with the anticolonial struggle. . . . Finally, the course of the war itself exploded a number of ideological myths which had helped hold together the old imperial structure. In particular, the fall of Singapore meant the crash of the illusions of British military invincibility in the face of "native" arms and of colonial loyalty to the empire in hours of crisis. (*Politics,* 28)

In 1939, when the Second World War began, the classic work of the Negritude movement, Aimé Césaire's *Return to My Native Land*, appeared. That year also marked the appearance of Jean Rhys's *Good Morning, Midnight*. The years from 1939 to 1966 have been referred to as the period of Rhys's "silence" and her "rediscovery." However, during the 1940s Rhys continued to write. By 1945 she had written a second book of short stories, *The Sound of the River*, which did not find a publisher. Some of the stories were published in the sixties and seventies. At that time as well, she was halfway through a novel, an early version of *Wide Sargasso Sea*. She also wrote poetry. Despite difficult personal circumstances and the lack of publication of her work, Rhys did write some and read extensively during her "silent" period. The personal and professional difficulties that she experienced are undoubtedly critical and offer important insights in understanding the shape of her writing career.

But the historical conjuncture of Jean Rhys's silence with the eruption of anticolonial politics and literature within the Caribbean and throughout the world must be considered in order to understand questions of her identity, her "place," and the structures of her fiction. Jean Rhys's locational identity, a West Indian Creole, which made possible her subjective identity as colonial, woman, and Outsider in the metropolitan context, drew its meaning from the political fact of colonialism. When Jean Rhys reemerges as a writer in 1966, the world has changed in profound ways. The writing of West Indian, African, and other anticolonial writers has altered permanently the landscape of "English literature." In the decade 1948–58, as George Lamming notes, "a dozen or so novelists in the British Caribbean [produced] some fifty books to their credit or disgrace" (*Pleasures*, 29).[7] In that same year, the influential Caribbean Artists Movement was formed in England. John La Rose also started a new publishing house in London, New Beacon, using as his company's "ancestor and inspiration" the *Beacon* of 1930s Trinidad. Political and social upheavals have destroyed the structures of colonialism, and several of the West Indian nations have gained or are moving toward constitutional and cultural independence. It is impossible that these political, social, and cultural conditions would not have affected significantly the structure of Rhys's fiction, her writing in general, and her perception and articulation of her identity and place. It is within this historical context that Jean Rhys's "difference" is intelligible.

The Creole and West Indian Writing

The question of Jean Rhys's place is most provocatively posed by Caribbean writer and scholar Jean D'Costa:

> Critics at three corners of the triangular trade lay claim to Jean Rhys. In England scholars read her as "British woman writer," painter of grim urban settings and social subtypes, catching time, place, mood, and the values that upheld a fading imperial world: England after Victoria, before Hitler. To American critics her work speaks mostly of woman-as-victim, although they recognize her insight into British society. In the Caribbean Rhys is the exponent of the "terrified consciousness" . . . of the ruling class. For all three groups, Rhys presents problems of classification which disguise problems of interpretation and acceptance. How can the author of "Let Them Call It Jazz," the creator of Christophine, and the satirizer of Hester Morgan be sincerely British? It is permissible to mock from within, but surely not to stand outside wanting to be Black, hating "being white and getting like Hester" [in *Voyage in the Dark*],

hating the faces "like . . . blind rabbit[s]"; . . . faces "the colour of wood-lice." Then, too, Rhys is not Everywoman's feminist: the Rhys heroine is devoured as greedily by other women as by men. Caribbean readers, more concerned with class, race, and history than with the politics of sex and gender, may well question the significance of Mr. Mackenzie, or of René the gigolo. ("Jean Rhys," 390)

Within the Caribbean, the period of Rhys's reemergence, the decades of the 1960s and 1970s, formed a crucial moment in the evolution of regional / nationalist culture and politics. As in the 1930s, the political and social currents were inseparable from the artistic and intellectual. Cultural and political struggles were being waged in terms of the trinity of "identity, race and protest," most starkly manifested in the Black Power movements and a more visible emergence of Rastafarianism (Nettleford, *Mirror, Mirror*). Kamau Brathwaite's seminal article "The Love Axe / 1: Developing a Caribbean Aesthetic 1962–1974" records some of the activities of the period. One crucial event was the expulsion from Jamaica of the historian Walter Rodney, author of the well-known work *How Europe Underdeveloped Africa* (1972). Another was the occupation of the Creative Arts Center of the University of the West Indies in Jamaica by a "group of students demanding the Westindianization of the cultural events at the Centre and greater student participation in and control of its administration." Yet another was the explosion of grassroots artistic and intellectual output as well as the February Revolution in Trinidad (23–24).

Debates about West Indian politics, culture, and literature flourished in journals, little magazines, student publications, and newspapers. What Brathwaite justly describes as "one of our great critical landmarks: a major essai into literary *ideas*, and the first to be written *in* the West Indies" (27), Sylvia Wynter's "Reflections on West Indian Writing and Criticism," appeared in the *Jamaica Journal* in 1968 and 1969. Gordon Rohlehr engaged in a cultural critique that established an aesthetic link between "folk" forms and "art" forms, as demonstrated in the title of such works as "The Calypso as Rebellion" (1970) and "Calypso and Politics" (1971). That period also saw the appearance of works by writers and critics such as Orlando Patterson (*Children of Sisyphus*, 1964), Wilson Harris (*Tradition, the Writer, and Society*, 1967), Louis James (*The Islands in Between*, 1968), Kenneth

Ramchand (*The West Indian Novel and Its Background*, 1970), among other foundational texts.

In concluding his historical assessment of the period, Brathwaite observes:

> We must recognize that our literature began on the slave plantation with imitation Euro-writing by Europeans and white creoles on the one hand, and the often unremembered sound-poems, stories and religious litanies of the slaves, on the other; that after slavery (c. 1838–1938) we entered the slough of colonial despond when very little creative work was produced among the literate and the existent folk culture was attacked/submerged. . . . The anticolonial consciousness of the period from 1900 produced our first authentic novels and witnessed the beginning of native newspaper work and publishing. The period of national consciousness marked by the publication of . . . V. S. Reid's novel, *New Day* . . . saw what is now regarded as the "Renaissance" of the West Indian writing, with over 100 novels appearing in print between 1950 and 1965. (32)

One of the central figures omitted from Brathwaite's account of this period is himself. His body of work as historian, cultural critic, poet, and founding member of the London-based Caribbean Artists Movement remains one of the most influential in Caribbean and postcolonial studies. His response to Wally Look Lai's reading of *Wide Sargasso Sea*, which established the terms of the debate about Rhys's place, must be read within the context that I have briefly outlined. An equally important context consists of the historical, sociological, and anthropological debates in the 1960s and 1970s about creolization, plantation society, and cultural pluralism in the Caribbean. Brathwaite himself is a central figure in this debate, which falls outside the scope of this study.[8]

It is within this confluence of intellectual, cultural, and political thought that Wally Look Lai's groundbreaking analysis of *Wide Sargasso Sea* makes a persuasive claim for its inclusion in the literary production of the West Indies:

> It is tempting . . . to construe *Wide Sargasso Sea* as simply a triumphant restatement of an old preoccupation, placed in a different social con-

text and presented with a greater complexity and sophistication. It is precisely this reading, however, which may have been responsible for the West Indian critic's reluctance to accept this novel as having any major relevance to West Indian life and experience, since on this interpretation there would be no real break between this novel and the earlier ones, and the West Indian social setting would be reduced to being a mere incidental background to the working out of an established concern with rejected womanhood. But . . . the real greatness of this novel lies . . . in the way [Rhys] made use of this theme in order to convey a totally different reading of experience. . . . It is with this more fundamental reading that we are concerned, for this is what constitutes the essentially West Indian nature of the novel. The West Indian setting, far from being incidental, is central to the novel; it is not that it provides a mere background to the theme of rejected womanhood, but rather that the theme of rejected womanhood is utilised symbolically in order to make an artistic statement about West Indian society, and about an aspect of the West Indian experience. ("Road," 18–19)

In response to Look Lai's observations, Brathwaite asserts that "we cannot begin to understand statements about 'West Indian culture,' since it is so diverse and has so many subtly different orientations and interpretations, unless we know something about the speaker/writer's own sociocultural background and orientation" (*Contradictory Omens*, 33). Embedded in the term "socio-cultural background and orientation" is the question of race. Look Lai is a West Indian of Asian ancestry, Rhys, European, and Brathwaite, African. Brathwaite argues that the "friendship" between Tia and Antoinette (the central act of mirroring that is so crucial to the structure of *Wide Sargasso Sea*) could never have existed because of the ways in which the white/European subjectivity in the West Indies has been historically constructed over and against that of the black Other/African. With respect to the ending of the novel (when Antoinette jumps from the burning house to Tia as a mirror image), Brathwaite notes,

The "jump" here is a jump to death; so that Antoinette wakes to death, not to life; for life would have meant dreaming in the reality of madness in a cold castle in England. But death was also her allegiance to the carefully detailed exotic fantasy of the West Indies. In fact, neither world is "real." They exist inside the head. Tia was not and never could have been her friend. No matter what Jean Rhys might have made Antoinette think, Tia was historically separated from her by this kind of paralogue:

"There is, I must confess, an involuntary feeling apparently implanted in the breasts of white men by nature herself, that black men are a race distinct and inferior to those whom providence has blessed with a fair complexion. This distinction of colour forms, indeed, such an impassable boundary between these two races of mankind, that it would seem to countenance the general supposition that Providence, in the wise dispensation of earthly affairs, has formed them to be hewers of wood and drawers of water to those of the favoured caste distinguished by complexions less dark." (36)

Brathwaite's critique clarifies the vital link between the use of characterization in Rhys's novel and the European colonialist discourse that invents subjectivities for black and white West Indians. It seems true to say that Rhys's is a Creole perspective which articulates the political values and the emotional and psychological investments embodied in this colonialist discourse. The ground of authority that empowers her writing is the social, political, and historical existence of colonialism and the colonialist/colonizing discourses, which remain even when the political structures have been removed. The "black people" of the Caribbean are, more often than not, recruited into the engendering of the Creole subjectivity. There is much in Rhys's writing to support this. As Rhys herself says, the position that her fiction or a character articulates is not necessarily hers. Yet if her own thinking is different from that of her texts and "characters," there are certain recurrent attitudes: the mulatto woman is often tragic, victimized, sometimes beautiful, and often silent. This is unlike the white female characters, who always resist at some level and who are never silent. The maids are always dark-skinned and are either very "good" (that is, loyal, loving, selfless, black mammy types) or very "bad" (indifferent, resentful, or hostile to the Creole). Black and mixed-raced people do not exist autonomously. The forms of (Creole) selfhood that Rhys's writing elaborates are racially inflected. The profoundly racialized, even racist, structure of her imagination insistently reveals itself in her use of West Indian "black people" as props to the Creole identity and as cultural objects.

My major point of disagreement with Brathwaite is that he sees *Wide Sargasso Sea* as "a fictional statement that ignores vast areas of social and historical formation. . . . White Creoles in the English and French West Indies have separated themselves by too wide a gulf . . . to give credence to the notion that they can, given the present structure, meaningfully identify or be identified with the spiritual world on this side of the Sargasso Sea" (38).[9] Yet, in terms of his writing as a whole, Brathwaite's position on white West Indians is more ambivalent than it may first appear. In *Roots* he notes: "When most of us speak of 'the West Indian,' we think of someone of African descent. When we think of 'West Indian problems,' 'the West Indian situation,' we are thinking of certain problems and a certain kind of situation which relate to a more or less easily identifiable majority group, sharing, at least, a common history of slavery. There are of course 'white people' in the West Indies, but these are regarded as either too far apart to count or *too inextricably mixed into the whole problem to be considered as separate*" (40; emphasis added).

It is the "inextricable" link that my study seeks to examine. Far from ignoring social and historical formation or separating herself, Jean Rhys's writing demonstrates that the "identity" of the Creole is made of the sociohistorical, discursive fabric of the colonial West Indies. The articulation of the Creole subjectivity is at one and the same time a discursive self-destruction articulated within the historical specificity of racialized slavery in the Caribbean. Rhys does not have a choice. One of the achievements of her fiction is that, as Brathwaite does in the excerpt quoted above, it calls attention to and opens up for examination the historical and discursive processes by which the white Self in the Caribbean is constructed over and against that of the black Other. It is even conceivable that Rhys's unpacking of that which constrains and contains racialized subjectivities in relations of dominance and parasitism functions as an indictment of that colonialist discourse, which is also called History. Her self-consciousness displays a critical awareness. I do not mean to suggest that this critical self-consciousness allows her to "transcend" the assumptions of this discourse to become antiracist or pro-black. Is this possible? My own position is that there is in all of Rhys's writing a knotted dialectic tension between the ontological negation/appropriation of "black people" and a formidably critical intelligence that understands and analyzes the constructed nature of the colonialist discourse that passes itself off as natural and transparent. This tension underwrites her fiction, in particular, in subtle, ironic, and fruitful ways. Her fiction also shows an understanding of the discrete but interconnected character of all forms of oppression.

In my analysis of *Wide Sargasso Sea*, I shall attempt to show that the structure of the novel and Rhys's own observations demonstrate that part of Brathwaite's position is not far removed from that of the author and her text. However, I shall argue that instead of weakening the credibility of the work, both the deployment and the unmasking of the colonialist discourse help to forge Jean Rhys's "truth."

If, in the 1960s, the sociopolitical struggles helped to shape critical response to Jean Rhys in the Caribbean, these events and the presence in England of West Indian writers decisively shaped her own perception of the West Indies and her writing. In terms of her nonfiction utterances, especially her letters and interviews, Rhys often displays a sense of antagonism, though not separation, with respect to the political and discursive events of the West Indies of that period. Although there has been a tendency to divide Rhys's writing into West Indian and non–West Indian, it is true to say that the West Indies is ever present in all her writing from 1927 to 1979, sometimes in overt, sometimes in occluded ways. From *The Left Bank* to *Smile Please*, Jean Rhys writes her West Indies in overt thematizing and allusions, ruptures, uses of songs and creoles, hidden and explicit historical referents, and the density of local and recognizable Dominican place names like Roseau, Rosalie, and La Plana/La Plaine often used to identify characters. The "black people," who are *objects* in Rhys's discourse, have become the *subjects* of the works written by post-1940s West Indian writers. Several of these and subsequent texts, most notably George Lamming's *In the Castle of My Skin*, were to rewrite the history of the West Indies from the position of the formerly silenced Others and to implicate, in the process, the complicity of the ruling class of white Creoles.

In 1960 Rhys refers to "West Indian"—the quotations marks are important—"people" whom she had not then read (*Letters*, 197).[10] The presence in England of the second generation of Caribbean writers—African, Asian, and mixed-race—*and their very identities as writers* would necessarily and radically expose the scaffolding that supported the Creole's discursive construction of the West Indies, a scaffolding whose material and design were made of the appropriated voices and identities of West Indian people of non-European or mixed ancestry. The emergence of these writers and the anticolonial thrust of their writing destabilize Rhys's sense of place. Her quotation marks emphasize that it is her own positionality as a "West Indian" writer that is now being called into question. The hitherto (apparently) inert material that structured the Creole's discourse has shifted.

Increasingly, Rhys's letters and interviews from the late 1950s to the 1970s return obsessively to the "ingratitude of black people." She observes: "I made up my mind to go back to live [in Dominica], but I was put off, after corresponding, by the turns things have taken there. I grew up with feelings of being surrounded by alien people, but I liked many of them. Now they say that the English are devils, though their culture is derived from English culture; the horrors of slavery are constantly referred to but they leave out all the good" (Thomas, 31). Rhys's invocation of the time-honored trope of the "ungrateful negro" coincides with the period in which hitherto silenced Caribbean groups are making themselves heard. Her complaint is an indication that such an action poses a threat to the Creole subjectivity whose identity derived in large part from a recruitment of the silenced, degraded black/mulatto Other into her own self-engendering.

Rhys's letters of the period also demonstrate an insistent desire to seek legitimacy for the articulation of the West Indian world from the Creole's perspective. In a letter to Francis Wyndham on 14 May 1964, she notes, "The place I have called Coulibri *existed*, and still does. It is now owned by a Syrian. . . . (I'm not making this up—it's true)" (*Letters*, 276). Rhys's concern with *her* "true" aesthetic portrayal of the West Indies is also seen in a March 1957 letter to Selma Vaz Dias: "I did a nonsense called *English Harbour* to calm myself. It's not quite nonsense as it is based on an old story about English Harbour in Antigua (partly true certainly). Nelson's headquarters where he was stationed in the West Indies. It's supposed to be haunted and the whole affair was dramatic—romantic and so on. . . . I've written it as a film script because that's the way I see it. . . . I don't believe anybody has the 'feel' of the West Indies as they were in the 17th 18th and part of 19th century at all. Should say perhaps the 18th, 19th and part of twentieth" (144).

In a letter to Morchard Bishop dated 7 April 1953, Rhys notes: "I've spent much time lately trying to persuade a cousin of mine, also a West Indian, that she can write creole songs and calypsos better than anyone I've struck" (*Letters*, 106). In another letter to Selma Vaz Dias that same year, Rhys suggested that these songs be published and argued for their authenticity. In addition, apparently in response to a query from Vaz Dias, she emphasizes the distinction between West Indian Creoles and "negroes":

> Please have a look at them and consider them and *please* believe me that they have an authentic ring about them which isn't too easy to get hold of, though the ersatz are cheap. . . . Surely *somebody* will see the difference.
>
> There is a sort of charm about the . . . West Indies as a whole and no other has got hold of it yet. It would be new.
>
> It isn't Noel Coward's Jamaica or Katherine Dunham's Martinique — It just has not been done or even attempted.
>
> I do think Lily might come very near it for it's in her blood. Her family have been in the West Indies for something like three hundred years. (All Creoles are not negroes. *On the contrary*). (108)

In her later years Rhys recorded some "creole songs" that she remembered from her childhood in Dominica (Jean Rhys Collection). She also worked hard to assist a fellow West Indian Creole, Eliot Bliss, in getting her work, *Luminous Isle*, republished. It was subsequently published in 1984.

In the United States and Britain perhaps the best-known commentary on Rhys's inscription of the "native" is that of Gayatri Spivak. With respect to the character of Christophine in *Wide Sargasso Sea*, Spivak observes:

> Christophine is tangential to this narrative. She cannot be contained by a novel which rewrites a canonical English text within the European novelistic tradition in the interest of the white Creole rather than the native. No perspective *critical* of imperialism can turn the Other into a self, because the project of imperialism has always already historically refracted what might have been the absolutely Other into a domesticated Other that consolidates the Imperialist self. . . . Of course, we cannot know Jean Rhys' feelings in the matter. We can, however, look at the scene of Christophine's inscription in the text. Immediately after the exchange between her and the Man, well before the conclusion, she is simply driven out of the story, with neither narrative nor characterological explanation or justice. ("Three Women's Texts," 272)

As it happens, we do know Rhys's "feelings in the matter." In a letter to Diana Athill dated 14 April 1964, Rhys states that Christophine was conceived primarily to fulfill the role of the obeah woman: "From the start it must be made clear that Christophine is 'an obeah woman'" (*Letters*, 262). In another letter to Athill on 20 February 1966, Rhys also points to a major flaw of her almost finished text: "The most seriously wrong thing with Part II is that I've made the obeah woman, the nurse, too articulate. I thought of cutting it a bit, I will if you like, but after all no one will notice. Besides there is no reason why one particular negro woman shouldn't be articulate enough, especially as she's spent most of her life in a white household." (297)[11]

The writer's emphasis on Christophine being "too articulate" is crucial since it is precisely the silence imposed on the West Indian Creole by Brontë that Rhys most fiercely attacks in *Jane Eyre* (see Chapter 2 of this study). There is a striking parallel between what Rhys sees as Brontë's dehumanization of the West Indian Creole and her own implicit assumption that the access of the "negro woman" to language and its articulation is a function of her intimacy with the white world. Yet, as a reader, Rhys's critique of her text suggests an awareness that, despite her intention to make this "character" merely instrumental, Christophine "produces effects incongruous with its social position and moments of vision incongruous with literary functionality" (Robbins, *Servant's Hand*, xi). It is also a measure of Rhys's insights as reader that she critiques her own writing for producing effects for which her own historical and political positioning cannot account. She observes in an interview with Mary Cantwell that "sometimes, a character will run away from me . . . and get more important than I intended" ("Conversation," 208).

As Spivak says, Christophine is "the first interpreter and named speaking subject" ("Three Women's Texts," 271). And in her exchange with the nameless husband prior to her being "driven out," Christophine *through the narrative structure* effectively gains access to the husband's thoughts and feelings and articulates them (*WSS*, 152–59). This textual strategy inverts one of the classic tropes of colonialist discourse, that of the imperial I/eye who positions, explains, and speaks for the "native." Further, as Benita Parry argues, "Christophine's defiance is not enacted in a small and circumscribed space appropriated within the lines of [the] dominant code, but is a stance from which she delivers a frontal assault against antagonists, and as such constitutes a counter-discourse ("Problems," 38). It seems to me that Parry is right to suggest that the subaltern can speak. But it is also true that Christophine is constructed according to the stereotypes of black promiscuity and the black mammy who privileges the white child over her own. In short, there are several points in the novel at which Christophine is put back in her "place."

The unspoken problematic underlying all the foregoing debates is the profoundly ideological and political question of reading and writing (that is, the discursive construction of) the West Indies and the ground that authorizes or validates its construction. When Jean Rhys writes to her editor in England in 1966 that no one will notice the textual and narrative problems posed by the too-articulate "negro" servant, she takes as given a certain kind of readership, which does not include people like the West Indian and Third World critics cited, or myself. Rhys's writing in England and Europe was *for* a metropolitan readership, and it engaged in a dual relation of participation and opposition in terms of the dominant Euro-centric discourse.

The White English Race and the Black White West Indian

The Creole writer's dual relation to metropolitan discourse is an analogue of the dually located character of the West Indian plantocracy in terms of the imperial center and the periphery. Europeans born or living in the West Indies, educated to conceive of England as "home," they were also culturally marked and excluded as inferior colonials. At the same time, they were racially and institutionally privileged in relation to the African people who existed as bound labor and subalterns. The white West Indian forms the intermediate category between the metropolitan subject and the "native" West Indian. Jean Rhys's self-fashioning is constructed both in terms of a dual relation to Europe and Eurocentric discourses and through the recruitment of the silenced or degraded "natives" as parts of her identity. Toward the metropolitan Subject, the Creole often articulates a position of liminality and a poetics of *ressentiment*. Toward the West Indian mulatto and black Others, the Creole demonstrates a sense of proprietorship that allows for the appropriation and recruitment of "race" as an accessory of power and a trope of otherness. This is most clearly articulated in an unpublished, undated essay entitled "The Bible Is Modern" (the handwriting suggests Rhys's later years):

God said, "Let there be Light and there was Light." There is something short, snappy and utterly modern about this sentence. You have only got to alter "God said" to "Said God," put a stop in the middle, and you could almost call it a quotation from the newest, starkest American novel.

The real English of this obviously is "In His great wisdom the Deity commanded that the firmament should be illuminated, and it was amply illuminated." Or you might say excessively, putting in the fantastic touch, "Allah, bestriding the universe with the sun in his right hand and the moon in the left, uttered these words to his chief attendant Gabriel, 'The constellations and the orbs shall march in their places.' So saying, he flung the sun and the moon into the firmament. Gabriel, obedient but disapproving stamped his foot, and there were the stars. Behold the earth and all the angels."

Instead of this, you get the stark, modern touch—"Let there be Light, and there was Light." In this marvellous Book, the Bible—which I am sure you have yet to discover—there are many such stories expressed in the modern manner. And, though it is obvious that the significance of this manner is entirely dependent on the intensity of feeling let us remember that we are dealing with primitive people who express themselves in the primitive way. These people are an Oriental people who have never learned to keep a stiff upper lip.

So buy the Bible. More modern than you know. . . .

You cannot understand it, unless you understand the English social system. It is a great crime to feel intensely about anything in England, because if the average Englishman felt intensely about anything, England as it is could not exist; or, certainly, the ruling class in England could not exist.

Thus you get the full force of a very efficient propaganda machine turned on the average Englishman from the cradle to the grave, warning him that feeling intensely about anything is a quality of the subject peoples or that it is old-fashioned, or that it is not done, or something like that.

The idea that books written in short, simple sentences depending for their effectiveness on the intensity of feeling of the author, are inferior books, follows automatically, because the whole solidarity of the English social system is extraordinary. It is based on the idea that the poor Englishman must not think very much, they certainly must never feel, and as for expressing their feelings—Never . . . When you think of the mentality of the average Englishman, all this is understandable. But then what is difficult for us black people [*sic*] to understand is the ingenious way they set about making money out of "God Said 'Let there be Light' and there was Light." (Jean Rhys Collection)

"The Bible Is Modern" clearly articulates the *ressentiment* of the Creole toward the metropolitan subject. Yet it goes beyond that to examine the interlocking formations of hierarchies based on imperialism, class, and "race" and the ideologies that legitimize literary and cultural productions. It also demonstrates that the construction of the domestic subject, the "Englishman," by strategies of differentiation, "us" and "them," is crucial to the imperialist project. The Rhys essay deconstructs the "authentic" Englishman and exposes its dependence on the strategies of othering of the "primitive" people and of the coercion of the nonelite domestic subject. It argues that the manipulation of the perceptual and psychological apparatus of the "Englishman" is designed to maintain the power and privilege of the ruling class. Benita Parry notes: "Through its network of cultural affirmations and denigrations, imperialist discourse offered to the English an imaginary mapping of their situation within the domestic social formation and of their relationship to the peripheries, and it did so in a language of social inclusiveness" ("Problems," 53).

Rhys's analysis of this "efficient propaganda machine" further lays bare the relationship between socioeconomic and discursive structures. The oppression of the domestic subject, the denigration of the "primitive" people, and methods of writing that naturalize or mystify these power relations are part of the "extraordinary solidarity" of the English social system. Therefore, "books written in short, simple sentences depending for their effectiveness on the intensity of feeling of the author" iterate the politics of Jean Rhys's writing practices. Her radical portrayal of the interlocking of social and discursive orders, her analysis of "race" as a social and cultural category and as a trope of power and resistance represent a critique of "Englishness" and its assumptions about individual, social, national, and racial character.

The crucial last paragraph engages with the British episteme at the point of its deepest contradiction: imperial imposition is achieved and remains in place by its dependence on its Others and through the manipulation of a Judeo-Christian ethic in the service of imperialist economic expansion. Rhys's appropriation of the term "black people" as political and ideological identification demystifies the constructed nature of whiteness and polemically embraces its other side, "blackness," as a site of creativity and resistance. Here Rhys's theory also shows affinities with white Creoles and mulattoes of the Spanish-speaking Caribbean. As Kamau Brathwaite notes, "The literary expression which came out of these white creoles (and mulattoes) was black based; they recognized that the only form of expression which could be used as a protest, or an authentic *alter / native* . . . was ex-African" (*Roots*, 209).

The Creole's Gender Identity

Among metropolitan critics, especially within the United States in the 1970s and 1980s, Jean Rhys is discussed primarily as a "woman writer." The privileging of the gendered identity sometimes relegates the West Indies and the "natives" to background, local color, emblems of Rhys's pathological psychology, and props. My concern with gender in this study rests on two central points. The first and more important is that Rhys's writing of a gender identity is based on a Creole identity and cannot be separated from the meanings of the "racial," historical, and sociolocational identities of the white West Indian. British critic Jane Miller says: "It took writers . . . who had grown up as colonials and become immigrants, to see that their situation as women, and the possibilities of change, could not be addressed outside an understanding of the effects of a class society, imperialism and racism on all forms of human relations. . . . To propose alternative ways for women to live their lives inevitably meant confronting class, race and economics" (*Women*, 209). Although this position is by no means sustained throughout Rhys's writing, I shall analyze in subsequent chapters some of the ways in which it is explored in her fiction. I shall also examine "the other side"—the usurpation of "race"/blackness in the service of gender.

My second point is that Rhys's writing, far from providing case studies of isolated, pathetic victims based on her personal experiences, scrutinizes the construction of gender in carefully detailed ways. Her analysis of gender is based on a critique of the social and discursive systems of power; and it shows clear links to the writing of her contemporaries. Her precursors, near contemporaries, and contemporaries include Gertrude Stein, Dorothy Richardson, Edith Sitwell, Marianne Moore, Amy Lowell, Rebecca West, Christina Stead, Katherine Mansfield, and others. Rhys's writing demonstrates important similarities to many of these writers. The clearest connection is a preoccupation with one major "theme" — the denigration of women. In *The Tunnel* (1919), Dorothy Richardson's protagonist, Miriam, comes to the conclusion that "life is poisoned for women, at the very source." Miriam asserts this after she reads an insulting entry listed under "Woman" in the encyclopedia. Virginia Woolf, who reviewed Richardson's book, also uses the same concern in her essay *A Room of One's Own* (1929). Rhys's "I Spy a Stranger," written in the 1930s, intertextually invokes these two texts.

An example of Rhys's nonfictional analysis of gender politics survives in an unrevised essay most probably written in the 1930s. This piece is driven by Rhys's preoccupation with gender, misogyny, the British social system, and writing. It is important to note her belief that writing has a subversive potential. Resistance, she suggests, can be carried out through writing that exposes and opposes the political and social arrangements. But she notes that writers, too, are constrained by the dominant ideologies. It is during this middle period of her fiction writing, a period marked by intense political and social upheaval in England and Europe, that Rhys articulates her most trenchant criticisms of the construction of woman. The essay bears the title *"The Ant Civilization: The Kingdom of the Human Ants; Part of a Lecture Given When I Was Drunk from Sadness[:] Woman."* The self-mockery notwithstanding, the controlling metaphor of the essay points to a concern with more than private anguish:

All women are individuals and they resist as long as they are alive the process which makes them into the neuter — the ant female. Even in England with heredity and environment pressing on them they still unbearably resist (unbearably to the onlooker). There is nothing more [characteristic] of the British civilization than the unhappiness of the woman and [the] difference between the young woman and the older woman. The young woman is often beautiful and eager with a touching humility and charm longing [*sic*] — the older woman is drab spiteful cruel the unused force and tenderness in her turning sour as one looks.

All the literature of escape (murder) all the thunderings of the British God Almighty [can't] stop the process. You see it as you walk (if you have eyes) and it's more of an eyesore than the hideous anthills they call houses (again over and over and over) you think how can these girls grow into these women. But the process is inevitable in the ant civilization—for there is nothing more antagonistic than the love of woman for a man and man for a woman to the ant civilization. . . .

Love of woman exists under [sufferance] in England[.] [I]f it exists instinctively (as it must) . . . [b]ehold it is broken under a Niagara of Literature—I believe that if books were brave enough the repressive education would fail but nearly all English books and authors slavishly serve the ant civilization. Do not blame them too much for the Niagara of repression is also beating on them and breaking their hearts—To live or not to live there is the [question.]

In an ant civilization individual love is anathema antisocial. It must be so—A woman is something—is a thing to have children by and enrich the antheap. To love the woman herself is a sin the greatest sin in the English [calendar]. From this all ills come. To love the man himself an unheard of eccentricity. Only less thundered against because as woman is the weaker less antisocial and dangerous. It is ridiculed not thundered against and the fact that it hardly exists in England is an example of the power of ridicule. (Jean Rhys Papers, Add. MS 57858)

Writing (and) the Creole

The Self

My debt to the body of work, especially by West Indian and Third World writers, that I have cited in the previous sections is obvious and enormous. The point of departure for my study is an attempt to examine in the structures of Rhys's writing the linguistic and rhetorical operations that work upon the relationship between the self in/and writing. In addition I attempt to analyze her writing within a consideration of the historical contexts and discourses as well as her own theoretical postulates, which can be culled from her letters, draft manuscripts, journals, diaries, and her unfinished autobiography. My main task in this section is to uncover the implicit literary and cultural theories that are embedded, sometimes occluded, in Rhys's own writing.

If some critics insist that Rhys is apolitical, writing out her personal demons, the obvious "autobiographical" nature of her writing and many of her own utterances seem to support this. For example, the writer says: "If you want to write the truth . . . you must write about yourself. It must go out from yourself. I don't see what else you can do. I am the only real truth I know. . . . If you try and write the truth then it remains the truth for all time. If not, then the things around you change and your work becomes dated" ("Fated," 5). I shall focus on another such comment that appears, on first reading, to be unequivocal:

> I can't make things up, I can't invent. I have no imagination. I can't invent character. I don't think I know what character is. I just write about what happened. Not that my books are entirely my life—but almost. . . . *Though I guess the invention is in the writing.* (qtd. Plante, *Difficult Women*, 52; emphasis added)

I would like to examine at length the word "writing." Insinuating her theories within the Mallarmean concept of the Book and the tenets of the medieval encyclopedia or the medieval guild, Rhys does articulate a belief in the enterprise of writing as an uncanny, transhuman, transhistorical, impersonal, and implicitly repetitive structure: "All of writing is a huge lake. There are great rivers that feed the lake, like Tolstoy and Dostoevsky. And there are trickles, like Jean Rhys. All that matters is feeding the lake. I don't matter. The lake matters. You must keep feeding the lake. It is very important. Nothing else is important. . . . But you . . . should be taking from the lake before you can think of feeding it. You must dig your bucket in very deep. . . . What matters is the lake. And man's unconquerable mind" (qtd. Plante, "A Remembrance," 247).

In *Difficult Women*, Rhys says, "I'm a pen, nothing but a pen [in someone's hand]. . . . It's only then that I know I'm writing well. It's only then that I know my writing is true. Not really true, not as fact, but true as writing. . . . You're picked up like a pen, and when you're used up you're thrown away, ruthlessly, and someone else is picked up" (31). In a letter to Francis Wyndham on 21 July 1960, the author states: " I used to think that all writing should be anonymous. Was I so far wrong? A bit unfair perhaps, to past strivings" (*Letters*, 190). She also observes in a letter to Morchard Bishop on 5 March 1953: "I don't believe in the individual Writer so much as in Writing. It uses you and throws you away when you are not useful any longer. But it does not do this until you are useless and quite useless too. Meanwhile there is nothing to do but plod along line by line" (*Letters*, 103).

However, in that same letter to Bishop, Rhys insists that a writer can only write about herself. In referring to Georges Bernanos's injunction that one should write about oneself with "inflexible rigor," Rhys observes, "I know that 'parler de soi' is not supposed to be the proper thing to do. Not in England. And not now. . . . I feel so fiercely about that. No one knows anything but himself or herself. And that badly" (104).[12] She notes also that a writer is ineluctably shaped by her lived experiences: "Books and plays are written some time, some place, by some person affected by that time, that place, the clothes he sees and wears, other books, the air and the room and every damned thing. It *must* be so, and how can it be otherwise except his book is a copy?" (101).

If writing is simultaneously personal and transhuman, it is also a prod-uct(ion) of human and historical agency. The Book is written by class interests, by the history of imperialism and colonialism, by racial and gen-der hierarchies, by concepts of insider and outsider, and by notions of good and bad literature. The practice of writing is deeply imbricated with the social and material world and is (over)determined by that context: "People write to make money. They write what they're told to write and what they'll get paid for writing and what people expect to read. There never has been any other sort. There never will be" (Green Exercise Book, Jean Rhys Collection, 12). In a letter to Morchard Bishop on 27 January 1953, Rhys is unequivocal about what she sees as the social control and coer-cion that shape artistic production. Referring to Maupassant's *Boule de suif*, Rhys observes, "I very much doubt whether any story seriously glorifying the prostitute and showing up not one but several English housewives, to say nothing of two nuns! — their meanness, cant and spite — would be ac-cepted by the average editor or any editor" (*Letters*, 99–100).

The self of which Rhys writes is variously inscribed as a double, an ontological split, a shared identity, an absence, anonymous, drifting away from itself, splintered into mirror images. These inscriptions of subjec-tivity draw on the symbolist phenomenon of *dédoublement* and Mallarmé's "elocutionary disappearance." The self is also figured as tragic mulatto, emergent consciousness, history in human form. This rhetoric of self figu-ration in Rhys's work incorporates the historical and the social, the con-crete and the numinous, the impersonal and the personal in ways that accord with Benita Parry's definition of self-writing: "the project [which] reconceptualize[s] subjectivity as ineradicably historical, occupying a diversity of positions, the site of multiple and competing identities that are never given but always achieved through social processes.... [I]t [is] always psychically and ideologically constrained, yet constitutive as well as constituted, and therefore not the captive of ideological systems or the passive object of structural forces" ("Contradictions," 42).

Rewriting is the major technical and textual strategy in Rhys's work. It functions in two ways. First, she writes and rewrites the same "facts," using them in different contexts. By so doing, it seems to me, she quite literally writes (the) life out of them, turning the biographical facts into fictions and the fictions into her own provisional and partial "truths." Second, through quotations, allusions, and other forms of intertextuality, Rhys rewrites many of the topoi and texts of European discourse on the West Indies. Why? In order to write her self, she has to write through the constructions of selfhood assigned to her within prior and dominant discourses, to read her way through them. Like Caliban, Rhys recognizes that "his Art is of such pow'r" to shape and name her subjectivity and her place. In rewriting, she is simultaneously critiquing existing readings and producing new ones. As Julia Kristeva observes with respect to intertextual writing as a whole, "The author refuses to be an objective "witness" — possessor of a truth he symbolizes by the word — in order to inscribe himself as reader or listener, structuring his text through and across a permutation of *other* utterances. He does not so much *speak* as *decipher*. . . . [The writer's enunciation] admits the existence of an *other* (discourse) only to the extent that it makes it *its own*" (*Desire*, 46). Rewriting then becomes citation and testimony.

Repetition and rewriting as strategies of resistance are interwoven with the use of memory and the imagination. The "I" that is written in the Rhys texts is a site of exploration and a process of becoming. She insists on the importance of trusting one's own imagination and memory as a means of resisting the recolonization of the self: "At the end one is forced back — away from other people away from books away from trees flowers & grass back & *down*. They say madness that way to madness no the madness is to resist the most powerful. With this eye I see & no other. I cannot see with other people's eyes. With my own eyes I must see. I cannot help what I see" (Green Exercise Book, Jean Rhys Collection, n.p.). As Judith Kegan Gardiner acutely observes, Rhys "anchors the fiction in her own life not simply because she cannot see outside it, but because she must validate her rejection of prior literary views . . . by comparing them with her memory and experience" (*Empathy*, 22).

Rhys's use of the nominative pronoun "I" and its significance to her writing is worthy of closer examination. Emile Benveniste's important work, *Problems in General Linguistics*, reminds us that "habit easily makes us unaware of [the] profound difference between language as a system of signs and language assumed into use by the individual. . . . [I] exists only insofar as [it is] actualized in the instance of discourse" (220). This distinction is of profound importance in Jean Rhys's discourse. Some examples of her uses of the "I" demonstrate this:

> It is not I who hate it is they who hate me — I am trying trying — If I could write [of] the story of my love and their hate. I say I but it is not the I you mean — it is another I who is everybody. (Green Exercise Book, Jean Rhys Collection, n.p.)

> I do not agree that there's nothing to defend myself against — I do not agree that my way of looking at life and human beings is distorted. I think that the desire to be cruel and to hurt (with words because any other way might be dangerous to ourself) is part of human nature. . . . Everybody's trying to hurt first, to get in the dig that will make him or her feel superior, feel triumph. . . . But I do not admit that because I am badly adapted to these encounters I'm therefore a mental deformity. . . .

> The I in above paragraph was impersonal — will now return to the personal, the all important I. Me. I. I. I. (*Letters*, 30–31)

> [The short story] is not (repeat *not*) autobiography, and not to be taken seriously. But the people here are terribly narrow minded and they gossip like crazy. . . . For them "I" is "I" and not a literary device. Every *word* is autobiography! (187)

The "I" of Rhys's fiction is a "literary device." It is also based on the concept that "it is in myself. . . . All. Good, evil, love, hate, life, death, beauty, ugliness. *And in everyone?* I do not know 'everyone.' I only know myself" (*Smile Please*, 161). The writing of the "I" is a performative gesture: "It's hard to explain how, when and where a fact becomes a book. I start to write about something that has happened or is happening to me, but somehow or other things start changing. It's as if the book had taken possession" ("Conversation," 208). It is the *process* of the writing itself which invents.

If the "I" is a literary device and the writing process inventive, it could be argued that it is the thematics of Rhys's writing which support the reading that her books are "about" her "life." In much of her writing the focus is on gender, class, money, books, and history. Some recurrent concerns are with animal imagery, sleep, withdrawal, the body, sex, sexuality, food, mirrors, and money. Eating, drinking, sleeping, having sex, and interacting with or withdrawing from the world—the practices of everyday life exaggerated, amplified, distorted, muted, in her words, "cut to the bone." As Rhys herself notes, her focus on these is informed by a theory of writing as a process which extracts from the quotidian and the ordinary that which is extraordinary and reveals the extraordinary in the seemingly ordinary: "There are two ways of writing. One way is to try to write in an extraordinary way, the other in an ordinary way. Do you think it's possible to write in both ways? . . . [W]hat one should do is write in an ordinary way and make the writing seem extraordinary. One should write, too, about what is ordinary, and see the extraordinary behind it" (qtd. Plante, *Difficult Women*, 52).

I would now like to quote again the passage in which Rhys says that she cannot invent:

> I can't make things up, I can't invent. I have no imagination. I can't invent character. I don't think I know what character is. I just write about what happened. Not that my books are entirely my life—but almost. . . . *Though I guess the invention is in the writing.* (qtd. Plante, *Difficult Women*, 52; emphasis added)

The self that Jean Rhys writes/invents can be read as a site where narratives of empire; ideologies of race and gender, memory, and imagination; and theories of reading and writing are all structured interdependently and sometimes contradictorily.

Writing the Self

During a career spanning more than fifty years, Jean Rhys repeatedly insists on the centrality of writing to her life. But if "the invention is in the writing," the apparently autobiographical pieces, which I shall examine in the following sections, invite us to focus on their performative function rather than on a mimetic desire to authenticate a "life" or a personality. In discussing how she proceeds as a writer, Rhys insists that her major task consists of giving life shape and form: "The things you remember have no form. When you write about them, you have to give them a beginning, a middle, and an end. To give life shape—that is what a writer does. That is what is so difficult" (Vreeland, "Jean Rhys," 225). As her interviews and letters and the Jean Rhys Collection show, Rhys wrote multiple drafts of each piece of work, always aiming to make it simpler: "She reworks a chapter as many as ten times, aiming always to say something more simply and clearly than she first managed, and sometimes, for an exercise, she will take a piece of complicated writing and rephrase it in the simplest way ('nearly always you find it improved').... She still detests what she calls 'descriptive writing,' and in all innocence offers as a good example of admirable style the line: 'Let there be light. And there was light' " (Hall, "Jean Rhys," 8).

Rhys describes the effort of writing as trying to "torture the thing into shape" (Black Exercise Book, Jean Rhys Collection, n.p.) and to search for the *mot juste*: "I thought very hard of each word in itself" (qtd. Plante, *Difficult Women*, 53). This concern extends even to her published work. In a letter to Selma Vaz Dias dated 12 November 1956, with respect to the dramatization of *Good Morning, Midnight*, Rhys notes, "Please don't think me pernickety but every word must be exact" (*Letters*, 139). In writing to Francis Wyndham on 8 July 1959, she states, "I have noticed that the wrong details can spoil a story.... I am pretty sure that most people notice details *without knowing it*. Anything false and bang goes the illusion and perhaps they don't know why" (170). Before giving permission for the reprinting of her early works, Rhys insisted on making alterations. Of *Voyage in the Dark* she observes, "The revisions ... are small but important—making it a better book—for now 1964" (*Letters*, 279–80).

The text that I will examine in this section comprises several draft manuscripts of "Leaving School: How I Became a Novelist" (Jean Rhys Collection). The guide to the collection provides notes on each manuscript, which I shall paraphrase below. The first draft of the manuscript is undated but believed to be circa 1974. It is heavily marked and includes alternative versions of several passages. The second manuscript is closely written and very heavily revised. The opening few paragraphs differ completely from the first. The third manuscript, "Two Beginnings" of "Leaving School," is dated March 1974. Although closely related to the two previous manuscript versions, these openings show differences from both in many details. The fourth manuscript, dated 14 September 1974, is heavily revised, with approximately one hundred and ninety words in the author's hand and with further changes by the typist. The fifth, also dated 14 September 1974, incorporates the revisions made in the previous manuscript and includes a full-page insert and adds several hundred words. Further additions, deletions, and revisions are made. The sixth, an undated carbon typescript of twenty-three pages, is very heavily marked in the author's hand and includes fragments of drafts for *Wide Sargasso Sea*. The seventh is undated and heavily revised and contains indistinct elucidations in Jean Rhys's hand. Part of an early draft, later published as "Overtures and Beginners Please," and part of the short story "Kismet" have been worked into this draft (Jean Rhys Collection).

Even the briefest analysis of these manuscripts shows that the "autobiographical" text is worked upon, "is tortured into shape" by the same procedures that are used in the novels and short stories. The invention in the writing processes the "life" into a fictionalized biotext whose "truths" reside not in their factual nature but in the constitution of a self through a concern with place and writing, which are two of the central tropes of Rhys's work. The draft manuscripts help us to see the process by which "Jean Rhys" becomes the subject of her writing.

My reading will focus on the manuscript numbered 54, the "final" draft, because it incorporates many of concerns that are the focus of my study. Writing her departure from the West Indies, the narrator/"Jean Rhys" recollects the event through the discourse of the English Romantic poet Byron and suggests the effect that moving to England had on her writing endeavors: " 'I am going to England, what shall I find there, no matter what, not what I sought, said Byron, not what I sought or what I seek.' This was the last poem I was to write for a very long time" ("Leaving School," Jean Rhys Collection, n.p.).

The self is linked not only to the West Indies, England, and writing but also to appearance or exteriority, as symbolized by the dress: "I remember so well the day when I lost all belief in myself. Dreary silence and cold mean caution took over. It was when she [her aunt] bought the ugly dress instead of the pretty one. . . . I stared at myself in the long glass, pale, hollow eyed, lifeless as if I were thinking 'Now what has happened to that girl, that not at all bad girl who was wearing the red dress?' In the teashop she told me that what I looked like didn't matter. It's what you are that matters. I thought 'Yes, supposing I get to be what I look like in that horrible dress'" (n.p.). Memory and self-recollection are written as strategic interventions in common assumptions about gender construction and the concept of depth subjectivity.

This concern is linked explicitly to other forms of political and social control: "Then we were outside in the hostile street and into the hated bus squashed up against perfect strangers, such millions of strangers in this place and the wheels said 'And *when* we *say* we've *always* won, and *when* they ask us *how* it's done.' You wouldn't dare say how you do it, not straight out you wouldn't, it's too damn mean the way you do it" (n.p.). The reference to the hostile streets and the bus that crunches out a syncopated rhythm of domination in "this place" suggests an outsider's awareness of the way power is diffused and mechanized as part of everyday activities. The unidentified "you" suggests a mystification of the sources of control that construct insiders and outsiders and keep the Outsider subordinated and estranged.

"Leaving School" writes two beginnings of "Jean Rhys's" writing career. The first is written in the narrator's exchange with her aunt when she moves to England:

"I have always thought that you ought to write." "Write? Write what? Poetry?" "Oh no something you can try to sell." . . . I presented her with a short story. . . . "This sort of thing never happened when I was in the West Indies," she said. "But you weren't there very long, were you?" I answered. Sensibly enough I still think. "I'll send it to that magazine, you know the one that tells you your faults, if they don't like it." The story bounced back quick together with a long list of shortcomings. Number seven—No plot, number eleven—Plot very unlikely were both marked with a cross. (n.p.)

The story of the West Indies written by Jean Rhys and read by English readers has a plot that is at once nonexistent and unlikely. This inscription of the metropolitan readers' contradictory responses to Rhys's early efforts, produced in 1974, is emblematic of the author's reading of European/English commentary on her writing of the West Indies as she knows it.

The second beginning is connected to Ford Madox Ford, whom Rhys credits with being the single most important influence on her writing. Ford's roles as writer, mentor, editor, collaborator, and supporter of young talent is well documented. His credentials as reader, writer, and critic are formidable. Comments by his companion, Stella Bowen, seem to be widely endorsed by his contemporaries and by Ford scholars: "He gave [other artists] much of himself; patient perusal and brilliant criticism of their efforts. . . . He had no professional secrets and would take any aspiring writer behind the scenes and explain exactly how he got his effects" (*Drawn from Life*, 80). When Jean Rhys was introduced to Ford about 1923 or 1924, she was introduced to an impressive range of literary and cultural theories sifted through the mind not only of Ford himself but of many of the European writers who produced some of the major literary and artistic works of the late nineteenth and twentieth centuries. The roll call of contributors to Ford's *English Review* and his collaboration with Conrad, James, and others testify to the zeitgeist in which Rhys developed her craft as a writer. At the time of their meeting, Ford was working on his tetralogy *Parade's End*.

In "Leaving School," an elliptical, allusive style, a rejection of biographical exactness and referentiality, the suppression of names, and the use of unattributed dialogue inscribe Ford's contribution to Jean Rhys's aesthetics and craft. "I am going to send this to a man who will be very interested. He thinks that some of these expatriate writers in Montparnasse are very important" (n.p.). This inscription is juxtaposed with a disingenuous questioning of the narrator's place, nationality, and "identity" in relation to Europe and the "man":

> I thought, Am I an expatriate? Expatriate from where? So began several months of writing short stories and having them torn to pieces or praised for reasons I did not understand. "Don't be so glib. Don't do this. Do that. Or Don't take the slightest notice of what I say or what anybody says if you are certain in yourself. . . . [T]ranslate one of my books into French. It's very good practice." "I don't know French well enough to translate your book," I said. "Then try la Maison de Claudine into English. Bring me all you can do of the first chapter tomorrow." (n.p.)

In juxtaposing the question about her putative nationality with an impressionistic account of how she learned the techniques of writing from

Ford, the narrator/"Jean Rhys" clarifies the relationship of her self and her writing to metropolitan Europe's cultural forms, articulating the convergence of history, politics, and aesthetics. The rhetorical question ("Am I . . . where?") suggests Jean Rhys's own awareness that the dominant ideologies of early-twentieth-century Europe constructed the West Indies of that period as a "nothing" in terms of European politics and culture. As Ford himself noted, Jean Rhys as an apprentice retained strict control over his tutelage, refusing certain forms and procedures of European writing while choosing others. In her conversation with Mary Cantwell, Rhys says: "I think French books helped me an awful lot. . . . They had clarity. Ford insisted—if you weren't sure of a paragraph or statement, translate it into another language. And if it looks utterly silly, get rid of it. Anglo-Saxon is rather messy. . . . [I read] [c]ontemporary French novels. . . . And I loved Maupassant, Anatole France, Flaubert" (208).

Writing the History of the Creole

As my frequent references in the last section attest, some of the most useful records of Rhys's theories of writing and her concepts of selfhood may be found in David Plante's "Jean Rhys: A Remembrance" and *Difficult Women*. Although Plante's portrayal of the writer is often harsh, insensitive, and sometimes plain wrong, I believe that Rhys critics owe him a debt of gratitude for providing us with important documents with respect to her theories and ideas. The critic's two pieces come out of his work with Rhys on *Smile Please*, her unfinished autobiography; and as such they may be read as companion pieces to the Rhys text. Plante's contribution to Rhys's text as amanuensis or coauthor raises several interesting challenges because of his opinions about Rhys as reader and writer:

> To have argued with Jean about her opinions would have been mad: she simply would not have understood if one had said, "But . . . don't you wonder *why* you say that about women?" In terms of psychology (she said she had never read Adler, Jung, or Freud, didn't know what they were about, and didn't want to know) or social studies (she wouldn't have understood what a social study was), she never asked why her female

characters acted as they did: they just did, as she did. There is about them a great dark space in which they do not ask themselves, removing themselves from themselves to see themselves in the world in which they live: Why do I suffer? *When Jean said she delved and delved into herself, I didn't understand*; it was certainly not to question her happiness, or more, unhappiness, in terms of the world she lived in, and certainly not her prejudices. (*Difficult Women*, 40; emphasis added) [13]

On Rhys as a reader, Plante says: "She admitted, with no sign of great regret, that she hadn't read Balzac, Proust, Fielding, Trollope, George Eliot, James, Conrad, Joyce. . . . She said it was very important for a writer to have read a great deal at some time in his life. I presumed this was when she was a girl in Dominica. . . . She must have read when she started to write, though I am not sure what. She spoke very highly of Hemingway, and she knew many modern writers at least well enough to comment on them" (45). [14]

Plante's comments about working with Rhys on the actual writing of *Smile Please* are also very important: "I began to help her to sort out the months and years of her life. . . . The more we got into the chronology, the more muddled Jean became, until, her hands to the sides of her head, she said, 'I can't go on, I can't. This isn't the way I work.' We never again attempted to make a chronology (32). He also says: "I sorted [the manuscript] out. Each time I came back it was messed up again. I would put it in order, with clips" (46).

Sonia Orwell's letter to Plante offers useful insights into the Plante-Rhys collaboration:

> [Rhys] told me time and time again how impossible it was for one writer not to, quite unconsciously, alter or rewrite another writer. . . . [H]er terror [was] that two writers never have the same "voice" and that, without meaning to, *you were in fact writing her book for her in a way she wouldn't have written it herself. . . . I think this explains why she wanted to talk about* writing *so much with you, and why she . . . so enjoyed doing this and again, perhaps you don't realize her generosity in this, why she wanted . . . to help you. It also explains how hard it was for you to get her to do any long stint of work. Her terror of you writing her book would overcome her. . . . Yet she always wanted to give you something: an idea . . . some knowledge she just might have that you didn't.* (*Difficult Women*, 66; emphasis added)

With respect to the published version of *Smile Please*, the editors usefully indicate that only the first half was completed to Rhys's satisfaction. (My analysis will concentrate on that section for this reason and also because it focuses my reading of Jean Rhys as a Creole reader and writer.)

If *Smile Please* presents certain difficulties relating to authorship, its process of production, and its status as "unfinished," the published text clearly repudiates the linking of "facts" and chronology with self-recollection. In spite of or perhaps because of its antiautobiographical approach, it is a crucial text for understanding the historical locations of Rhys's reading and writing practices. As Hélène Cixous asserts, "Every writer, every artist, is brought at one moment or another to work on the genesis of his / her own artistic being" (Sellers, ed., *Writing Differences*, 15).

Some critics have produced important, historically inflected readings of Rhys's work that take into account her social positioning as a female member of a small, white, upper-class elite in a nineteenth-century British West Indian colony. Robin Visel, for example, analyzes the dilemma of the white colonial woman, observing that the "white-settler woman and her descendants occupy a privileged position in comparison to their darker native or slave-descended sisters. . . . [T]he white settler woman can best be described as half-colonized. Although she too is oppressed by white men and patriarchal structures, she shares in the power and guilt of the colonists ("Half-Colonization," 39).[15] Yet *Smile Please*, while inscribing the "history" of one colonial woman writer, also questions the notion that "race," class, and gender are givens, are things-in-themselves. The Rhys text reveals that the process of identification and self-narration is also the project to analyze elements of the social and cultural history that make "identity" radically impure.

There is in *Smile Please* a profound ambivalence toward history itself, which is simultaneously invoked and undermined. Historical vectors clearly demarcate a frame of representation: the narrative covers familial, social, colonial, and imperial history from the 1820s through the 1830s and 1840s. It moves to the 1930s, though the time is not specified, when Rhys returned briefly to the West Indies; and the section on the West Indies "ends" in 1907 — the year she left for England. This account is being written by Rhys in the 1970s, with the focus being on memory and reflection, combined with a sense of loss resulting from the dismantling of colonial structures and the cultural assertions of "Black Power." This historical trajectory—from the 1820s to the 1970s—covers the slave society, post-slavery, and postindependence Dominica (West Indies). There are implicit and overt comparisons between then and now, meaning colonial and postcolonial West Indies; us and them, meaning white and black West Indians. At the same time, certain textual operations reveal a questioning of this frame. These operations include the fracturing, elision, and interpenetration of different historical times, the dis(re)membering of names and dates, the uses of specularity, spatial fragmentation, the construction of shared identities, and the concern with forgetting. In short, there is a rewriting of history and the self that fractures a unitary frame. This structure of ambivalence, which marks much of Jean Rhys's writing, exposes the fiction of an autonomous self constituted prior to or as an effect of the historical, social, and discursive matrices. It demonstrates the always dialectical and mobile relationship between self and society as well as the linguistic and rhetorical operations that work upon this relationship.

The Self

My reading of *Smile Please* is heavily indebted to the theories articulated by Michel Beaujour in his *Poetics of the Literary Self-Portrait*, as Rhys's work seems to accord with his "literary self-portrait"—the self-portrait of a "writer qua writer," a book among books. In *Smile Please*, the titles of chapters, the patchwork effect, the spatialization of events, the use of place, and the taxonomy of the Dominican culture upon which the writing depends eclipse the individual life.

The opening scene warns the reader of the impossibility of writing and reading the self. The image of the child's photograph being taken writes the split subjectivity whose unity is endlessly deferred. The self that is posed/exposed is always already different, always already lost. This vignette can be read as the evocation of the myth of origins of the narrated self and the self narrator. It also raises and dispels notions of interiority or subjective depth.[16] The importance of time and displacement in Rhys's self-writing is then suggested through the reference to the child looking at her photograph at a later date: "It was about three years afterwards that . . . I . . . looked at the photograph attentively, realising with dismay that I wasn't like it any longer. I remembered the dress she was wearing, so much prettier than anything I had now, but the curls, the dimples surely belonged to somebody else. The eyes were a stranger's eyes. The forefinger of her right hand was raised as if in warning. . . . [S]he wasn't me any longer. It was the first time I was aware of time, change and the longing for the past. I was nine years of age" (19–20).

From the first moment of writing, the writer is already two. The finger raised as in warning may suggest: reader beware! "Painting oneself," suggests Beaujour, "perhaps is . . . an unstable and fleeting moment since the proposition inverts itself with the realization that the subject cannot paint himself and thus ends up in dispersal and in the effacement of the subject's predicates: what remains then is intransitive *writing* rather than a mimesis of the self" (336). The writer dooms herself simultaneously to displacement, absence, and death as the writing moves beyond individual memory and horizon to become a microscosm of the culture. In *Smile Please* Rhys's concern with the self is articulated through books, writing, "black people," and history.

Books

The second chapter, entitled "Books," inscribes the concern with meaning making and self making in Jean Rhys's reading and writing practices: "Before I could read, almost a baby, I imagined that God, this strange thing or person I heard about, was a book" (27). Any attempt to grasp the "meaning" of this statement and its relevance to Rhys's "life" seems to fail, to be incomplete, or to raise more questions than it answers. The utterance remains undecidable. However, were we to read her "autobiography" for what it suggests to us about Jean Rhys as reader and writer—her writing strategies, aesthetic theories, and ideological positions—this statement may be read "otherwise." The Book as God, as transcendental signified, the Alpha and Omega, the origin, meaning and end of the world, provides the framework and one of the motivating principles of Rhys's reading and writing practices. It is for this reason that intertexuality is the fundamental condition of her work.

The Book refers to the whole conglomeration of symbolic systems: the symbolic order. It comprises everything that is ordered as discourse and all the techniques of dissemination, communication, and interpretation. In particular, Rhys's work addresses reading in all its meanings, writing in all its processes and practices. The self is constituted by and constitutive of the universe of the Book. Reading "Jean Rhys," then, demands that we analyze not her "life" but Rhys as a sign within the Book, as a reader of the Book, and, equally important, as a writer whose work contributes to the Book. And we also need to question her positionality in terms of the Book—where she positions herself and why.

In this brief chapter, a page and a half, the narrator recalls her voracious reading habits as a child, listing titles of books that were present in her home: "*The Heroes, The Adventures of Ulysses, Perseus and Andromeda* . . . the Encyclopaedia Britannica that I never touched, a large Bible and several history books . . . novels . . . Milton, Byron . . . Crabbe, Cowper, Mrs. Hemans, also *Robinson Crusoe, Treasure Island, Gulliver's Travels, Pilgrim's Progress*" (27).

Almost all the important events of the narrator's "life" are told through reference to books. Texts, in short, shape the "life" of the narrator. Memories and recollections are also filtered through history-as-text and the presence of the past. She recalls the dining room of her home with the picture of Mary Queen of Scots going to her execution: "The crowd behind her was male, also dressed in black. I have often seen the narrow eyes, their self-satisfied expressions" (24). Childhood memories, applying makeup, learning about sex and life, observations about her mother, important family events, births and deaths—all are told through references to particular books, poems, plays, or magazines: "It is at Bona Vista that I have my first clear connected memory. . . . [M]y two brothers and elder sister were acting their version of Red Riding Hood" (23). "One of my most vivid memories of my mother—she was sitting under the Seville orange tree at Bona Vista stirring guava jam over a coal-pot with a wooden spoon in one hand and Marie Corelli's *The Sorrows of Satan* in the other" (36). The recollection of her Aunt Jeannette cites Omar Khayham's work and Fitzgerald's "bad translation" (70). The death of her paternal grandmother is recounted through books: "Her last present to me was a novel about Richard Brindley Sheridan and his love for Elizabeth Linley. . . . I suppose this was to let me know she realised I was growing up" (71). Recalling the birth of her younger sister, which shifted much of the attention away from her, the narrator observes, "I was alone except for books" (26). There are books about makeup: "Also several books warning us of the dangers of make-up. . . . Years afterwards, as I slap on make-up regardless, I think I am still defying those books"(37). "Knowledge" of England came from books: "I thought a great deal about England, not factually but what I had read about it" (63).

In the chapter entitled "The Facts of Life," unable to sort out the problems of "life," the narrator tells us that she becomes immersed in books:

"So as soon as I could I lost myself in the immense world of books, and tried to blot out the real world which was so puzzling to me. Even then I had a vague, persistent feeling that I'd always be lost in it, defeated. However books too were all about the same thing, I discovered, but in a different way. I could accept it in books and from books (fatally) I gradually got most of my ideas and beliefs" (62–63).

"Black People"

Meta, the bad black servant, first appears at the conclusion of the second chapter, which introduces the protagonist's relationship to European books. Meta dislikes the narrator and dislikes her even more with a book. The nurse warns her that reading will cause her to lose her sight. The next chapter, titled "Meta," begins, "Now it is time to talk about Meta, my nurse and the terror of my life. . . . [A] short, stocky woman, very black and always, I thought, in a bad temper. I never saw Meta smile. She always seemed to be brooding over some terrible, unforgettable wrong" (29). As Toni Morrison notes with respect to the deployment of an Africanist discourse, "The other side of nursing, the opposite of the helping, healing hand, is the figure of destruction . . . whose inhuman and indifferent impulses pose immediate danger" (*Playing*, 84).

It is significant that Meta's cruelty is not only physical and psychic but also discursive, as manifested in her lies and her storytelling practices, which offer a counterdiscourse to the European books: "It was Meta who talked so much about zombies, soucriants, and loups-garoux (werewolves). . . . She also taught me to fear cockroaches hysterically. . . . Even Meta's stories were tinged with fear and horror. They all ended like this: 'So I went to the wedding and they say to me What you doing here?' I say, 'I come to get something to eat and drink.' He give me one kick and I fly over the sea and come here to tell you this story" (30–31).

If the "very black" Meta and her stories inspire "terror," "fear," "horror," embedded in Meta, the bad nigger/nurse/storyteller, is its antithesis, the good nigger/nurse/storyteller Francine, whose "stories were quite different, full of jokes and laughter, descriptions of beautiful dresses and good things to eat. But the start was always a ceremony. Francine would say 'Tim-tim.' I had to answer 'Bois sêche,' then she'd say, 'Tablier Madame est derrière dos' (Madam's apron is back to front). She always insisted on this ceremony before starting a story and it wasn't until much later, when I was

64 : *History, Reading, Writing*

reading a book about obeah, that I discovered that 'Bois sêche' is one of the gods" (31). The narrator says that Francine disappeared from her life without saying a word and hurt her terribly. It was, however, Meta, whom she calls the "Black Devil," who damaged the narrator irreparably, scarring her for life with her lies, her stories, and her cruelty: "The damage had been done. Meta had shown me a world of fear and distrust, and I am still in that world" (32).

The rhetoric of the black Other as hateful and destructive and as good, loyal servant is contained by and in the knowledge of the white subjectivity. This "Africanist discourse," through which the narrated self disarticulates *and* re-members her "life" in the West Indies, punctuates the text. As Homi Bhabha points out, the white self is "tethered to . . . his dark reflection . . . that splits his presence, distorts his outline, breaches his boundaries . . . disturbs and divides the very time of his being. This ambivalent identification of the racist world . . . turns on the idea of man as his alienated image, not Self and Other but the Otherness of the Self inscribed in the perverse palimpsest of colonial identity" ("Interrogating Identity," 187).

In *Smile Please* the black Other occupies a wide range of discursive locations contingent upon the desires or the positions from which the narrated self speaks. One of the most interesting specular uses of the black Other is seen in the section called "My Mother": "Once I heard her say that black babies were prettier than white ones. Was this the reason I prayed so ardently to be black?" (42). Her mother, at the same time, objects to her handing out bread and money to a procession of men, who "were old and often not very well." This duty was insisted upon by her father. The narrator says, "One of them was very different from the others. He bowed, then walked away through the garden and out of the gate at the other end with the loaf under his arm, so straight and proud, I couldn't forget him afterwards" (44). The narrator later recalls an occasion when, observing her mother closely, she saw that she seemed obstinate and lonely: "From across the room I knew she was like someone else I remembered. I couldn't think who it was, at first. She was like the old man walking out of the gate with a loaf of bread under his arm, patient, dignified" (45).

In *Difficult Women*, David Plante records Rhys's comments about the same event: "I remember a black man in Dominica. . . . My father made me give loaves of French bread . . . and sixpence to poor black men who came to us. . . . I recall this black man walking away from us, the loaf under his arm, and his dignity. His dignity and his unconquerable mind. . . . 'Live and take comfort. . . . thou hast great allies; thy friends are exultations, agonies, and love, and man's unconquerable mind'" (19–20). The quotation is taken from William Wordsworth's poem first published in *Morning Post* on 9 November 1802 after the death in France of Toussaint L'Ouverture. The last lines of the ode read: "Though fallen thyself, never to rise again, / Live and take comfort, / Thou has left behind / Powers that will work for thee; air, earth, and skies / There's not a breathing of the common wind / That will forget thee: thou hast great allies; / Thy friends are ex- ultations, agonies, / And love, and man's unconquerable mind" ("To Tous- saint L'Ouverture," *Poetical Works*, 286). Significantly, Wordsworth celebrates Toussaint's heroism only after he is dead.

The anonymous black man of Jean Rhys's childhood memories is writ- ten in *Smile Please* as a reflection and substantiation of her mother's dignity and stoicism and in *Difficult Women* as romanticized recollection. Rhys's re- call of the man is processed through the English Romantic poet's fetish- ization of the dead Haitian revolutionary leader. This narcissistic and met- onymic use of the "noble," "dignified" black suggests a contradictory iden- tification that disrupts the presentation of autonomous selfhood. If the discourse of the Creole subject does epistemic violence to the anonymous black man, the black presence mediates the Creole's narrative construction of self.

In the chapter entitled "Black / White," the narrator observes, "I re- member the Riot as if it were yesterday. I must have been about twelve. . . . I heard far away a strange noise like animals howling but I knew it wasn't animals, it was people and the noise came nearer and nearer" (47). The riot is then explained as this time not being a threat to her family: "This particular riot was aimed at the editor of the local paper. His house was near ours. He had written an article attacking the power of the Catholic priests in Dominica. The crowd was some of the faithful who intended to stone his house, frighten him and prevent him ever writing about reli- gion again" (48). In terms of Jean Rhys's "biography," there is no record of a riot in Roseau (where Rhys lived before leaving for England) in 1902 or 1906, depending on whether Rhys was using 1890 or 1894 as her birth date. The "religious riot" in 1847 that she writes of in her early short story "Again the Antilles" (1927) was aimed at the editor of the newspaper for his stand against Catholicism. The inscription of the riot may also invoke the "Guerre Negre" of 1844. The strategy of suppressing names, distorting "facts," and misremembering dates is a central feature of Rhys's writing, as I have tried to show.

In this instance, by inscribing the self experientially in the event of a riot, which stands as a potential and ever-present threat of black animality and violence against her family, Rhys rewrites and consciously distorts historical "facts" to produce a working invention/inventory for the self in terms of history and "black people": "I could not forget the howling sound and there's no doubt that a certain wariness did creep in when I thought about the black people who surrounded me" (48). The refusal of historical concreteness and the construction of a fictional biotext that privileges memory ("I remember the Riot as if it were yesterday") inscribe the narrator as a ventriloquist's dummy made up of a repertoire of assumptions embedded in the sociotext. As Beaujour observes: "The self-portrait, as an encyclopedic *speculum*, is a memory that mediates between the individual and his culture. This memory is especially *attached* to the place where there is a clash in the problematically enunciated relations between the microcosmic monad and the linguistic and cultural macrocosm. . . . [It] tends as much to hollow out and contest the empirical individual's memory, by dispersing it amid the contested *topoi* of its culture, as it does to fill it artificially by recentering it on the Other" (*Poetics*, 35).

Throughout *Smile Please*, the Creole identity is sustained by the simultaneous love and hatred of "black people." The narrator makes a distinction between those "black people" she "knew well," that is, her servants, and those who were strangers. She also tells of a colored girl's intense hatred of her because she was white. Like Meta, this unnamed colored girl scarred the narrator for life: "This was hatred—impersonal, implacable hatred. I recognised it at once and if you think that a child cannot recognise hatred and remember it for life you are most damnably mistaken" (49).

Other stereotyped images of the black Other include uninhibited sexuality, physicality, and a proximity to nature and to the animal: "Side by side with my growing wariness of black people there was envy. I decided that they had a better time than we did, they laughed a lot though they seldom smiled. They were stronger than we were, they could walk a long way without getting tired, carry heavy weights with ease. Every night someone gave a dance. . . . We had few dances. They were more alive, more a part of the place than we were" (50). This us/them depiction of "black people," which rivals Carlyle's, is linked to questions of morality, "family values," and gender roles as these constitute the self of the Creole. The white woman's education — her initiation into conventional standards — is constructed over and against, even as it depends upon, the excluded, sexually promiscuous, not-quite-human blacks:

> [T]here wasn't for them, as there was for us, what I thought of as the worry of getting married. In those days a girl was supposed to marry, it was your mission in life, you were a failure if you didn't. . . . That fact that I knew several old maids who seemed perfectly happy, indeed happier and livelier than the married women, didn't affect the question at all. I dreaded growing up. I dreaded the time when I would have to worry about how many proposals I had, what if I didn't have a proposal? This was never told me but it was in every book I read, in people's faces and the way they talked.
>
> Black girls on the contrary seemed to be perfectly free. Children swarmed but negro marriages that I knew of were comparatively rare. Marriage didn't seem a duty with them as with us.
>
> All this perhaps was part of my envy which rose to a fever pitch at carnival time. (51; emphasis added)

If "black people" are closer to life energies and nature, they can also deal death through their ingratitude. The account of the librarian's death operates yet another stereotype, the "ungrateful black," even as it fetishizes the "black hands" as a signifier of black people's function as producers of labor:

> When years later I paid a short visit to Dominica I went to the library of course. Instead of being empty it was crowded, a long queue before the librarian's desk. At first I thought it was a very touching sight, all the black hands, eagerly stretched out, holding books. Then I noticed how ill the librarian, whom of course I knew, looked. As people filed past her she'd take the book, stamp it and give it back. No one looked at her and no one thanked her. They seemed to think that she was a machine and indeed there was something robotlike about the way she was working. Book after book and with each one she seemed to get more tired, look more ill. I wasn't at all surprised when I heard a few days later that she was dead.

I seem to be brought up willy-nilly against the two sides of the question. Sometimes I ask myself if I am the only who is; for after all, who knows or cares if there are two sides? (64)

Smile Please also writes the black Other as a source of ridicule and contempt. In the chapter entitled "The Religious Fit" the narrator recalls trying to teach the overseer, John, to read, incurring the jealousy and resentment of his wife. Her "help" also has other consequences: "It turned out that Émile [John's friend] had asked for my hand in marriage and promised her, if she would consent, a present of a large yam. I never heard the last of that yam. 'You're only worth a yam,' they would say, shrieking with mirth. My mother said, 'Well, you insisted on going to John's house against my advice' " (85–86). The narrator's desire to help the black Other, as part of her religious fit results in familiarity breeding contempt.

Dominican History

The political history of Dominica and the West Indies, the institutions and patterns of power, and the economic superstructure also articulate self and other in *Smile Please*. The narrator refers to the West India regiment comprised of predominantly black soldiers and recalls an occasion when some of them "bucked the system" by sitting in the front row, reserved for whites, in the racially segregated Anglican Church: "Like Queen Victoria I had fallen in love with the uniform. Dressed like that it would be impossible not to be brave, impossible not to be bold, reckless and all the things I admired so much" (89). The recollection of the soldiers is linked to a fictionalized account of the administrator Henry Hesketh Bell, whose tenure in Dominica lasted from 1899 to 1905: "We had at that time a very energetic administrator called Mr. Hesketh. That was part of his name anyway" (89). Historian Joseph Borome describes Bell in similar terms: "Energetic, possessed of a lively imagination, self confident and shrewd, Bell set a standard for dynamism and accomplishment." Borome also observes that he was accused of "fostering racial prejudice" by establishing a social club for whites only and excluding most colored people from government house receptions ("Crown Colony," 139). *Smile Please* juxtaposes the recollection of the soldiers with an account of the narrator's invitation to a "fancy-dress dance" at the governor's house and her desire, which was not satisfied, "to be a zouave" (90). The recall of the social milieu of the elite members of the Dominican society is processed through the rebellious consciousness of a child emblematized by her admiration for the black soldiers and their uniform.

In the chapter entitled "St. Lucia" the narrator recalls: "The memory from St. Lucia of a long line of women carrying coals to the ship. Some of them looked very strained up and tired, carrying those huge baskets. I didn't like to think of them, but I hadn't asked any questions. I knew someone would say 'They're very well paid,' and another, 'Yes, but women are cheaper'" (56). If this memory alludes to the capitalist exploitation of African Caribbean women as cheap sources of labor, and its justification by those who benefit from the system, the text also writes the "other side" — what the narrator sees as the destruction wrought after the white governing class in the West Indies was displaced: "Soon after our visit to St. Lucia there was a big fire in Castries, and as all the houses were wood, it did a lot of damage. But as far as I knew it was built up again. I was very shocked when I heard someone recently, after they had made a trip to the West Indies, talk of Castries as a shanty town. I supposed they call Roseau a shanty town too, now. I didn't know whether to answer 'It isn't true!' or 'We didn't do that!' So, as usual, I said nothing" (56). There are also references to the political events that in 1940 led to the change in Dominica's status from being one of the Leeward Islands to one of the Windward Islands.

My analysis of the vignettes in *Smile Please* reveals the deployment of a colonialist discourse in its systematic use of dehumanized black figures and an unquestioning acceptance of the economic superstructure that enables and is enabled by the production of "difference." In this regard, Brathwaite's observation about the writing of some West Indian Creoles seems apt: "White West Indian writers . . . are not yet prepared to allow their art to erode the boundaries set up around their minds by the physical/metaphysical plantation, and so do not yet recognize . . . that the plantation has transformed itself into other, new mercantilist forms, in which they are enslaved as surely as the descendants of their former bondsmen. It is only when this comes to them as crisis . . . that the white West Indian writers will find their voice" (*Roots*, 208).

I would argue that, with respect to *Smile Please*, there are some crucial and interlocking points that attenuate such an analysis. First, in reading and writing the subjectivity of "Jean Rhys" through the Book/writing, the black Other, and the history of Dominica, the text exposes the ontological and epistemological paradigms that produce discursive power. It does this by bringing to the fore the cultural and political conditions, the place(s) and demography, through which the Creole's self, reading, writing, and history are construed. At the same time, it exposes the paradox at the heart of the discourse that constitutes the racialized colonialist episteme: Rhys's "black people" is seen to be an artifact, the Other, in which the self of the Creole is heavily invested and apparently grounded. Yet this allegedly grounded Other occupies multiple and contradictory positions within the sociodiscursive space, dependent upon the needs and desires of the Creole subject. This dispersal of the self into the cultural and discursive framework forces an engagement, not with "Jean Rhys," but more with the historical locations of systems of signification that interdict the acts of reading and writing and the constitution of subjectivity. "What is of interest to the self-portraitist, as a writer," Beaujour says, "is the process of construction and deconstruction of places, the classification, inventory, interlocking, and unlocking of images. . . . This is why the . . . contents tend to conform to cultural and mythical stereotypes (without ever reaching such a limit)" (*Poetics*, 199).

Rhys's stated intention in *Smile Please* is clear: "I wanted to write about my life. I wanted to write my autobiography, because everything they say about me is wrong. I want to tell the truth. I want to tell the truth, too, about Dominica. No it's not true that we treated the black people badly. We didn't. . . . Now they say we did. . . . They won't listen. No one listens" (Plante, *Difficult Women*, 19). Yet instead of an "autobiography" that explains how being born white and raised in the West Indies accounts for Jean Rhys's "psychology," "life," and "themes," as a response to the "lies" told about the author, *Smile Please* enacts the historical and discursive procedures by which the Creole self/"Jean Rhys" becomes a trompe-l'oeil. The reader, seeking a mimetic representation of the essential Jean Rhys, is deceived, comes away empty handed. Gail Pool sees this as a failure of the text. She concludes, however, that her reading of *Smile Please* results in her calling into question the nature and concept of autobiographical writing in Rhys's work as a whole: "That the book is not in itself successful is, I think, evident, and the reasons for its lack of success relate interestingly to the way that Rhys's fiction works. . . . [W]hat we discover moving back from the autobiography to the fiction, which uses much of the same material, is how little we know about Jean Rhys personally. . . . [A]s a result of reading *Smile Please*, I began to question the autobiographical aspects of her work" ("Life's Unfinished Form," 69, 73).

The text fulfills a discursive necessity, not a descriptive one. In *Smile Please* the elliptical instead of expository style and the transformation of the individual "Jean Rhys" into a historical construct display a subject engendered by colonial structures, whose various locations and identities depend upon imperializing fictions of "black people," the West Indies, and History. The excavation of subjugated knowledges, naming and making visible mechanisms that depend for their effectiveness and affectivity on their remaining invisible and unspoken, fractures the colonialist discourse, which *Smile Please* appears to reproduce. By exposing the fault lines and the fissures of the discourse it repeats, Rhys's text lays bare the crisis of the white West Indian's enslavement to "the metaphysical plantation," to which Brathwaite points.

The Creole's Reading of History

It is through the paradoxical emphasis on self and self-recollection and the redeployment of European "history" that Rhys's writing most overtly and even aggressively constructs a West Indian subject position. In a particularly vehement assertion, Rhys says, "I don't think that English people have the slightest idea of the real West Indies in the 1830's. Or now for that matter!! (I read the most ludicrous lies every day almost). I do know — it's in my blood" (unpublished letter to Selma Vaz Dias, December 1963, Jean Rhys Collection). In describing as "ludicrous lies" English historical and contemporary representation of the West Indies and privileging knowledge carried "in [her] blood," Rhys challenges History (as European discourse) and posits history as that which is secreted within her experience, memory, and imagination. One of the fundamental obsessions of Jean Rhys's writing is an insistence on the symbiotic relationship between history and self-writing and the attempt to reconceptualize both, in Edouard Glissant's terms, as "consciousness at work" and as desire. She uses and reworks historical and autobiographical data as a means of resisting the cannibalizing of West Indian history by the dominant European narratives, while producing the Creole's version of that history. Her writing is consumed by the determination to free the self and the West Indies, as she knows and imagines both, from their containment within dominant discourses of European history and of subjectivity. As Wilson Harris notes, the history of the West Indies is both a "history of crisis [and] a living process of individuation rather than . . . an expendable and fortuitous creed. . . . If I were asked to give . . . the direction in which I would like the West Indian novel to move, my reply would be towards *an act of memory*" ("Unresolved Constitution," 45). Michelle Cliff also observes: "As Caribbean writers, we need to recognize the extremes we were brought up under, have internalized, which may charge our work as well as censor us" ("Caliban's Daughter," 38).

When Rhys invokes her West Indian identity, she assumes the role and function of historiographer. The writer culls data on the West Indies from Europe's historical, "eyewitness," and narrative texts, redeploying or undermining these according to her knowledge, memory, and imagination. Rhys recognizes that the West Indies that she knows "in [her] blood" is undocumented, nowhere available in England and Europe of the early twentieth century, the time and place in which she began her work. Yet throughout her long career she claims, with striking resoluteness and tenacity, the right to imagine her own past, the right to reinterpret the Caribbean as she knows it.

The rewriting of History does not deny its materiality or power, nor does it overturn entirely its assumptions. The Creole's relationship to this discourse, as I suggested earlier, is variously one of questioning, denial, undermining, or complicity—never total rejection. Rhys's reading of metropolitan accounts of the West Indies engages with the central functions of affiliation and intertextuality in constructing what Edward Said terms "the reservoir of accredited knowledge," which underwrites the authority of imperialist and colonialist discourses. A very brief and schematic historiography of some of the foundational European "eyewitness" and "historical" texts on the West Indies will serve to illustrate this point. These seventeenth-, eighteenth-, and nineteenth-century works prominently display their ideological function in the maintenance and expansion of the imperial order.

One of the earliest known texts is Jean-Baptiste Du Tertre's *Histoire Génerále des Antilles Habitées par les Francoises* (1667). Elsa Goveia, in her groundbreaking *Historiography of the British West Indies*, describes it as the "most important single work of the new [seventeenth-century] phase of historical writing" on the West Indies (19). It forms the pretext for Jean-Baptiste Labat's *Voy-*

ages aux Isles de l'Amerique (Antilles). Labat grants authority to his precursor's text while highlighting some of its defects: "My confrère, Père Dutertre, was the first of our Frenchmen to make known the islands of America. His work was admirable at the time it was written. . . . But, as obviously he did not see everything for himself, he wrote on many matters from the reports of others." Labat promises to record all matters precisely as he "saw, learned, or practiced them" (qtd. Roberts, *French*, 93).

The Labat text forms one the major pretexts for James Anthony Froude's *The English in the West Indies: The Bow of Ulysses* (1888). Froude's text repeatedly invokes Labat, sometimes quoting and footnoting sections of the precursory text. Froude explicitly filters his own "eyewitness account" through the prism of the Frenchman's text, written more than two hundred years prior to his own visit to the West Indies: "I was anxious to see how far Labat's prophecy had been fulfilled. . . . Labat had not exaggerated the beauty; I could say for myself, like Père Labat, the island was all that man could desire. '*En un mot, la vie y est delicieuse*' "(57). Froude also compares the West Indies to Walter Scott's novels: "As to natural beauty, the West Indian Islands are like Scott's novels, where we admire most the one which we have read the last" (158). As the book's subtitle makes clear, Froude's text also uses as its point of origin the ultimate precursory writing on the West's encounter with its savage Others.

In the 1980s Teresa F. O'Connor invokes Froude as an authoritative eyewitness: "James Froude visited the West Indies, including the island of Dominica, and wrote a book about his trip. That book . . . was much disputed after its appearance because of its negative depiction of the blacks there. . . . Froude's description of the sight of Dominica, which is not essentially different from earlier travelers', will serve to show what the island looked like during Rhys's youth" (*Jean Rhys*, 14).

Lafcadio Hearn, in *Two Years in the French West Indies* (1890), refers to Du Tertre and collects data about and reconstructs the "life" of the by then legendary Père Labat. Hearn places his own reading of the West Indies within English/metropolitan epistemology and referentiality: "But the secrets of these woods have not been unexplored; one of the noblest writers of our time has so beautifully and fully written of them as to leave little for any one else to say. He who knows Charles Kingsley's 'At Last' probably knows the woods of Trinidad far better than many who pass them daily" (79–80).

Frederick Ober, an ethnographer, invokes Anthony Trollope (*The West Indies and the Spanish Main*) as his precursor and cites "Humboldt . . . quoting Cicero" as the authority and source of authentication on the language spoken by the Caribs. He also finds "evidence" for his firsthand discovery of the West Indies in a European text: "Seeking farther, I found in an ancient volume, a French work published in 1658, conclusive evidence in place of what was with Humboldt mostly conjecture. It says . . ." (*Camps*, 101). The French work to which he refers is Charles de Rochefort's *Histoire Naturelle et Morale des Antilles de l'America* (1658), translated as *History of the Caribby Islands* (1666). Labat (and subsequent writers) accused Rochefort, who did not visit the Caribbean, of plagiarizing Du Tertre's work and publishing his book first: "The Minister Rochefort, who never saw the islands of America with his own eyes, did not hesitate to write a history which would be tolerable enough, since he copied from Père Dutertre; but he entirely spoiled his narration with descriptions far removed from truth, his ideas being to make things seem more agreeable, and the better to conceal his theft" (qtd. Roberts, *French*, 93). Alec Waugh in *Sugar Islands* (1949) invokes Ober as an authority on the Dominican Caribs.

It is in the engagement with this discourse that Rhys shows strong affinities with most, if not all, West Indian writing, which uses as one of its most important pretexts European imperialism and its representational language. As John Frow argues in another context, "Textual events are not arbitrary in relation to the system which structures their occurrence. . . . [T]hey cannot be reduced to its terms since they may exceed them, but what makes them possible is *this* system, not any other" (*Marxism*, 1). West Indian intellectual thought and practice that self-consciously negotiates writing as a socially constructed and enforced activity goes back to the nineteenth century at least. Froude's *The English in the West Indies* elicited a response from Caribbean linguist J. J. Thomas in his *Froudacity: West Indian Fables by James Anthony Froude* (1889). Thomas uses the term "fables" to expose the fantastic fabrications of the "historical" and "eyewitness accounts" of the West Indies by the English historian. Thomas's focus on Froude's "singular contempt for accuracy" exposes and analyzes the desires that underwrite the historian's account. Other early West Indian writers who challenged the myths of Europe include Edward Wilmot Blyden (*Christianity, Islam, and the Negro Race*, 1887), Louis Joseph Janvier (*L'égalité des races*, 1884), and Hannibal Price (*De la réhabilitation de la race noire par la république d'Haiti*, 1900).

The approaches to imperial history and writing may vary among different West Indian practitioners, but the engagement with it is constant. Some examples of the post-1940s writers' positions are in order. George Lamming asserts that "the function [of imperialism] is to annihilate the human person . . . so that his source of energy may be converted into a commodity for profit. The West Indies . . . did not evolve out of this system, nor did they degenerate into this system. They were actually created by it. And upon the basis of this creation, a structure of education and a whole kingdom of values was founded. It is not enough to know this as a fact of history; it must be imaginatively grasped and creatively mastered at the deepest levels of our reflective self-consciousness" ("West Indian People," 65). Jan Carew notes: "My research into the early periods of Caribbean history shows many distortions and many omissions, and . . . these fictions that we accept as fact are repeated like incantations" (Interview, 37). John Hearne states elliptically: "History is the angel with whom all we Caribbean Jacobs have to wrestle, sooner or later, if we hope for a blessing" (*Carifesta Forum*, vii). Derek Walcott's provocatively titled essay, "The Muse of History," offers yet another perspective:

> [Some] writers reject the idea of history as time for its original concept as myth, the partial recall of the race. For them history is fiction, subject to a fitful muse, memory. Their philosophy, based on a contempt for historic time, is revolutionary, for what they repeat to the New World is its simultaneity with the Old. Their vision of [the hu]man is elemental. . . . Yet the method by which we are taught the past, the progress from motive to event, is the same by which we read narrative fiction. In time every event becomes an exertion of memory and is thus subject to invention. The further the facts, the more history petrifies into myth. Thus . . . we grow aware that history is written, that it is a kind of literature without morality, that in its actuaries the ego of the race is indissoluble and that everything depends on whether we write this fiction through the memory of hero or of victim. (2)

With respect to Jean Rhys, I shall examine briefly the precision with which her writing intervenes in precursory discourse on the West Indies by comparing her fictional rendering of two events written as historical "facts" by the colonial governor of Dominica, Hesketh Bell, whom she fictionalizes in *Smile Please*. His *Glimpses of a Governor's Life* (1946) is based on journal entries that he wrote in Dominica between 1901 and 1905. Rhys's vignette, "Heat," appeared in 1976. The two events treated by both texts are the death of an Englishman at Dominica's Boiling Lake in December 1901 and the eruption of the Soufrière volcano on St. Vincent in 1902. Both these events are juxtaposed in Rhys's short story.

Bell's journal entry for 5 December 1901 states, "Wilfred Clive . . . arrived yesterday." The next entry, dated 11 December, reads:

> A very dreadful thing has happened. Poor Clive has been killed in the Boiling Lake.
>
> He left us yesterday morning, to make the excursion and it seems that he engaged a couple of men at Laudat, to act as guides. Only one of the three has returned. This man says . . . [t]hey were standing on the border of the inner crater when, suddenly, an immense volume of steam arose from the water, intensely impregnated with sulphur. He was standing some thirty or forty feet above Clive and the other guide and saw them fall to the ground. He himself then became entirely overcome by the fumes but regained consciousness after a few moments. . . .
>
> This is indeed a terrible occurrence, and I fear that all hope of the survival of Clive and of the unfortunate guide must be abandoned. (46–47)

In Rhys's "Heat" the narrator recalls the date of the Soufrière volcanic eruption, 8 May 1902, as the day "ash had fallen" and recounts the fear of a possible eruption of the Dominican Boiling Lake. Her knowledge of the Boiling Lake is tied to the death of a young Englishman, which she remembers:

> Our volcano was called the boiling lake. . . . In the churchyard . . . was a large marble headstone. "Sacred to the memory of Clive —, who lost his life at the boiling lake in Dominica in a heroic attempt to save his guide." Aged twenty seven. I remember that too.
>
> He was a young Englishman, a visitor, who had gone exploring with two guides to the boiling lake. As they were standing looking at it one of the guides, who was a long way ahead, staggered and fell. The other seized hold of the Englishman's hand and said "Run!" . . . After a few steps the Englishman pulled his hand away and went back and lifted up the man who had fallen. Then he too staggered and they both fell. The surviving guide ran and told what happened. (CS, 295)

The fictional and the "factual" accounts show certain similarities; the most important are that both use secondhand sources and interpretation of events to invent a narrative.

With respect to the eruption of the Soufrière volcano, Hesketh Bell's journal entries from 4 May 1902 record premonitions and accounts of disaster. On 25 May he writes:

> We hear now that the sole survivor of the whole population of St. Pierre is a negro prisoner who was under sentence of death. He was confined in an underground cell, once used as a bomb proof magazine. . . .
>
> All sorts of stories are, of course, being circulated in connection with this terrible catastrophe. St. Pierre has always had a reputation, in the West Indies, as being a very gay city in which morals, among some sections of the population, were very lax. The lower classes of the coloured people had become increasingly irreligious, and we are told that scenes of a sacrilegious nature were seen during the recent carnival. . . . So incensed and scandalized by these occurrences was the Bishop of St. Pierre that he is said to have left the city in indignation and to have foretold Divine punishment. Whether this story be true or not, the fact remains that the destruction of St. Pierre has been of a most extraordinary nature, strongly reminiscent of that of the Cities of the Plain. (59)

In "Heat" the Rhys narrator remembers the "gossip" that started immediately after the volcano: "That went on for years so I can remember it well. St. Pierre, they said, was a very wicked city. It had not only a theatre, but an opera house, which was probably wickeder still. Companies from Paris performed there. But worse than this was the behaviour of the women who were the prettiest in the West Indies. . . . The last bishop who had visited the city had taken off his shoes and solemnly shaken them over it. After that, of course, you couldn't wonder" (296–97).

In both texts, "stories" and "gossip" discursively reconstruct the natural catastrophe as a cautionary tale of social evils, the innate morality of the "lower orders," and the effect of the wrath of a religious leader. The Rhys text, however, which specifically links questions of gender to "immorality," is both a rewriting and a critique of the former. By blurring the lines between what is borrowed and what is invented, between facts and fiction, the Rhys text exposes the mechanisms by which History and Truth are constructed by the dominant ideologies. Firsthand knowledge and "eyewitness accounts" are displaced and shown to be fictitious. The re-presentation of European history and texts can be read as an ironic rewriting of Europe's invention of its Others. The Creole's reading of European writing on the West Indies is a performative act of cultural criticism.

The narrator of "Heat" says that, as she grew older, "I heard of a book by a man called Lafcadio Hearn who had written about St. Pierre as it used to be . . . but I never found the book and I stopped looking for it" (297). The narrator may not have found the book, but we know that Jean Rhys did read Hearn's text because it is intertextually reworked in *Wide Sargasso Sea*. It is possible to read this narrator's statement as suggesting that the book about St. Pierre (and the West Indies) as it used to be cannot be found because it does not exist, so the narrator decides to stop looking for it. The narrator finds instead old newspapers and magazines, with "the English version of the eruption," which excised information about Martinican social life and focused on the one man who had survived. Like the Hottentot Venus, "He was now travelling round the music-halls of the world being exhibited. They had taught him a little speech. . . . I read all this and thought but it wasn't like that, it wasn't like that at all" (297). Read together with Bell's narrative, Rhys's text is an example of the metaphorical ficitionalizing of the colonialist history of the West Indies, a project that engages so many writers of the region. Rhys's reading and rewriting call attention to how "the English side" is considered synonymous with History. She therefore aims to tell "the other side," from her own perspective.

The formal and structural dismantling of precusory texts "about" the West Indies also shows Rhys's awareness that the construction of imperialist and colonialist discourses is not an individual writer's project. This implicit assumption is of a piece with Virginia Woolf's assertion that *Robinson Crusoe* ("set" in the West Indies) "resembles one of the anonymous productions of the [English] race itself rather than the effort of a single mind" — in short, the myth of Europe (*Common Reader*, 86). There is also the assumption, nevertheless, in some of Rhys's writing that individual European writers' motives can be self-serving. In a draft manuscript of "Pioneers, Oh, Pioneers," which clearly echoes the work of James Fenimore Cooper and Willa Cather, the thoughts of an Englishman on the "superstitions" of the "natives" of the West Indies are portrayed: "[Dr. Cox] thought about the bell which so many people said sounded when you got off the tracks in this curious island — peopled by white morons and black apes . . . but still the most beautiful of the lot. The bell must be some nocturnal insect, he thought, and imagined himself tracking it down, classifying it, naming it. 'Then when I am dead and pushing up the daisies I won't be quite forgotten,' he thought" (Jean Rhys Papers, Add. MS 57859, 28).

All writing is rewriting. It is the reader who makes the writer. These caveats occupy center stage in Jean Rhys's work: citations, titles of precursory texts, hidden and overt allusions and references abound. More often the focus is on unidentified authors; texts that cannot be found; excerpts that are half-forgotten or inaccurately remembered; incomplete quotations, fragments, anachronisms, erroneous attributions, palimpsests; the suppression or distortion of individual names, titles, texts, and historical events. These procedures suggest a rereading and rewriting of dominant discourses of empire, gender, and subjectivity. The errors, misinterpretations, and misreadings of Rhys's writing repeat and foreground the mechanics of colonialist, imperial, and patriarchal discourses. What has been presented as objective, authoritative knowledge, upon retextualization, is exposed as partial, distorted, and often false.

In her interventions in precursory or canonical models or both, Rhys enters critically into existing configurations of discourse and alters systems of meaning, repeating and revising the primary texts of imperial Europe. Recognizing that she is present in European texts as an absence, she questions the systemic functioning of her own silencing and hollows out an affective space for her critical reflection.

It is *Wide Sargasso Sea* that most clearly articulates the construction of the Creole subjectivity and her relationship to the West Indies and to Europe. It is for this reason that I shall begin my analysis of the individual novels with this text. As Jean D'Costa acutely observes, *Wide Sargasso Sea* predates conceptually all other Rhys texts ("Jean Rhys," 394). The figure of the "madwoman in the attic" appears in *After Leaving Mr. Mackenzie* (1931), *Good Morning, Midnight* (1939), and "I Spy a Stranger" (written in the 1930s and 1940s). On 20 February 1966, when *Wide Sargasso Sea* is near completion, Rhys writes:

> I came to England between sixteen and seventeen, a very impressionable age and Jane Eyre was one of the books I read then.
>
> Of course Charlotte Brontë makes her own world, of course she convinces you, and that makes the poor Creole lunatic all the more dreadful.

I remember being quite shocked, and when I re-read it rather annoyed. "That's only one side — the English side" sort of thing.

(I think too that Charlotte had a "thing" about the West Indies being rather sinister places — because in another of her books "Villette" she drowns the hero . . . on the voyage to Guadeloupe, another very alien place — according to her).

Perhaps most people had this idea then, and perhaps in a way they were right. Even now White West Indians can be a bit trying . . . (not only white ones) but not quite so awful surely. They have a side and a point of view. (*Letters*, 296–97)

2 : The 1840s to the 1900s
The Creole and the Postslavery West Indies

The Creole is of course the important one, the others explain her. . . .
Take a look at Jane Eyre. *That unfortunate death of a Creole! I'm fighting*
mad to write her *story.*
(Letters, *157*)

Wide Sargasso Sea

Rhys's biggest quarrel with Charlotte Brontë is over the inscription of the mad white West Indian woman. In a letter to Selma Vaz Dias on 9 April 1958, Rhys argues that Bertha Mason is impossible because the Victorian novelist did not work hard enough to develop a "character" that was true even to the "world" of *Jane Eyre*:

> I've read and re-read *Jane Eyre*. . . . The Creole in Charlotte Brontë's novel is a lay figure—repulsive which does not matter, and not once alive which does. She's necessary to the plot, but always she shrieks, howls, laughs horribly, attacks all and sundry—*off stage*. For me . . . she must be right *on stage*. She must be at least plausible with a past, the *reason* why Mr. Rochester treats her so abominably and feels justified, the *reason* why he thinks she is mad and why of course she goes mad, even the *reason* why she tries to set everything on fire, and eventually succeeds. . . . I do not see how Charlotte Brontë's madwoman could possibly convey all this. (*Letters*, 156–57)

While writing her own novel, Rhys, in correspondence with her editors and with Selma Vaz Dias, insistently challenged Brontë's portrayal of the West Indian Creole. Some examples are instructive. Rhys refers to Bertha Mason as an "impossible monster" (*Letters*, 149). She notes that she "was vexed at [Brontë's] portrait of the 'paper tiger' lunatic, the all wrong creole scenes, and above all by the real cruelty of Mr. Rochester" (262). However, Rhys also points to her admiration for the Victorian writer: "I have a very great and deep admiration for the Brontë sisters. How then can *I* of all people, say [Charlotte Brontë] was wrong? Or that her Bertha is impossible? *Which she is*" (271). Brontë herself was unhappy with her own technical and moral portrait of Bertha, accepting that her character's humanity was not fully realized: "It is true that profound pity ought to be the only sentiment elicited by the view of such degradation and equally true that I have not sufficiently dwelt on that feeling: I have erred in making horror too predominant" (qtd. Thorpe, "Other Side," 101).

Rhys further asserts: "I believe and firmly too that there was more than one Antoinette. The West Indies was . . . rich in those days *for* those days. . . . The girls [West Indian Creole women who married Englishmen] . . . would soon once in kind England be *Address Unknown*. So gossip. So a legend. If Charlotte Brontë took her horrible Bertha from this legend I have the right to take lost Antoinette. And, how to reconcile the two and fix dates I do not know — yet. But, I will" (271).

The shifting of dates is crucial, as Mark McWatt explains. *Marmion*, newly published when Jane is given a copy toward the end of the novel, appeared in 1808, whereas the date for the Emancipation Act is 1833. Bertha Mason was already confined to the attic of Thornfield Hall by the first decade of the nineteenth century, whereas Antoinette Cosway in *Wide Sargasso Sea* was still a child in the 1840s. In terms of *Jane Eyre* the literary references in *Wide Sargasso Sea* are equally anachronistic: "Jeannie with the Light Brown Hair" was written by Stephen Foster in 1826; Tennyson's "Miller's Daughter" was not well known until the 1840s; most of Byron's poetry and all of Scott's novels (noticed by Antoinette's husband on the bookshelf at Granbois) appeared after 1800 ("Preoccupation," 12–13). These shifts and changes show the process by which Rhys deliberately locates the events of her novel in the West Indies of the 1830s and 1840s.

Wide Sargasso Sea, as a rereading and rewriting of *Jane Eyre*, seeks to articulate the subjective and locational identity of the West Indian Creole of the postslavery period. It also imaginatively reinvents a category evacuated of social and political meaning in the 1950s and 1960s, the period of writing when colonial structures are being dismantled. Structurally and ideologically, then, *Wide Sargasso Sea* is deliberately anachronistic. An unpublished letter to Selma Vaz Dias in October 1957 makes explicit some of the guiding principles of Rhys's crafting of this novel—the link between facts and fiction, history and writing; the importance of anchoring fiction to specific social and historical events; how "facts" become legends; getting to a "truth" through the reconstitution and re-ordering of facts and the use of imagination:

One sentence in your letter to me is significant. You write "Of course it will be a fictitious Mrs. Rochester." But, don't you see, Charlotte Brontë's Mrs. Rochester is also fiction. The flash that came, linking up with much that I'd heard and know was that *this fiction was founded on fact or rather several facts*. At that date and earlier, very wealthy planters did exist, their daughters *had* very large dowries, there *was* no married woman's property act. So, a young man who was not too scrupulous could do very well for himself and very easily. He would marry the girl, grab her money, bring her to England—a faraway place—and in a year she would be an invalid. Or mad. I could see *how* easily all this could happen. It *did* happen [and] more than once. So the legend of the mad West Indian was established. . . . There have been one or two novels about this. One was called "The Little Girl from Dominica." It was silly Prettified out of existence. Still there was the same old legend. . . .

My difficulty is first: to get back more than a hundred years ago. . . . Second that the West Indies I write of has vanished completely—even the West Indies I knew has vanished. There is not even much record of it. . . .

They had their own civilization but it has gone. . . . How can I make it seem true? Now—Yet I must try. . . . I could make it plausible, but that's not good enough. It must be true or sound true. That is not so easy. (Jean Rhys Collection)

Rhys's reworking of historical data, cultural references, and literary allusions suggests that, in rewriting the Victorian novel, she is calling into question the entire Book, the metatext of the dominant, metropolitan discourse. In order to demonstrate the implausibility and the "lie" of the English portrayal of the West Indian Creole woman, Rhys performs the cultural criticism that insinuates Brontë's text into the larger discursive practices; and she reads the precursory novel as a production of its cultural and social ethos. Furthermore, Rhys's text works upon a repertoire of strategies and discursive acts engendered by British imperial control of the West Indies. Another important pretext for the West Indian novel, as I mentioned in the previous chapter, is Lafcadio Hearn's *Two Years in the French West Indies*, specifically the chapter entitled "Un Revenant." Rhys borrowed this title for the first writing of what would become *Wide Sargasso Sea*. In a letter to Francis Wyndham on 22 July 1962, she says: "I wrote this book before!—Different setting—same idea. (It was called 'Le Revenant' then.) . . . I tried to rewrite 'Le Revenant' but could not . . . however I discovered two chapters . . . and have used them in this book" (*Letters*, 213).[1]

The first few pages of *Wide Sargasso Sea* imaginatively reconstruct the personal effects of slave emancipation on members of the white plantocracy. The first-person narrative of the young girl is thickened by manifold presences, "confused voices" (named and unnamed), and embedded historical referents. The novel opens with a reference to Annette's exclusion from the white community and the suicide of their neighbor, Mr. Luttrell. Both personal tragedies are grounded in the historical order. First, Annette, as a young, attractive widow in the small white community poses a further threat to the other family units even as the sociosystemic structure of the plantocracy is being broken down by the ending of slavery. Second, part of the hostility toward Annette stems from her being a French West Indian woman in a British West Indian colony. This alludes to the centuries-long feud between the French and the English in the eastern Caribbean, about which historians such as Joseph Borome have also written. In the case of Mr. Luttrell, his suicide is a result of his failure to receive the compensation promised by the British government. As noted earlier, West Indian planters were voted twenty million pounds sterling to compensate for the loss of their slaves. In both this novel and *Voyage in the Dark*, Rhys writes a Creole account suggesting that, though promised, the compensation was not always received.

If an old order is passing, the emergent order bears its marks and is deeply imbricated in the old. As Lenox Honychurch asserts, "Slavery had ended, but the problem of labour and the creation of a new society had just begun" (*Dominica*, 94). In *Wide Sargasso Sea* the allusion to the Garden of Eden as a beginning is simultaneously written as intimations of Apocalypse: "Our garden was large and beautiful as that garden in the Bible—the tree of life grew there. But it had gone wild" (*WSS*, 19). Unlike the biblical garden, the West Indian postslavery "beginning" is not "sui generis," but is born out of the nightmare of history. All the human relationships are marked by slavery and the plantation society, and all are constructed, for the most part, within these parameters. Christophine, we are reminded, was a wedding gift to Annette. These relationships are also marked by a complicated web of intense dependency. Annette says: "Christophine stayed with me because she wanted to stay. She had her own very good reasons you may be sure. I dare say we would have died if she'd turned against us and that would have been a better fate" (21). With respect to the other freedpersons, " 'They stayed,' she said angrily, 'because they wanted somewhere to sleep and something to eat. . . . Godfrey is a rascal. These new ones [white planters and merchants who came after the abolition of slavery] aren't too kind to old people and he knows it. That's why he stays' " (22).

When Antoinette says "These were all the people in my life" (22), the text has already folded into the substance of the character's life centuries of West Indian history, calling attention to the continuity between slavery and postslavery conditions—the presence of the past. The narrative also demonstrates that to "write her a life" does not mean to write Antoinette's singular life, but to write into being the life of the Creole woman in terms of its conditions of possibility in the West Indies of the 1830s and 1840s. The Creole woman is made of the historical substance and its representational language. The history of the West Indies, then, does not provide the context for a reading of the novel nor does it even provide its content or theme. This history comes to be the process of the text's self-determination. Imagery, events, and characters and their interrelationships are figured as history itself.

In this regard, the process of naming and identifying the narrative characters is of vital importance. In terms of the main characters, Antoinette's name does not appear until several pages into the novel, and the context in which it appears is significant: "We can colour the roses as we choose and mine are green, blue and purple. Underneath, I will write my name in fire red, Antoinette Mason, née Cosway, Mount Calvary Convent, Spanish Town, Jamaica, 1839" (53). The date, the year after full emancipation, is significant, as I have tried to show. The colors that Antoinette uses to emblematize her self, to represent her identity (and to foretell and remember her fate), are the very same colors from which her husband will recoil when he first arrives in the West Indies: "Everything is too much. . . . Too much blue, too much purple, too much green. The flowers too red. . . . And the woman is a stranger" (70).

In addition, mother and daughter, Annette and Antoinette (the French and English versions), bear the same name. Tia is a diminutive of Antoinette/Antoinetta. The husband is nameless. Daniel Cosway suffers from a simultaneous lack and excess of proper names. The exploration of the semiotic and ontological status of names is carried out in the novel through a retelling of history. The characters on whom I shall focus in the following sections are Antoinette, the nameless husband, and Daniel.

Antoinette — Writing a Life and a Death for the Creole Woman

The subjectivity that functions under the sign of Antoinette inhabits various ontological, figural, and aesthetic realms, all operating at different levels of textuality. For example, in Part One, Antoinette writes her life in the convent as anamnesis: "It is easy to imagine what happened to those two, bar accidents. Ah but Louise! . . . Anything might have happened to you, Louise, anything at all, and I wouldn't be surprised" (55). When is she remembering her classmates in the convent? Is it while she is in the attic of her husband's house? In Part Three, when she is in her husband's house in England, she challenges the reader who may be reading her at this point of her story/life as the madwoman in the attic: "He [her half brother] looked at me and spoke to me as though I were a stranger. What do you do when something happens to you like that? Why are you laughing at me?" (184). There are no quotation marks in the text. These words are "spoken" to the reader. They "jump out," so to speak. Who, then, is Antoinette? When does she tell her story? And to whom? Does she survive her own death to speak her "truth," to tell her side of the story? These moments in the text pose "the writing itself as a problem without a solution, or whose solution is dissolution" (Chambers, *Room*, 159). The problematic of textuality can be read as an explicit intentional and constitutive aspect of the structure and characterization of *Wide Sargasso Sea*.

One of the most striking relationships in the novel, as many critics have pointed out, is that between Antoinette and Tia. In his valuable critique, which I cited in Chapter 1, Kamau Brathwaite argues strongly that a friendship between the two girls is implausible. He asserts, "No matter what Jean Rhys might have made Antoinette think, Tia was historically separated from her" by the ideological barriers embedded in the colonialist discourses of white supremacy (*Contradictory Omens*, 36). I would like to draw on this perception of Tia and Antoinette to propose a somewhat different (though related) reading of this relationship. I shall pay particular attention to two key moments: the burning of Coulibri and the final installment of her dream, in which Antoinette, in England, sets her husband's house on fire and then sees her self reflected as Tia in the pool at Coulibri. But first I shall examine the ways in which the text structures and contextualizes the relationship by analyzing the brief vignette that precedes the inscription of the meeting of the two girls:

> One day a little girl followed me singing, "Go away white cockroach, go away, go away." I walked fast, but she walked faster. "White cockroach, go away, go away. Nobody want you. Go away."
>
> When I was safely home I sat close to the old wall at the end of the garden. . . . I never wanted to move again. . . . Christophine found me there when it was nearly dark. . . . She said nothing, but next morning Tia was in the kitchen. . . . Soon Tia was my friend and I met her nearly every morning. (23)

An unidentified black is a source of menace and a threat to Antoinette. As I've tried to show, in much of Rhys's writing there exists only the Manichaean division of "good blacks" — those who serve — and "bad blacks" — those who are hostile, threatening, unknown. If Christophine understands Antoinette's isolation and her need for companionship and a playmate, the relationship between the two girls, framed as it is by the incident above, begins on an ominous note. The social divisions of black and white and the enabling *and* disabling tropes of the "good black" and "hostile black" have already constructed the terms of the Antoinette/Tia relationship. Even when they become "friends," the relationship is based on the production of difference through the racialist stereotypes of the hardy, physically superior, animallike, lazy negro: "Tia would light a fire (fires always lit for her, sharp stones did not hurt her bare feet, I never saw her cry). . . . [A]fter we had eaten she slept at once. I could not sleep, but I wasn't quite awake as I lay . . . looking at the pool" (23). (The lazy black, who only desires to sleep after eating, is a common trope of colonialist discourse. In some parts of the West Indies, the term "niggeritis" has been facetiously coined to refer to this purported deficiency among West Indians of African ancestry.) The sensitive white child, on the other hand, contemplates nature, seduced by the "rêve exotique."

The marks of "race" that structure the Antoinette/Tia relationship undermine the *narrative* suggestion that it is a friendship. The *text* insists upon the racial divisions even as it appears to be "transcending" them. Here I am borrowing Ross Chambers's distinctions. The narrative function, he suggests, must be processed by the textual function: "A 'narrative function' that respects the power structure serves as a form of disguise for a 'textual function' whose operation is more covert, but ultimately more significant, and serves as an appeal to the 'readerly' activity of interpretation, thereby subverting notions such as those of the autonomous subject or the discursive 'transmission' of information" (*Room*, 13). The "narrative function" enacts a sentimental fiction of friendship between the black and white girls even as the "textual function" demystifies and undercuts it. In this way the Rhys text displays its own contradictions, offering its own internal critique.

At the level of theme and narrative, the friendship is terminated when Tia cheats Antoinette out of her pennies. The already fragile relationship ends acrimoniously, their quarrel marked by more racialist epithets and abuse, this time explicitly traded between the two girls:

> "Keep them then, you cheating nigger. . . . I can get more if I want to."
> That's not what she hear, she said. She hear all we poor like beggar. We ate salt fish—no money for fresh fish. That old house so leaky, you run with calabash to catch water when it rain. Plenty white people in Jamaica. *Real white people, they got gold money. They didn't look at us, nobody see them come near us. Old time white people nothing but white nigger now, and black nigger better than white nigger.* (24; emphasis added)

The three pennies that Tia unfairly takes from Antoinette (which, significantly, were given to her by Christophine, a former slave) are placed within a consideration of the ideologies of "race," class, empire, and colony. The death of her planter father and the ending of slavery reduce Antoinette and her family to penury, from white to black. "Real white people" have money. The racial superiority of the whites depends upon the economic ascendancy achieved by unpaid black labor. Without money, Antoinette's family become niggers, isolated from the rest of white society. As Frantz Fanon says, "In the colonies the economic substructure is also a superstructure. The cause is the consequence; you are rich because you are white, you are white because you are rich" (*Wretched*, 40).

Like the three pennies, the dress is a crucial trope. "I searched for a long time before I could believe that [Tia] had taken my dress. . . . She had left me hers and I put it on . . . and walked home . . . hating her" (25). A focus on dress is threaded through the narrative to inscribe an examination of the roles of Creole woman within the racialized hierarchies of the plantation society of the nineteenth-century West Indies. When Tia switches the dresses, leaving Antoinette her shabbier one, the text reverses in a microcosmic way, the white-over-black paradigm, destabilizing categories of victim/victimizer, haves/have-nots. Tia's action consummates the discursive invention of Antoinette as a "white nigger." Forced to put on Tia's dress, Antoinette, the poor white, takes on the mantle of the nigger.

When Antoinette goes home in Tia's dress, her mother has guests who "wore such beautiful clothes." Embarrassed by her daughter's appearance, Annette insists that the dress be burned. One of her guests, we will later learn, is Mr. Mason, Annette's future husband. As Antoinette forces on an old dress, Christophine predicts that trouble is imminent and that the notion that slavery has ended is farcical: "Trouble walk into the house this day. Trouble walk in. . . . No more slavery! She had to laugh! 'These new ones have Letter of the Law. Same thing. They got magistrate. They got fine. They got jail house and chain gang. They got tread machine to mash up people's feet. New ones worse than old ones—more cunning, that's all'" (26). Historian Thomas Holt cites incidents in which the treadmill as a form of punishment was used even in the postslavery period, causing serious injury and even death (*Problem*, 65). Woodville Marshall also argues that the freedpersons were "disappointed that the emancipation apparently promised by the Abolition of Slavery Act of 1833 had not come, and [they were] continually harassed by masters who attempted by various legal and illegal contrivances to reduce the small portion of 'free time' which the Abolition Act had decreed" ("'We Be Wise,'" 14–15).

The linking of the account of the dress with Christophine's comments on postslavery "slavery" is crucial. It will be their dress that signals the restoration of the Creole mother and daughter to the status of the planter class, removing them from the category of "white niggers."[2] Their reinstatement into the elite membership of the plantocracy, embroiled in postslavery disputes with the laboring classes, will be the prime motivation for the burning of their home, Coulibri. It is during the fire that Antoinette and Tia will meet again in an intensely charged scene that also foreshadows the ending of the novel. The night following the incident with Tia, Antoinette has the first installment of her dream, which repeats itself three times and culminates in the burning down of the husband's house in England. Antoinette says, "I woke next morning knowing that nothing would be the same. It would change and go changing" (*WSS*, 27). The first change is that Annette works to provide new dresses for herself and her daughter. With the change in their appearance, their lives change. The poor white Creole woman changes her economic position and isolation by "improving" her appearance, by changing her dress, enhancing her beauty, and thereby activating a social life. Annette's active social life leads to marriage with Mr. Mason. Her marriage to the Englishman saves Annette from social and economic ruin and leads to tragedy.

Instead of being an erasure of history, the relationship between Tia and Antoinette is a direct engagement with the roles that have been historically and discursively assigned to black and white people in the West Indies. The relationship exposes the precarious, unstable, yet powerfully destructive mechanisms of the colonial structure. The name-calling, the verbal abuse, and the theft/switch dramatize the violence that inheres in the system of domination upon which the West Indian plantation society was constructed.

If in the postslavery period the relationship between West Indians of African and European ancestry is charged and volatile, the West Indian Creole woman's encounter with the English is estranged and deeply problematic. The textual representation of their conflicts and divergent views corresponds to historical referents: shortly after their marriage, an unnamed speaker observes that Mr. Mason came to the West Indies "to make money as they all do. Some of the big estates are going cheap, and one unfortunate's loss is always a clever man's gain" (30). Mr. Mason represents a new breed of English merchants and imperialists who still seek to dominate the economic life of the colonies and to coerce the labor force into working to ensure their wealth, even after plantation slavery has formally ended. Annette's repeated requests that they leave the island (Jamaica) in this unsettled period and her references to Mr. Mason's newly acquired property in Trinidad and Antigua underscore her awareness of the conflicts between laboring classes and capitalist interests and the ensuing human costs. She tells her husband: "An agent could look after this place. For the time being. . . . You are not a poor man. Do you suppose that they don't know all about your estate in Trinidad? And the Antigua property? They talk about us without stopping. They invent stories about you, and lies about me. They try to find out what we eat every day" (32). Mr. Mason's rejection of Annette's point of view is based on his assumption that his knowledge of "black people" is superior to hers. His refusal to respect the Creole woman's knowledge and understanding of her society helps to set in motion the violent clash that culminates in the burning of Coulibri.

An extended dialogue between Aunt Cora, another West Indian Creole woman, and Mr. Mason foreshadows this clash:

> Myra, one of the new servants, was standing by the sideboard, waiting to change the plates. . . .
>
> My stepfather talked about a plan to import labourers—coolies he called them—from the East Indies. When Myra had gone out Aunt Cora said, "I shouldn't discuss that if I were you. Myra is listening."
>
> "But the people here won't work. They don't want to work. Look at this place—it's enough to break your heart."
>
> "Hearts have been broken," she said. "Be sure of that. I suppose you all know what you are doing."
>
> "Do you mean to say—"
>
> "I said nothing, except that it would be wiser not tell that woman your plans—necessary and merciful no doubt. I don't trust her."
>
> "Live here most of your life and know nothing about the people. It's astonishing. They are children—they wouldn't hurt a fly."
>
> "Unhappily children do hurt flies," said Aunt Cora.
>
> Myra came in again looking mournful as she always did though she smiled when she talked about hell. (35)

Mr. Mason's belittling of the workers as lazy children naturalizes the planter's desire for economic prosperity based on their labor. As Aunt Cora suspects, Myra is listening to the conversation at the dinner table and tells the workers of Mr. Mason's plans. This is suggested, not stated. When the household becomes aware that the people had surrounded the house, Myra was still present: "I heard her speak to Myra and I heard Myra answer her" (38). However, when the fire starts and Annette goes to Pierre's room, she realizes that Myra has left: "The little room was on fire and Myra was not there. She has gone. She was not there" (39). When Aunt Cora responds aphoristically, "That does not surprise me at all," the reader is meant to recall her insistent warning to Mr. Mason to avoid discussing his plans for hiring new workers in Myra's presence.

In this episode understatement, suggestion, and allusions dramatize some commonly held attitudes of the planter class, during and after slavery, toward the people who worked for them. James Shipman, writing in the 1820s, says of the West Indian plantocracy:

> Their table is surrounded by domestic servants . . . where perhaps for want of other subjects, they introduce the favourite topic, the conduct of negroes, and their particular management of them. On these occasions every thing relative to them is freely discussed. . . . This being the real state of the case, can it be wondered at, that the negroes are increasing their knowledge of civil affairs? Don't we know that servants have got *eyes* and *ears* as well as ourselves? And that it is natural enough for them . . . to rehearse the observations of their masters, when those have a particular reference to themselves? (qtd. Brathwaite, "Contradictory Omens," 14)

In *Wide Sargasso Sea* the moment of the attack on Coulibri symbolically marks the end of the marriage between Mr. Mason and Annette, who had repeatedly warned her husband of the dangerous state of affairs: "She was twisting her hands together, her wedding ring fell off and rolled into a corner near the steps" (39). It is also when Annette's sick son Pierre dies or at least "looked dead." If Annette is saddened and feels betrayed by Myra's departure from her sick son, she is angered by her husband's refusal of her knowledge:

> "She left him, she ran away and left him alone to die," said my mother, still whispering. So it was all the more dreadful when she began to scream abuse at Mr. Mason, calling him a fool, a cruel stupid fool. "I told you," she said, "I told you what would happen again and again." Her voice broke, but still she screamed, "You would not listen, you sneered at me, you grinning hypocrite, you ought not live either, you know so much, don't you? Why don't you go out and ask them to let you go? Say how innocent you are. Say you have always trusted them." (40)

Annette's attack on her English husband exposes the inadequacy of his beliefs and his willed ignorance of the people on whose labor he depends.

He is rendered momentarily powerless in the face of the myths that he had taken as knowledge of "black people." In the confusion that follows, Mannie, one of the servants, "pushed Mr. Mason aside" as they struggle to escape the burning house.

With respect to the burning of Coulibri, some metropolitan critics, invoking the imperial history of the West Indies, bemoan the "violence of black people" and the suffering they cause to the whites. Louis James reads it as a fictionalized account of the historical burning of the Genever/ Geneva estate in 1844: "It was a night the like of which Jean Rhys was to recreate in *Wide Sargasso Sea*—the leaping red flames in the dark, the menacing black faces, the screams of the horses, and, beyond the flames, the great tropical night and the mountains" (*Jean Rhys*, 47). The "menacing black faces" reduce human beings to things, on the same ontological plane as horses, the tropical night, and the mountains. Nancy Casey Fulton, echoing Carlyle, sees the whites as victims of black freedom and betrayal: "Despite . . . spiritual closeness, external ties with the blacks are severed with Emancipation. The former slaves, intoxicated with freedom, abandon the helpless plantation owners" ("Exterminating," 344). The inscription of the people as a faceless, undifferentiated mass of black brutality also appears in the novel: "There were so many of them I could hardly see any grass or trees. . . . They all looked the same, it was the same face repeated over and over, eyes gleaming, mouth half open to shout." They mock the "black Englishman," Mannie, who helps the family and the "damn white niggers" (*WSS*, 42).

However, unlike the critical literature, the novel's depiction of the African-derived people as an undifferentiated mass of black hate, terror, and betrayal is counterpointed by the articulation of their political positions and their conflicting attitudes with respect to the fire. Some refuse to let the family and servants go, noting that they would report the incident to the police. One woman responds that they should let them go and say that "All this an accident and they had plenty witness. 'Myra she witness for us.' 'Shut your mouth,' the man said. 'You mash centipede, mash it, leave one little piece and it grow again. . . . [*sic*] What you think police believe, eh? You, or the white nigger?' Mr. Mason stared at him. He seemed not frightened, but too astounded to speak" (43–44). The unnamed colored man, through parabolic language, articulates a radical awareness that predatory forces must be fought ruthlessly in their multifarious forms and directions. His rhetorical question about the police underscores his awareness that forms of jurisdiction and justice are in the service of the Creole ruling class. A little later, when one woman cries at Annette's obvious distress, the same unnamed man "with a cutlass" poses another rhetorical question: "You cry for her—when she ever cry for you? Tell me that" (44).

This intensely charged episode, as I mentioned, emblematizes the post-slavery disputes about labor conditions between the plantocracy and the working people in the West Indies. In this historical moment, the ruling class, in order to secure its socioeconomic position and to control labor, sees punitive and coercive measures such as immigration and Asian indentureship as a viable response to the "laziness" of the African people. The freedpersons respond with material violence as part of their viable means of struggle and resistance at this point. It is within this context that the mirroring of Antoinette and Tia is dramatized. It is in this time and this place that the Creole desires and needs the black Other, whose "friendship" would transcend the violence of the sociopolitical struggles:

> I saw Tia . . . and I ran to her, for she was all that was left of my life as it had been. We had eaten the same food, slept side by side, bathed in the same river. As I ran, I thought, I will live with Tia and I will be like her. Not to leave Coulibri. Not to go. Not. When I was close I saw the jagged stone in her hand but I did not see her throw it. I did not feel it either, only something wet, running down my face. I looked at her and I saw her face crumple up as she began to cry. We stared at each other, blood on my face, tears on hers. It was as if I saw myself. Like in a looking-glass. (45)

In Antoinette's last interaction with Tia, the black child was "a cheating nigger" (24). Here she is "part of [Antoinette's] life," her mirror image, her Other. She needs Tia as the mirror to reflect her self-identity back to her whole, intact. Terry Eagleton asserts: "Where human subjects politically begin, in all their sensuous specificity, is with certain needs and desires. Yet need and desire are also what render us nonidentical with ourselves, opening us up to some broader social dimension; and what is posed within this dimension is the question of what *general* conditions would be necessary for our particular needs and desires to be fulfilled. Mediated through the general in this way, particular demands cease to be self-identical and return to themselves transformed by a discourse of the other" (Eagleton, Jameson, and Said, *Nationalism*, 37–38).

What Antoinette receives back from her Other is a crumpled face. What would Tia's embrace have meant? For Tia it would have meant, among other things, an acceptance of her "thingness," her role as chattel — socially dead and nothing more than a container for the Creole's unbroken self-image. Tia's violent attack repudiates the Creole's needs and gesture as acts of simultaneous coercion and erasure. This scene, made up of need and rejection, pain and pathos, tears and blood, anatomizes the intimate violence that inheres within the Creole's cathexis to the black Other and Tia's refusal of this role. The historical context that the textual operations so carefully construct determines the impossibility of friendship between the two. The representation of their interaction is a precise delineation of what never was, what could never have been, and, most important, why not. The writing of a "real" friendship between the two girls would have depended on an erasure of history. What the text offers instead is an unmasking of that history in its human form and a tragic example of its effects.

When they meet again it is in Antoinette's final installment of the dream, which precedes the burning of the husband's house in England. When Antoinette jumps to reconnect with Tia as her mirror image, we know, as Brathwaite reminds us, that "the 'jump' here is a jump to death; so that Antoinette wakes to death, not to life; for life would have meant dreaming in the reality of madness in a cold castle in England. But death was also her allegiance to . . . the West Indies. In fact, neither world is 'real.' They exist inside the head. Tia was not and never could have been her friend. No matter what Jean Rhys might have made Antoinette think, Tia was historically separated from her" ("Contradictory Omens," 36). In a letter to Francis Wyndham on 22 August 1962, Rhys says, "A lot that seems incredible is true, the obeah for example, the black girl's attack. I've stuck because it should have been a dream truth and I've tried to make it a realistic truth" (*Letters*, 214). It is possible to argue that Rhys's comments and the textual and structural operations of *Wide Sargasso Sea* are not that far removed from Brathwaite's central assertion. Both writers and Rhys's text show that the relationship between the two functions as a dream truth, a kind of death, because a "real" relationship would have been impossible.

If Tia is a mirror image of Antoinette writ small, there are several points at which Annette and Antoinette mirror each other. Both are Creoles who marry Englishmen. Annette says to Mr. Mason about the West Indies, "You won't believe in the other side" (*WSS*, 32). Antoinette repeats with slight variation the same words to her husband, "There is always the other side, always" (128). Both women possess great physical beauty, which is largely responsible for their selection as wives. The importance of their bodies to their husbands is depicted in their ability to dance: "Annette is such a pretty woman. And what a dancer. . . . Yes, what a dancer" (29). When Mr. Mason decides to marry off Antoinette, he wants to know whether she had learned to dance and observes, "That won't be the difficulty. I want you to be happy, Antoinette, secure, I've tried to arrange [it], but we'll have time to talk about that later" (59). Mr. Mason's cryptic comments refer to her arranged marriage. (It is on this night that Antoinette has her second installment of the dream.) The husband says of Antoinette later: "When at last I met her I bowed, smiled, kissed her hand, danced with her. I played the part I was expected to play" (76). Both women's marriages are based on the economy of the slavery and postslavery societies, with their bodies as a site of negotiation in this economy. Both die without the security that money was meant to bring. Both die outside the action of the novel. The sameness of the women is also rendered in their physical expressions: "A frown came between her [Annette's] black eyebrows, deep—it might have been cut with a knife" (20). "The frown between her [Antoinette's] thick eyebrows, deep as if it had been cut with a knife" (138). One of Annette's keepers forces her to drink alcohol as a means of forgetting her pain: "He poured her some more and she took the glass and laughed, threw it over her shoulder. It smashed to pieces" (134). In the ship in which she is being taken to England, Antoinette longs for escape: "I smashed the glasses and plates against the porthole. I hoped it would break and the sea would come in" (181). Structurally and textually, Antoinette tells Annette's story in Part One and again in a truncated form to her husband, in order to explain herself and dispute Daniel's account.

Questions of sexuality, gender, "race," and power also link Annette, Antoinette, and Amélie. Antoinette attacks her husband for sleeping with Amélie by pointing to the connections between his sexual abuse of power and that of the planters during slavery, suggesting that it is the structure of dominance that makes their actions parallel and exploitative:

"I thought you liked the black people so much . . . but that's just a lie like everything else. You like the light brown girls better, don't you? You abused the planters and made up stories about them, but you do the same thing. You send the girl away quicker, and with no money or less money, and that's all the difference."

"Slavery was not a matter of liking or disliking," I said, trying to speak calmly. "It was a question of justice."

"There is no justice. . . . My mother whom you all talk about, what justice did she have? My mother . . . and a black devil kissing her lips. Like you kissed mine." (146–47)

If Antoinette is Tia/Annette/Amélie, she must also come to terms with the identity her husband has invented for her—Bertha, imprisoned in the upper room of his house in England. In renaming Antoinette Bertha, the husband does not succeed in changing her, but in splitting her identity. This split subjectivity becomes the fate that she must confront. When she goes to Christophine for a potion to make her husband love her, she cannot take Christophine's advice to leave him. Antoinette understands that she cannot run away from the imposed identity, the doppelgänger. She must confront and explode it. Her future lies in her past: "I must know more than I know already. For I know that house where I will be cold and not belonging, the bed I shall lie in has red curtains and I have slept there many times before, long ago. How long ago? In that bed I will dream the end of my dream" (111).

When Antoinette is in the upper room, her insistent questioning links her identity to place and purpose. She bemoans the lack of a looking glass but recognizes that the mirror marks an alienation from the self: "There is no looking-glass here and I don't know what I am like now. I remember watching myself brush my hair and how my eyes looked back at me. The girl I saw was myself yet not quite myself. Long ago when I was a child and very lonely I tried to kiss her. But the glass was between us—hard, cold and misted over with my breath. Now they have taken everything away. What am I doing in this place and who am I?" (180). If the mirror cannot reveal the self, it is the social and discursive events that constitute her identity. When Antoinette opens the door of her room, she says she is not in England but in a place made of cardboard—that is, between the pages of a book.

Entrapped in the universe of the Book, Antoinette recognizes that "time has no meaning. But something you can touch and hold like my red dress, that has a meaning" (185). The red dress, an emblem of the West Indies, tells her what she has to do. The meaning of her life is contained in the dress. A symbol of fire, violence, blood, and death, it prefigures the burning down of the husband's house: "I looked at the dress . . . and it was as if the fire had spread across the room" (187).

Antoinette's dream takes over and encapsulates the movement of her "life." Her persistent questioning of her self and her mission parallel her refusal of the imposed identity of Bertha, which is threatening and in pursuit: "It seemed to me that someone was following me, someone was chasing me, laughing. Sometimes I looked to the right or to the left but I never looked behind me for I did not want to see that ghost of a woman they say haunts this place" (187). She refuses to "see" this ghost of a woman (Bertha). By deferring the confrontation with her object-image, she strategically moves away from that imposed identity which would extinguish her presence. Her recognition of the difference and distance between her self and the madwoman in the attic articulates the slippage between the representation of the sign and her own consciousness. This marks a moment of resistance.

Her inevitable confrontation with the doppelgänger occurs only after she goes into the Red Room, a shrine to the wealth, figured as an idol, that her husband accrued through trading in her life. And the moment when Antoinette finally comes face to face with Bertha is also the moment when she starts the fire ("She was surrounded by a gilt frame" suggests Antoinette's looking in the mirror): "It was then that I saw her—the ghost. The woman with streaming hair. She was surrounded by a gilt frame but I knew her. I dropped the candle I was carrying and it caught at the end of a tablecloth and I saw flames shoot up. As I ran or perhaps floated or flew I called help me Christophine help me and looking behind me I saw I had been helped. There was a wall of fire protecting me" (188–89).

Protected by the wall of fire, Antoinette looks at the red sky, which contains her life. Beckoned by her husband and by Tia, she makes the choice of jumping and calling out Tia's name. The jump into the mirror image of Tia and Coulibri suggests a symbolic return to the West Indies, even as it deliberately repeats the burning of Coulibri as a gesture of resistance. Yet it was that moment too which marked the violent separation of

Tia from Antoinette. The cathexis between Antoinette and Tia, as Self/ Other, Narcissus/Echo, the separation and the intimacy all work toward the construction and de(con)struction of the white Creole woman. Like the "Jean Rhys" figure in *Smile Please*, Antoinette's identity is the complex historical and political conditions in human form.

The Nameless Man as a Construct of History and the Book

The "character" of the husband is the most "fully developed." More than two-thirds of the novel is told from his point of view. His narrative appears to be dominant; yet it is his nothingness which the novel insists upon. He enters as a nameless person. In a letter to Diana Athill on 20 February 1966, Rhys says, "I carefully haven't named the man at all" (*Letters*, 297). His last words before disappearing from the action of the novel call attention to his nothingness: "That stupid boy followed us, the basket balanced on his head. He used the back of his hand to wipe away his tears. Who would have thought that any boy would cry like that. For nothing. Nothing . . ." (*WSS*, 173). The husband tells us that the little boy had been crying for him. The repetition of "nothing" further reinforces the sense of nothingness and suggests a dissolution of the self. He does not appear in the last section. These final words spoken by the husband are crucial, as Rhys herself notes in a letter to Francis Wyndham on 14 May 1964: "Last night I . . . got what I thought four or five lines right, fixed inevitable and not to be changed as they were the last lines of part II I was pleased — because four lines right can mean a lot. Well — this morning I woke up to this song ['Everything's been done before'] and the words 'Madame Bovary' and realised at once that these lines were not the words but the situation at the end of Madame Bovary, her death" (*Letters*, 276).

The husband's "death" is implicit in his beginning, and the process by which he is revealed as Nothing becomes the most important part of his "character." His entrance in the novel is a beginning with no introduction, no a priori explanation, no overt textual "setting up," no thematic preparation or signal to the reader. This is an inscription of the structural origins of the narrative and history of imperial Europe, which designates the West Indies as a blank space on which to inscribe the desires of the European man. As Frantz Fanon has noted, "The settler makes history; his life is an epoch, an Odyssey. He is the absolute beginning" (*Wretched*, 51). In the mind of Europe, prior existential reality is rendered as silence, severed from meaning. It is this which enables Europe to speak for its Others. In the West Indian text and context this beginning must be read simultaneously as error and History. Part One ends with Antoinette's dream, which foreshadows her doom. Part Two opens with the husband's words: "So it was all over, the advance and the retreat, the doubts and hesitations. Everything finished, for better or for worse" (65). The images are at once martial and marital. Whatever "it" was has been overcome. And the victor has the privilege of constructing his history and his truth and imposing it as Truth and History. The violence done to what went before is epistemic and linguistic.

When the husband arrives at the honeymoon house, he notices "Byron's poems, novels by Sir Walter Scott, *Confessions of an Opium Eater*. Some shabby brown volumes, and on the last shelf, *Life and Letters Of* . . . . The rest was eaten away" (75; Rhys's ellipsis). Homi Bhabha argues that the discovery of the book, a scene that is insistently repeated after the nineteenth century in colonial texts, is "at once, a moment of originality and authority. . . . The discovery of the book installs the sign of appropriate representation: the word of God, truth, art creates the conditions for a beginning, a practice of history and narrative" ("Signs," 166). Walter Scott and Lord Byron are two English writers whose writing showed clear connections to the enterprise of empire.[3] Percy G. Adams states that Scott recommended for publication William Williams's *The Journal of Penrose, Seaman,* and Byron "was fascinated by it." William Williams spent a year in Jamaica as a painter. His work, which for many years was considered factual, is a fiction that incorporates one of the most powerful myths in European discourse on the Caribbean — the castaway in a distant, lonely place (Adams, *Travel Literature,* 133–34).

After observing the title *Life and Letters Of* . . . , the husband rereads a letter he has written to his father. (In the Rhys text, the letter follows directly in italics.) He observes: "I wondered how they got their letters posted. I folded mine and put it into a drawer of the desk. As for my confused impressions they will never be written. There are blanks in my mind that cannot be filled up" (*WSS*, 76). The husband's placing of his letter in the drawer of the desk suggests that his life and letters will meet a fate similar to that of the book entitled *Life and Letters Of* . . . . In the same way that a precursory writer's life and letters has been eaten away, the husband's life and text will decompose at the end of his narrative into a "Nothing." The nameless husband is built up, analyzed, and cited in order that he might be annulled, reabsorbed into the Eurocentric discourses of narrative and history. In this way, his epistemological and ontological ground is simultaneously asserted and undermined. His nonappearance in Part Three highlights rather than undermines the power with which the nameless Englishman is invested. His dissolution into the "master narrative," structured as a powerful absence, still constitutes, though it does not determine, Antoinette's fate. His invisibility is a sign of the power of the ideologies by which he is constituted.

In the presentation of the husband, the text also examines the contradictions that inhere in an ideology of cultural superiority, rationality, and control by exposing the individual and social results of its practice. One of the achievements of the narrative structure is that the husband's story provides insights and gives the reader access to precisely those sites where the husband most lacks insight into himself. His "perception" of the West Indian people, their Otherness, the landscape, derives not from his interaction but from prior "knowledge," which invents the West Indies as uncivilized and wild, a place to make money, where the blacks are inhuman and the Creole whites are contaminated and strange: "She never blinks at all it seems to me. Long, sad, dark alien eyes. Creole of pure English descent she may be, but they are not English or European either" (67). "For a moment [Antoinette] looked very much like Amélie. Perhaps they are related, I thought. It's possible, it's even probable in this damned place" (127). "I wouldn't hug and kiss [black people]. . . . I couldn't" (91). These "personal" feelings of antipathy are undermined in several ways. When the husband makes this last remark, he notes that Antoinette laughed for a long time but would not tell him why she laughed (91). His later sexual encounter with Amélie must be read in light of his own words. The text also satirizes the stereotyped depiction of the "lazy black." When he wakes on the first morning of his visit to Granbois, Antoinette tells him that she had sent Christophine away twice already (with his breakfast, which she had prepared). He notes, even as he is still in bed drinking her "delicious coffee," that she "looks so lazy. She dawdles about" (86). Antoinette later tells him: "I'm very lazy you know. Like Christophine. I often stay in bed all day" (86).

The husband notes that the difference between himself and Antoinette made it impossible for him to feel love for her: "As for the happiness I gave her, that was worse than nothing. I did not love her. I was thirsty for her, but that is not love. I felt very little tenderness for her, she was a stranger to me, a stranger who did not think or feel as I did" (93). Part of his estrangement from Antoinette derives from their mutually exclusive definitions of "reality" as well as his own inability to assert superiority by controlling her perception.

> She often questioned me about England and listened attentively to my answers, but I was certain nothing I said made much difference. Her mind was already made up. Some romantic novel, a stray remark never forgotten, a sketch, a picture, a song, a waltz, some note of music, and her ideas were fixed. About England and about Europe. I could not change them and probably nothing would. Reality might disconcert her, bewilder her, hurt her, but it would not be reality. It would be only a mistake, a misfortune, a wrong path taken, her fixed ideas would never change.
>
> Nothing that I told her influenced her at all. (94)

Antoinette's refusal of the husband's England and Europe, her recalcitrance in the face of his "reality," provides the impetus for his desire to kill her: "Die then. Sleep. . . . I wonder if she ever guessed how near she came to dying. . . . Desire, Hatred, Life, Death came very close in the darkness. Better not know how close" (94). When Christophine later challenges him and charges that he wanted to "break . . . up" Antoinette, the husband says to himself: "It was like that. . . . It was like that. But better to say nothing" (152). The identity of the husband is constituted by the history and narrative of Europe and is dependent upon the "breaking up" of Antoinette, the Creole woman.

One event that simultaneously strengthens and weakens the husband's position is the arrival of Daniel's letter, which tells him that he had been lied to by Antoinette's family. After reading the letter, his initial desire, which he disavows, is to trample Antoinette (99). The husband wonders how to "discover truth" and wanders into the forest. He comes to "the ruins of a stone house. . . . Under the orange tree I noticed little bunches of flowers tied with grass." He sees a little girl who screams and runs away: "She sobbed as she ran, a small frightened sound." When Baptiste finds him, the West Indian man tells the husband that a priest, Père Lilièvre, lived there a long time ago. The husband wants to know whether there was a ghost there, and Baptiste says he knows "nothing about that foolishness." The husband describes Baptiste's face as savage and reproachful. He notes that when questioned about not liking the woods at night, Baptiste pointed to a light (104–6).

The carefully recounted details—the references to "Père Lilièvre," the light, the ruins of an old house, the paved road, the orange tree, the little girl's fear of the white man—suggest the legend of Père Labat as written by Lafcadio Hearn in 1890. Hearn rewrites the legend of Père Labat based on oral accounts, his own reading of Père Labat's narrative and biography, and his "knowledge" of West Indian people. It is important to note how Labat's *life* in the West Indies in the seventeenth and eighteenth centuries becomes a *legend* by the late nineteenth century when Hearn is writing. According to the legend, Hearn says, the ghost of Père Labat haunted the mountains carrying a lantern: "Everybody is afraid of seeing it. . . . And mothers tell their children, when the little ones are naughty: . . . I will make Pè Labatt come and take you away" (*Two Years*, 153). The light often came from the direction of the Morne d'Orange. Hearn collates the various oral accounts, and in seeking to test their "truth," he turns to a precursory written text:

> And who was Père Labat,—this strange priest whose memory, weirdly disguised by legend, thus lingers in the oral literature of the colored people? Various encyclopaedias answer the question, but far less fully and less interestingly than Dr. Ruft, the Martinique historian whose article upon him in the *Études Statisques et Historiques* has that charm of sympathetic comprehension by which a master-biographer sometimes reveals himself a necromancer,—making us feel a vanished personality with the power of a living presence. . . . Jean Baptiste Labat must be ranked among the extraordinary men of his century. (157)

For Hearn, Labat shaped the history and "helped" the people of Martinique. He observes that "all the wonderful work the Dominican accomplished has been forgotten by the people; while all the witchcrafts he warred against survive and flourish openly; and his very name is seldom uttered but in connection with superstitions,—has been, in fact, preserved among the blacks by the power of superstition alone" (174).

In *Wide Sargasso Sea*, when the husband returns to the house after his adventure in the woods, he too seeks confirmation of his "knowledge" and "experience" in precedent, as recorded in a European text. He reads *The Glittering Coronet of Isles* in order to find an explanation for what he has "seen" at the priest's ruined house and for Baptiste's strange behavior. The text reassures him that "negroes as a rule refuse to discuss the black magic in which so many believe." The account ends with "It is further complicated by . . ." (*WSS*, 107; Rhys's ellipsis). Later, after taking the obeah drink and sleeping with Antoinette, the husband, confused and frightened, returns to the ruins of the priest's house almost as an act beyond his conscious will: "I do not remember that day clearly, where I ran or how I fell or wept or lay exhausted. But I found myself at last near the ruined house and the wild orange tree. Here with my head in my arms I must have slept" (139).

Since the anonymous Englishman must purchase and maintain his identity with the currency of European epistemology, discourse, and dominance, his struggles to regain his loss of predicates in the West Indies demand that he subordinate the place and people to this paradigm. One of his most important efforts in this regard is that of changing Antoinette's name, codifying the Creole according to the logic of domination and desire. Antoinette understands the meaning of the gesture: "Bertha is not my name. You are trying to make me into someone else, calling me by another name. I know, that's obeah too" (147). When Antoinette tells him that changing her name is a form of obeah too, she calls attention to what Sartre describes as "that other witchery . . . Western culture" (Preface, *Wretched*, 19). The husband is as much enchanted by the "obeah" of European supremacy as Antoinette is by a belief in the cultural practices she attributes to Christophine. He himself is rendered subject to an ideology of control, without necessarily having a choice. In his encounter with Christophine, he

> said loudly and wildly, "And do you think that I wanted all this? I would give my life to undo it. I would give my eyes never to have seen this abominable place."
>
> [Christophine] laughed. "And that's the first damn word of truth you speak. You choose what you give, eh? Then choose. You meddle in something and perhaps you don't know what it is." (161)

When Christophine ironically challenges him to choose, she is implying that he cannot.

The West Indian novel insists that the imperial tradition—out of which the husband emanates and into which he dissolves—depends for its existence on the reconstitution of Others as creatures of European will and a belief in Europe's right of appropriation. Yet, at the same time, it anatomizes and displays the ravages of such a system on the person who appears to be privileged and dominant. As many theorists have shown, the objectification of Others demands first and foremost the objectification of the Self. The Rhys text constructs the husband as "Nothing" and the West Indian landscape as a not-nothing to which, ironically, access is denied. Shortly after his arrival at the honeymoon house, he notes: "What I see is nothing—I want what it *hides*—that is not nothing" (87). Virginia Woolf also points to the imperializing desires deeply embedded in the education of privileged Englishmen—the narcissism, the will to domination, and the inevitable tragedy that it breeds:

> They are driven by instincts which are not within their control. They too, the patriarchs . . . had endless difficulties, terrible drawbacks to contend with. Their education . . . had bred in them [great] defects. True, they had money and power, but only at the cost of harbouring in their breasts an eagle, a vulture, forever tearing the liver out and plucking at the lungs—the instinct for possession, the rage for acquisition which drives them to desire other people's fields and goods perpetually; to make frontiers and flags; battleships and poison gas; to offer up their own lives." (*Room*, 38)

The husband recognizes ultimately that he can ensure his dominance only by returning to England and taking Antoinette with him. His decision is written as an act that privileges his ego. The word "I," as an hierarchical marker, appears fifteen times, while Antoinette is drawn as a stick figure. Yet his conscious thoughts refuse what his drawings convey—his decision to return to England with Antoinette as captive:

> He scowled at me then, I thought. I scowled too as I re-read the letter I had written to the lawyer. However much I paid Jamaican servants I would never buy discretion. I'd be gossiped about, sung about. . . . Wherever I went I would be talked about. . . . I drank some more rum and, drinking, I drew a house surrounded by trees. A large house. I divided the third floor into rooms and in one room I drew a standing woman— a child's scribble, a dot for a head, a larger one for the body, a triangle for a skirt, slanting lines for arms and feet. But it was an English house.
> English trees. I wondered if I ever should see England again. (163)

Of the last section before the husband disappears into nothingness, Rhys says:

> It seemed so hopeless—so plodding. Then . . . I got right away from it and wrote what I call poetry and suddenly saw that I must lift the whole thing out of real life into—well *on* to a different plane. . . . *Then* I got this idea of making the last chapter partly "poetry"—partly prose—song. . . . I may not have done it. If not—well—I wonder if I can do it any other way—now. . . . I wonder too if I am terribly excited about something that has been done ago—James Joyce tried to make sound I know like Anna Livia Plurabelle [*Finnegan's Wake*] but this is of course lighter, different—a musical comedy compared to grand opera. (*Letters*, 277–78)

The automatic writing in this section (164–73) includes the husband's thoughts and feelings as constituted by Shakespeare, the histories and legends of the West Indies, Antoinette's songs and stories, Christophine's words, and his hates and desires: "Words rush through my head (deeds too). Words. Pity is one of them. It gives me no rest. Pity like a new-born babe striding the blast. I read that long ago when I was young—I hate poets now and poetry. As I hate music which I loved once. Pity is there none for me? Tied to a lunatic for life" (164). Christophine's words come back to haunt him even as he thought he had forgotten her. They beckon him to reject his "knowledge" as false and to embrace what he "sees" and feels in the West Indies: "As for her, I'd forgotten her for the moment. So I shall never understand why, suddenly, bewilderingly, I was certain that everything I had imagined to be truth was false. False. Only the magic and the dream are true—all the rest's a lie. Let it go. Here is the secret. Here. (*But it is lost, that secret, and those who know it cannot tell it*)" (167–68).

The husband draws consolation from his knowledge that "History" is on his side—a history that erases or deforms the Other: "It's a long, long line. She's one of them. I too can wait—for the day when she is only a memory to be avoided, locked away, and like all memories a legend. Or a lie . . ." (172; Rhys's ellipsis). His "madness" becomes Antoinette's imprisonment in the cardboard house of the Book, which she sets ablaze. In *Wide Sargasso Sea* the "character" of the Englishman, which appears to be the most "fully developed," is inextricably tied to a concern with Empire—imperial desires, imperial fictions, imperial aggression, imperial history.

John Hearne was one of the first critics to elaborate on the broader tropological and historical significance of Rhys's rewriting of the English canonical text:

> Its originality lies in taking the characters from an established work ... back from their literary beginnings and fashioning, credibly, the unwritten history of creatures whom a previous author had invented. Its validity depends on a *book* from elsewhere, not on a basic, assumed life.
>
> And yet, is this not a superb and audacious metaphor of so much of West Indian life? Are we not still, in so many of our responses, creatures of books and inventions fashioned by others who used us as mere producers, as figments of their imagination; and who regarded the territory as a ground over which the inadmissable [*sic*] or forgotten forces of the psyche could run free for a while before being written off or suppressed? ("The Wide Sargasso Sea," 323)

"They Call Me Daniel . . . but My Name Is Esau"

One of the most distinctive features of *Wide Sargasso Sea* is its use of narrative voices. As Jean D'Costa states, "Jean Rhys takes gossip, voice, and viewpoint to extraordinary lengths to fashion a new form: the multiple first-person narratives that make up the account of the first Mrs. Rochester in *Wide Sargasso Sea* have no precedent other than the necessity of a new sensibility and imagination" (D'Costa, "Bra Rabbit," 256). Rhys herself affirms the complexity of her novel in a letter to Francis Wyndham on 14 September 1959: "Because I tried to put in some of my love of the place where I was born (I shifted their honeymoon to Dominica) and some of my loathing of cruelty and hypocrisy all sorts of other characters have crept in" (*Letters*, 172). Rhys also tells Selma Vaz Dias in a letter of 30 August 1966 that "this book is complicated and a bit like a patchwork" (237). Embedded in the husband's narrative are counterdiscursive texts that he writes but cannot read. An examination of these fissures his discourse. In order to fully read Antoinette's life, we must read against the grain of his story. To read "the other side" of the story is to read what the husband's text cannot know that it does not know. The aporias of the husband's narrative are the ground of possibility for the "carnival" of voices, the multivocality, which helps to create the text of *Wide Sargasso Sea*.

One of the voices/subjects embedded in the husband's story is that of a man, a mulatto, who calls himself Daniel Cosway. If the husband has no name, Daniel has no name *and* an excess of names (at least two surnames). He signs his letter to the husband "Daniel Cosway." Antoinette asserts angrily: "He has no right to that name. . . . His real name, if he has one, is Daniel Boyd. He hates all white people, but he hates me the most" (*WSS*, 128). The figure of the mulatto who hates the Creole or whose paternity is uncertain or denied recurs in Rhys's writing. (This figure appears in *Smile Please*, *Voyage in the Dark*, and "Again the Antilles.") The ambiguity or lack of a surname — the Name of the Father, especially in its linkage to "race" and "race hatred" — problematizes the ontological realm occupied by proper names within the context of social systems formed by the institution of slavery.

"Pater incertus est" and a concern with "illegitimacy," as these are embodied in the mulatto figure, are central themes in the discourses of the white plantocracy of the West Indies. The major themes are racial contamination and economic threat. These are often figured as the loose sexual behavior of white men, which is a function of the innate promiscuity of black women, and the general animality of the black Other. Unquestionably, one of the most influential and eloquent ideologues of the Creole class is the eighteenth-century Jamaican planter, politician, lawyer, and writer Edward Long:

> A promiscuous intercourse and an uncertain parentage, if they were universal, would soon dissolve the frame of the constitution, from the infinity of claims and contested rights of succession: for this reason, the begetting an illegitimate child is reputed a violation of the social compacts. . . . The detestation in which [the transgressors] have been held by the English laws . . . may be inferred from the spirit of their several maxims: "A legitimate child is he that is born after wedlock." "The offspring of promiscuous conjunctions has no father." "Marriage ascertains the father." "Bastards are not endowed with the privilege of children." "No man's children."
>
> The institution of marriage, is doubtless of as much concern in the colony, as it is in the mother country. (*History*, 2:325–27)

In a lengthy and impassioned argument justifying the laws enacted in the 1760s to limit white men's financial support of their children by African women, Long reveals how sexual segregation and the prohibition of "miscegenation" are recruited into the enforcement of legal, juridical, and economic systems of governance that ensure that white men as a class retain power and wealth and maintain imperial control. He concludes that "it might be much better for Britain, and Jamaica too, if the white men in that colony would abate of their infatuated attachments to black women, and, instead of being 'grac'd with a *yellow offspring not their own,*' perform the duty incumbent on every good citizen, by raising in honourable wedlock a race of unadulterated beings" (2:327). Long also observes that "intemperance and sensuality are the fatal instruments which, in [the West Indies], have committed such havoc, and sent their heedless votaries in the prime of manhood to an untimely grave. It is owing to these destructive causes, that we perceive here such a number of young widows, who are greedily snapped up by distressed bachelors, or rapacious widowers" (2:285–86).

The noted historian Lowell Joseph Ragatz (to whom Eric Williams dedicated his *Capitalism and Slavery*), in his influential work *The Fall of the Planter Class in the British Caribbean* (1928), argues: "The white man in tropical America was out of his habitat. Constant association with an inferior subject race blunted his moral fibre and he suffered marked demoralization. His transitory residence and the continued importation of Africans debased life. Miscegenation, so contrary to Anglo-Saxon nature, resulted in the rapid rise of a race of human hybrids. Planter society was based upon whites and blacks, removed to unfamiliar scenes, and their unhappy offspring. The saddest pages of imperial history relate the heartrending attempts to effect adjustment between these discordant elements" (5).

Wide Sargasso Sea reinscribes this discourse as unattributed common knowledge, accepted "truths," and customs. Shortly after Annette's second marriage, anonymous, unidentified voices (of white women) gossip about Father Cosway's licentious ways: "Emancipation troubles killed old Cosway? Nonsense—the estate was going downhill for years before that. He drank himself to death. . . . And all those women! She never did anything to stop him—she encouraged him. Presents and smiles for the bastards every Christmas. Old customs? Some old customs are better dead and buried" (*WSS*, 28–29).

Daniel Cosway, as he calls himself, inscribes his subjectivity as an effect, a personal consequence, a lived embodiment of these "old customs." Daniel's narrative, through the letters and conversations with the husband, works the economy of discursive conventions on West Indian slave and postslavery societies. Gordon Lewis's account of playing the stereotype on the part of African people during slavery is useful as an understanding of Daniel's posture: "The slave recognized the psychological need of the stereotype in the master mentality and cleverly exploited it for his own ends. . . . To deliberately feed the master's expectations . . . to delude the master into a false sense of security; to adopt an air of exaggerated deference before the white person, really a disguised form of insolence; above all, to disguise one's own true feelings, since no one, least of all whites, could be trusted: all became part of the game, of putting on ole massa" (*Main Currents*, 181). Daniel manipulates the Englishman through appeals to the accepted assumptions of the decadence of the Creole men, the availability of the bodies of the slave/black/mulatto women, concerns with the moral impurity of West Indian whites, and the superiority of the English. The form of Daniel's first letter, its flattery and feigned piety, is meant to appeal to this last—the narcissistic belief in the superiority of the English:

Dear Sir. I take up my pen after long thought and meditation but in the end the truth is better than a lie. I have this to say. You have been shamefully deceived by the Mason family. . . .

You ask what proof I have . . . I am your wife's brother by another lady, half-way house as we say. Her father and mine was a shameless man and of all his illegitimates I am the most unfortunate and poverty stricken. . . .

This young Mrs. Cosway is worthless and spoilt, she can't lift a hand for herself and soon the madness that is in . . . all these white Creoles come out. . . .

Then it seems to me that it is my Christian duty to warn the gentleman that she is no girl to marry with the bad blood she have from both sides. . . .

I hear you young and handsome with a kind word for all, black, white, also coloured. . . .

I sit at my window and the words fly past me like birds—with God's help I catch some.

A week this letter take me. . . . So quickly now I draw to a close and cease my task. (95–98)

When the husband does not respond, the obsequiousness and flattery disappear. Daniel threatens the husband with scandal and demands that he visit him. The husband complies.

Daniel Cosway/Boyd/No (Father's) Name can be read as the return of the repressed with a vengeance:

> He went on talking, his eyes fixed on a framed text hanging on the dirty white wall, "Vengeance is Mine."
>
> "You take too long, Lord," he told it. "I hurry you up a bit." . . .
>
> "They call me Daniel," he said, still not looking at me, "but my name is Esau." (122)

Daniel, by naming himself Esau, is establishing prior claim to the wealth of the White Father by reason of birth. The trope of the disadvantaged first son, robbed of birthright and blessing, ironically alludes to the laws of primogeniture, which played such an important role in the plantation societies of the West Indies.[4] The second son was often sent to make his fortune in the West Indies by marrying into the plantocracy, as was the case with the husband: "Dear Father . . . I have a modest competence now. I will never be a disgrace to you or to my dear brother the son you love. No begging letters, no mean requests. None of the furtive shabby manoeuvres of a younger son. I have sold my soul or you have sold it" (70). When Daniel calls himself Esau in the presence of the husband, with his eyes on the text of the Father, he is suggesting that the second son (in-law) has unfairly gained his birthright.

> All I get is curses and get-outs from that damn devil my father. My father old Cosway, with his white marble tablet in the English church at Spanish Town for all to see. It have a crest on it and a motto in Latin and words in big black letters. I never know such lies. . . . "Pious," they write up. "Beloved by all." Not a word about the people he buy and sell like cattle. "Merciful to the weak," they write up. Mercy! The man have a heart like stone. Sometimes when he get sick of a woman which is quickly, he free her like he free my mother, even he give her a hut and a bit of land for herself (a garden some call that), but it is no mercy, it's for wicked pride he do it. . . . I know by heart all the lies they tell—no one to stand up and say, Why you write lies in the church? (122)

Daniel's assertion mimes and repeats the husband's narrative: the scorned-son motif and the husband's own condemnation of the West Indian planters. When he marries Antoinette, it is not the marriage ceremony that is privileged but the meaning of the stone tablets: "I remember little of the actual ceremony. Marble memorial tablets on the walls commemorating the virtues of the last generation of planters. All benevolent. All slave-owners. All resting in peace" (77). Daniel, by explaining his situation to the husband, is staking a claim for his inheritance. The site of negotiation for this is the body of the slave owner's daughter, Antoinette. Daniel's last derisive words to the husband suggest a sexual and racial "contamination" of his wife: " 'Give my love to your wife—my sister,' he called after me venomously. 'You are not the first to kiss her pretty face. Pretty face, soft skin, pretty colour—not yellow like me. But my sister just the same . . .' " (126; Rhys's ellipsis). The sexual innuendo is further suggested in what the husband sees as he leaves Daniel's house: "A black and white goat tethered near by was staring at me and for what seemed minutes I stared back into its slanting yellow-green eyes" (126).

Should Daniel's story be believed or should it not? How credible is it? What evidence does the text provide to support it? What are its claims to "truth" and historical veracity? Can these questions be answered? If the referentiality and signification of the character are called into question by the semiotic status of his names, what meanings may be produced by a reading of the signifier Daniel Cosway/Daniel Boyd/Daniel No (Father's) Name/Esau? In short, how do we read his narrative? Daniel and his story have been largely ignored or considered problematical by critics.[5] Mark McWatt notes: "It is claimed that Bertha Mason is 'a typical example of . . . the ruthless exploitation of a minor character in a novel of persuasion.' But if there is any validity to this kind of charge surely it can be made about some of the minor characters in *Wide Sargasso Sea*—Daniel Cosway, for instance, can perhaps be seen as a mechanical device for stoking the fears and doubts of Rochester concerning his wife; and Amélie a mechanical device for emphasizing the breakdown of the marriage" ("Preoccupation," 16).

I believe that, at the level of narrative, McWatt's assertion can be easily justified. Daniel is a shadow of the husband, a displaced phantasm, a surrogate. In their attitude toward Antoinette, the frontier between black and white, West Indian and English, is asserted and uncertain. Both Daniel and the husband are emanations of a repressed history of violence, linked to sexuality, gender, and economics, which has been written out of imperial history. Daniel, as the subaltern of the Englishman, is contiguous and distant, Self and Other. It is significant that the husband is the only person within the textual "world" with whom he communicates directly. Daniel is also the ever-present mulatto figure as a container for the white self and an object of scorn. His sexual innuendo may also allude to the paranoiac construction of the "black" man's perpetual desire for the white woman's body.

But the textual and structural operations of the novel complicate the issue. The ambiguity engendered by his simultaneous lack and excess of proper names allows us to read his narrative—the register of language, the discourses he deploys, the rhetorical tactics—as representative of a kind of speaker whose story (history) repeats and fissures the historical and cultural representations which the husband, as a kind of speaker, articulates as "knowledge" and by which he is constituted. Daniel is also made of this discourse, but differentially. Daniel's narrative intratextually operates upon and critiques that of the husband through repetition, inversion, parody, and contrapuntal complementarity. Furthermore, his story contradicts Antoinette's and remains a probability. He gives seemingly incontrovertible facts about Antoinette and Annette, asserting a kind of epiphenomenal knowledge of their family background as West Indian Creoles. His story as told to the Englishman cannot be disproved. It can only be denied or disbelieved. Whether it is accepted or rejected, it remains an important dimension of the narratives through which the subjective and sociolocational identities of the Creole woman are constructed in the slave and postslavery societies of the Caribbean.

Wide Sargasso Sea, a work in which the West Indies of the 1840s impinges upon and elucidates the England and West Indies of the 1950s and 1960s, seems to be underwritten by the Creole's desire to reclaim hegemony over the literary representation of the West Indies and "black people." The racialist usurpation of the voices, acts, and identities of "black people," so central to Rhys's writing as a whole, is the psychological cement in the architecture of this novel: Tia as cheating, hostile nigger and container for the self; Amélie as the lusty mulatto wench who hates the Creole; Daniel as the hateful mulatto and mirror image for the husband; Christophine as nurse, black mammy, and obeah woman who privileges the white child's needs over her own and, at times, infantilizes the Creole woman; the deletion of any autonomous "life" for the black and mulatto characters. Yet the unorthodox presentation of an anatomy of the "life" of the Creole woman in terms of the history of the West Indies and the deconstruction of its own assumptions, which pervade *Wide Sargasso Sea*, ensure that the work raises more questions than it answers.

Voyage in the Dark

My analysis of *Voyage in the Dark* will be based on a reading of the novel that includes its original ending, as it is in this ending that the text brings together the West Indies of the 1840s with Europe of 1914. In a letter of 18 February 1934 to fellow writer Evelyn Scott, Rhys says: "I don't know if I've got away with it. I don't know. It's written almost entirely in words of one syllable. Like a kitten mewing perhaps. The big idea. . . . [S]omething to do with time being an illusion. . . . [T]he past exists—side by side with the present, not behind it. . . . What was—is. I tried to do it by making the past (the West Indies) very vivid—the present dreamlike (downward career of girl)—starting of course piano and ending fortissimo" (*Letters*, 24).

The use of monosyllabic language, linked to the emphasis on the plasticity and sensory value of language to enact the coevalness of time, represents a form of rewriting of the dominant to make it bear the burden of "difference." This strategy shows affinities to Deleuze and Guattari's reading of Kafka. The language of a minor literature, they argue, "stops being representative in order to now move toward its extremities or its limits." Deterritorialization of language opens it up to an intensive use which "makes it take flight along creative lines of escape . . . [and produces] sober syntactical invention simply to write like a dog." Or, in Rhys's case, like a kitten (*Kafka*, 23–26).

The first-person narrative of *Voyage in the Dark* tells the story of a young Creole woman, Anna Morgan. Anna's apparently transparent story, told through the use of simple language, enhances the sense of her naivete and youth, her displacement. Her inability to fit the West Indies and England together suggests a loss of temporal (historical) referents: "Sometimes it was as if I were back there and as if England were a dream. At other times England was the real thing and out there was the dream, but I could never fit them together" (8).

An important corollary to this is that Anna apprehends experiences through her senses, feelings, body, and memory: "Somebody was playing the piano—a tinkling sound like water running. I began to walk very slowly because I wanted to listen. But it got farther and farther away and then I couldn't hear it any more. 'Gone for ever,' I thought" (10). "I was always sad, with the same sort of hurt that the cold gave me in my chest" (15). "When you have fever you are heavy and light, you are small and swollen, you climb endlessly a ladder which turns like a wheel" (33). When Anna encounters unpleasant or painful experiences, she does not "tell" her response but is often shown reacting in a delayed mode. Each painful emotional blow is first deflected and the effects on her rendered in slow motion (e.g., being compared to a stone, the cigarette-burning incident, Vincent's letter). Sometimes there is a sliding back into memory of the West Indies.

Anna is structured ontologically as divided self, loss, absence, and silence—in the sense that she cannot "communicate." She is not present and accountable. She is in one sense, therefore, not a reliable narrator: "I wanted to talk about it [the West Indies]. I wanted to make him see what it was like. And it all went through my head, but too quickly. Besides, *you can never tell about things*" (53; emphasis added). The narrator's assertion suggests a recognition that experiences, feelings, perceptions cannot be transmitted through words. We can read Anna's assertion as a warning that her narrative knows that there are things that it cannot say, gaps it cannot fill, that "things," especially the things that matter, cannot be communicated. Words, Anna also says, have no meaning: "I am bad, not good any longer, bad. That has no meaning, absolutely none. Just words. But something about the darkness of the streets has a meaning" (57). Anna's own utterances suggest that her function is hardly to *communicate* her story. Instead, her story writes the differential in the power of language articulated by her and by the other voices in the text.

Anna's subjectivity is engendered by an interpenetration of discourses of history, gender, "race," class, and empire. *Voyage in the Dark* assembles aspects of imperial politics and history as well as contemporary cultural artifacts (such as popular songs, advertisements, films, and books) to provide the framework through which the narrator's story is transmitted. A crucial passage, as several critics have noted, is the intertextual use of Zola's *Nana*, an anagram of Anna: "I was lying on the sofa reading *Nana*. It was a paper-covered book with a coloured pictured of a stout, dark woman brandishing a wine-glass. She was sitting on the knee of a bald-headed man in evening dress. The print was very small, and the endless procession of words gave me a curious feeling—sad, excited and frightened. *It wasn't what I was reading, it was the look of the dark, blurred words going on endlessly that gave me that feeling*" (9; emphasis added).

The words on the page are "lost" on Anna in terms of their grammatical and discursive "meaning," but they affect her in terms of her senses and feelings. It is through their affective power that they are transcoded into image. As an uninitiated reader, she will not grasp the words on the page as "meaningful," but the words have already positioned her. The effect of the Book on the reader is infinitely more potent than her reading of it could be. (Anna reads other books, more or less, in the traditional way. What is important here is the account the text gives of her response to this foundational book, which is the one by which she is most defined and which will become, in a sense, her story.)

The reference to the picture on the cover is richly allusive. The figuration of Nana and her function as a sexualized aesthetic object, as Sander L. Gilman has demonstrated, dramatizes the complicated act of reading and the construction of the reader: "The portrait of *Nana* is also embedded in a complex literary matrix. . . . The figure of Nana first appeared in Emile Zola's *L'Assommoir* (1877). . . . Manet was captivated by the figure of Nana (as was the French reading public), and his portrait of her symbolically reflected her sexual encounters presented during the novel. Zola then decided to build the next novel in his Rougon-Macquart cycle about the figure of Nana as a sexualized female. Thus in Zola's *Nana* the reader is presented with Zola's reading of Manet's portrait of Nana" ("Black Bodies," 253).

The "stout, dark woman . . . sitting on the knee of a . . . man in evening dress" (*Voyage*, 9), which Anna observes, suggests Manet's portrait, in which "Nana is presented being admired by a well-dressed-man-about-town" (Gilman, "Black Bodies," 251).

Maudie observes, "I bet you a man writing a book about a tart tells a lot of lies one way and another. Besides, all books are like that—just somebody stuffing you up" (*Voyage*, 10). Books are part of the mechanism that initiates individuals into the social system. Anna's "reading" of the text is followed immediately by her meeting with Walter, who will further the initiation process. When Maudie tells him that "the girls call [Anna] the Hottentot" (12), this suggests that Anna is constructed not only as a sexualized object but specifically as a black sexualized object. Gilman argues that the figure of the Hottentot or the sexualized black is hidden in the figure of the white prostitute of Manet's painting: "We know where the black servant is hidden in *Nana*—within Nana. Even Nana's seeming beauty is but a sign of the black hidden within. All her external stigmata point to the pathology within the sexualized female" (251).

Voyage's excavation of the tropes of racialized sexuality in the literary and plastic arts of European male artists and its reinscription of these will be examined in what follows. The construction of Anna as a "blackened," sexualized object in Walter's presence helps to define the male/female, white/black, master/slave dialectic of their relationship. It simultaneously privileges, complicates, and undermines the historicity of these constructions. In a conversation with Walter Anna recalls:

> "I saw an old slave-list at Constance once," I said. "It was handwritten on that paper that rolls up. Parchment, d'you call it? It was in columns—the names and ages and what they did and then General Remarks."
>
> . . . Maillotte Boyd, aged 18, mulatto, house servant. The sins of the fathers Hester said are visited upon the children unto the third and fourth generation—don't talk such nonsense to the child Father said— a myth don't get tangled up in myths he said to me . . . . (52–53; Rhys's ellipses)

During sex with Walter, the name Maillotte Boyd repeats itself in her mind: "*Maillotte Boyd, aged 18. Maillotte Boyd, aged 18. . . . But I like it like this. I don't want it any other way but this*" (56; Rhys's ellipsis). The presence of "history" during an apparently intimate moment collapses the past into the present even as it exposes the fiction of private, individual subjects connected to each other through unmediated desire or romantic love. Anna does not "lie back and think of England" but re-members the commodified body of the West Indian slave woman on the auction block. The physical connection between Walter and Anna is placed under erasure, allowing the repressed Other, the body of the nineteenth-century mulatto slave woman, to return via and between the repressing forces: the white woman's body, constructed as pure, over and against the lascivious black/colored woman and the body of the English upperclass gentleman.

The textual arrangement exposes the suppressed third term in the "triangle of desire," which upholds the apparent binary opposition of the individual white West Indian woman and the English gentleman. It writes the equivalence of the "free" (but poor, thereby implicating class divisions) twentieth-century white woman with the nineteenth-century enslaved colored woman as an effect of the interlocking ideologies of "race" and sexuality, empire and colony, gender and class. The past/"history" of the West Indies provides the ground for Anna's present (relationship with Walter). The text inscribes historical and social practices as subjectivity. The "sins" of Anna's slave-owning fathers and their commodification of the slave woman's body recoil upon the daughter as "past" and "present" converge and the "I" is shown to be the "Other." Anna, then, may be read as a product of the European systems of knowledge and governance that construct the West Indian slave woman, the prostitute, and the poor white woman as sexualized objects. In this way, the colored West Indian woman becomes not a surrogate body upon which to write the gender and class oppression of the white woman, but the Self is written as sharing an identity with its Other.

But there is a *but*. Anna, who is astute, if naive and disempowered, recognizes the implications of her recall of Maillotte Boyd. She says, "But I like it like this. I don't want it any other way but this." Does this suggest the narrator's belief that while the political and the historical constitute the "personal," they cannot exhaustively account for the interaction between individuals? Does it suggest masochistic self-abasement? Is it a blind spot of the text?

Favorite terms for the "Jean Rhys woman" have often been "weak and passive." However, an analysis of the nature of the relationship between the two demonstrates that Walter, like the husband in *Wide Sargasso Sea*, is as much rendered subject to the hierarchies of domination and subjection as Anna is. Rhys in her "autobiography" writes the real-life relationship that provides the basis for *Voyage in the Dark*. She writes it not in terms of "facts" but in terms of an analysis of the class distinctions that separated the protagonists and the fictions (romances) that shaped their relationship: "It still annoys me when my first object of worship is supposed to be a villain. Or perhaps the idea at the back of this is that his class was oppressing mine. He had money. I had none. . . . He was like all the men in all the books I had ever read about London" (114).

Walter works in the City (the British equivalent of Wall Street in the United States). "I work in the City. I work very hard," he says. "You mean somebody else works hard for you" is Maudie's reply (14). Walter and Anna's first "date" is marked by a privileging of their class differences and a satirizing of the pretensions of Walter's class and those who uphold the hierarchy. When the waiter brings the wine, the men's response is scrutinized and parodied by Anna's text:

> "This wine is corked," Mr. Jeffries said.
> "Corked, sir?" the waiter said in a soft, incredulous and horror-stricken voice. . . .
> "Yes, corked. Smell that."
> The waiter sniffed. Then Mr. Jeffries sniffed. Their noses were exactly alike, their faces very solemn. The Brothers Slick and Slack, the Brothers Pushmeofftheearth. I thought, "Now then, you mustn't laugh. He'll know you're laughing at him. You can't laugh." (19–20)

The reference to people of privileged classes and social status pushing her off the earth echoes *After Leaving Mr. Mackenzie* when Julia feels that she is looking over the edge of the world (see Chapter 3).

If Anna understands the construction of class as a system of exclusion, she is also aware that restrictions on female sexuality are socially constructed imperatives: "I'm not a virgin if that's what's worrying you. . . . [I]t doesn't matter, anyway. . . . People have made all that up." Walter, on the other hand, insists that it "is the only thing that matters" (36). He, unlike Anna, believes in and reproduces the values that define gender as a category of social organization. Anna's blasé attitude about virginity notwithstanding, he understands that her exchange value will be damaged by the "loss" of her virginity.

The use of mirroring techniques dramatizes the "meanings" of their after-sex interaction: when Walter pays her for sex, Anna, *through the looking-glass*, sees him surreptitiously putting the money in her purse. Looking in the mirror, Anna sees not a physical reflection of herself but the coming into being of a social subjectivity, *produced by Walter's action*. The self that is reflected back at her and that she comes to be is a woman who is used and paid for sex. Anna's ambivalence is underscored: "I meant to say 'What are you doing?' But when I went up to him instead of saying, 'Don't do that,' I said, 'All right, if you like—anything you like, any way you like.' And I kissed his hand" (38). Her own angry response dies in her throat and she accepts the self that has been constructed for her. In psychosexual terms, she is dependent, abject, almost grateful. This scene demonstrates the reciprocal relationship of representation and reality and the production of subject positions by social interaction. The function of the mirror is to make Anna participate in treating herself first and foremost as a sight, an object. This scene also suggests that human agency depends upon the location of the subjectivity within the social economy. Once Anna becomes illicitly sexualized and grasps the image of herself that Walter's action constructs, she transgresses the ideologies of gender that he upholds and that can only be maintained by transgression.

When Anna tells Walter, "I want to be with you. That's all I want" (50), he is annoyed and compares her to the Sisyphean stone. Walter believes in the bourgeois ethic of self-making and self help. He tells her about her predecessor in his life, which underscores the temporary nature of their relationship and the fact that Anna, as a commodity in the sexual economy, is replaceable. But he is kind enough to help her by paying for singing lessons: "What I want, Mr. Price, is an effective song for a voice-trial. *Softly Awakes My Heart As the Flowers Awaken*—that's a very effective one. Everybody says the man's bound to get tired and you read it in all books. But I never read now, so they can't get at me like that, anyway. ('My darling Walter . . .')" (74; Rhys's ellipsis). Anna is caught between what the books and "everybody" say about the nature of her relationship with Walter and her belief in romantic love. The title of the song she chooses for her lesson bespeaks the (woman's) heart opening up to "love" like a flower awakening. This image evokes Walter's "deflowering" of her, which makes her his according to the popular notions of sex, love, and gender. His financial support further concretizes her sense of belonging to him. The pervasive effect of the symbolic and social order on the individual ensures that even as Anna tries to "get on" by taking singing lessons, the substance of her work—the song—reproduces the mystified ideology of romantic love and seeps back into her relationship with Walter.

Anna's reading on love and sex and woman is positioned against that of other women in the novel. She believes that she understands the importance of clothes as a means of social and gender control: "About clothes, it's awful. Everything makes you want pretty clothes like hell. People laugh at girls who are badly dressed. . . . And the shop-windows sneering and smiling in your face" (25). She buys clothes with most of the money she receives from Walter *before* she sleeps with him. She thinks that her clothes will change what she is, make her more like him: "*Out of this warm room that smells of fur I'll go to all the lovely places I've ever dreamt of. This is the beginning*" (28). This backfires. She incurs the wrath of the landlady, who gives her notice and implies that Anna has obtained money by sleeping with a man. Later she calls Anna a tart. The landlady's false accusation mocks her attempts at moving up socially by means of clothing and points to the paradoxical constraints of gender. A well-dressed man, with money, is successful. A well-dressed woman, without money, is a tart. When Anna is about to sleep with Walter for the first time, it is the false, accusatory words of the landlady that echo in her mind as she goes up the stairs in his house: "'*Crawling up the stairs at three o'clock in the morning,' she said. Well, I'm crawling up the stairs*" (37).

The other women with whom Anna interacts understand that as "girls" their exchange value as commodified objects is precariously low. They also understand, as Walter does, that they must attempt to get money in order to save themselves socially. Maudie, a poor chorus girl, recalls being told by a man: "Have you ever thought that a girl's clothes cost more than the girl inside them? . . . You can get a very nice girl for five pounds, a very nice girl indeed; you can even get a very nice girl for nothing if you know how to go about it. But you can't get a very nice costume for her for five pounds. . . . People are much cheaper than things. . . . Some dogs are more expensive than people. . . . And as to some horses" (45–46). Maudie realizes that her chances of "finding" a man depends on having enough money to buy the right clothes. Laurie insists that there is no friend like money in the bank. Ethel decides to exploit Anna because of her naivete and her fur coat. These women are single, unattached, poor, and not young. They all, in various ways, depend on men for money. The women's "identity" is a function of their female bodies and sexuality.

Anna's self and narrative are sites where contradictory discourses on sex, gender, class, romance, and history converge and intermingle. And, as I have argued, the analysis of gender in Rhys's writing is dependent upon the historical locations of the Creole, and therefore complicated by "race" and colonialism.

Voyage in the Dark is perhaps first and foremost a wealth of historical, literary, and cultural intertexts. There are references to Columbus's journals, Zola, Manet, Aubrey Beardsley, Poe, Puccini, Stephen Foster, *The Rosary*,

The Iron Shroud, films like *Three-Fingered Kate*, songs, advertisements, and travel writing on the West Indies. The pervasive references to advertisements in this novel (and the short stories of the period) suggest Rhys's critique of one of the major "vehicles of imperial propaganda" in early twentieth-century England. (MacKenzie, *Propaganda*, 16). The metatext against which the Rhys novel is strategically positioned is the history and narrative of empire. I say "strategically" because the intertextual references to literary precursors are often based on misreadings, misquotes, imperfect recall, the suppression of individual writers' names, and anachronisms. In terms of "history," Anna is in England in 1914 as a teenager, but her stepmother's and uncle's texts place them firmly within the 1830s–1840s postslavery period in the West Indies. The final section of the original ending, when Anna recalls the carnival, does this explicitly. By placing her fiction athwart the historical and literary narratives of empire, by misquoting, borrowing, and conflating, Jean Rhys evacuates for purposes of analysis the fictitious/constructed character of this discourse and examines the mechanisms by which it is naturalized.

One of the genres to which the novel ceaselessly refers is eighteenth- and nineteenth-century travel writing on the West Indies. The function of the travel genre in the ideological management of "race" and empire has been effectively demonstrated by several critics. The title *Voyage in the Dark* is suggestive of the "voyages," journals, "eyewitness accounts," "histories," and letters of eighteenth-century European writing on the West Indies. It can be read as a *récit de voyage* from the periphery to the center. The Other voyages into the dark center of the Self and returns the gaze. Percy Adams observes that "the story with a naive but astute foreign observer was one of the most popular fictional forms of the eighteenth century" (*Travel Literature*, 115). Anna, who is "naive but astute," always already the Other, remains outside of the English culture in which she is a stranger. Like the European texts and narrators, who assumed their own transparency, Anna's text appears straightforward and innocent.

In its rewriting of these discursive acts, *Voyage in the Dark*, among other things, calls attention to and parodies the construction of the English gentlewoman who visited or lived in the West Indies, evoking such texts as *Lady Nugent's Journal* (1907), A. C. Carmichael's *Domestic Manners and Social Condition of the White, Coloured, and Negro Population of the West Indies* (1833), Clara Bromley's *A Woman's Wandering in the Western World* (1861), and Janet Schaw's

Journal of a Lady of Quality (1921). This is most clearly seen in the character of Hester, Anna's stepmother: "[Hester] had clear brown eyes which stuck out of her head if you looked at her sideways, and an English lady's voice with a sharp, cutting edge to it. Now that I've spoken you can hear that I'm a lady. I have spoken and I suppose you now realize that I'm an English gentlewoman. I have my doubts about you. Speak up and I will place you at once. Speak up, for I fear the worst. That sort of voice" (*Voyage*, 57–58).

Hester tells Anna that she is going to give a present to the rector's daughter of two jumbie beads set in gold and made into a brooch: "The niggers say that jumbie-beads are lucky, don't they?" (58). The English gentlewoman is appropriating the "superstitious" cultural artifact of the Other, increasing its monetary value by setting it in gold, and giving it to someone connected to a representative of one of the most hallowed British institutions, the Church of England. This short exchange becomes a synecdoche for imperialist exploitation tied to religion, capital, race, and gender. This linkage typifies many imperialist texts, as Laura Brown notes: "The association of women with the products of mercantile capitalism and particularly the obsession with female adornment is a strong cultural motif" ("Romance," 52–53).

The conversation about jumbie beads is followed by silence in which Anna's thoughts juxtapose a concern with her own financial situation, which is dependent on Walter, and an advertisement in the newspaper: "I kept on wondering whether she would ask me what I was living on. 'What is Purity? For Thirty-five Years the Answer has been Bourne's Cocoa.' Thirty-five years. . . . Fancy being thirty-five years old. What is Purity? For Thirty-five Thousand Years the Answer has been . . .'" (59; Rhys's ellipses). The wordplay on "Purity" and "thirty-five" further demystifies the interlocking ideologies of gender, race, and empire: "Purity" (cocoa) is an advertised consumer product, obtained through imperialist exploitation of East African raw material, "refined" in the metropolis for consumption in the mother country. Companies creating and supplying the new tastes for colonial products placed much emphasis on the forms of new advertising techniques that emerged in the late nineteenth century: "They were concerned to sell not only their own product but also the world system which produced it. The most aggressive and innovative advertisers of the day were companies dependent on the imperial economic nexus, in tea, chocolate, soaps and oils, tobacco, meat extracts, shipping and later rubber. They set out . . . to illustrate a romantic view of imperial origins, a pride in national possession of . . . the imperial "estates" (MacKenzie, *Propaganda*, 16). "Purity" is also a hallowed tradition of gender oppression and commodification through its concern with controlling women's bodies and sexual activities. If the laws about purity are validated by time, the passage of time, in terms of aging ("thirty-five years old"), signals the deterioration of the woman's value. Ostensibly moral valences, which seek to naturalize the forms of oppression in which they are grounded and by which they are enabled, are determined by the monied and the powerful within specific, dominative sociohistorical systems. They are, however, circulated in a language of fixed and eternal verities, as advertisements for the "natural" and time-honored right of the powerful to rule and oppress. Anna's location as a "blackened" Creole gives added resonance to the term "purity," which bases the notion of purity and "true womanhood" on racial, gender, and class differences.

This scene prefaces Hester's reading of a letter from Anna's Uncle Bo that is purportedly about Anna. It deals with money, gender, the construction of "race," England and the West Indies, and the formation of cultural hierarchies and practices. The letter and Hester's response focus the clash of contradictory readings of the West Indies and of England by the Creole and the English. Bo, a representative of the West Indian planter class, feels that Hester has cheated Anna out of her inheritance and must therefore take responsibility for supporting her financially. Although he is Anna's favorite uncle, he makes it clear that her "identity" is as much a function of property as it is of blood relationship: "If you feel that you don't wish her to live with you in England, of course her aunt and I will have her here with us. But in that case I insist—we both insist—that she should have her proper share of the money you got from the sale of her father's estate. Anything else would be iniquitous" (*Voyage*, 61).

Hester's version of the story counters Bo's and focuses on the "way English people are cheated into buying estates that aren't worth a halfpenny" (62). She also feels that Anna's father, an Englishman who remained in the West Indies for more than thirty years, lost touch with reality because he had grown to dislike England and what he considered to be the hypocrisy of the English. The idea that an Englishman would not like England is unthinkable. Such a feeling Hester construes as madness or a kind of death: "When he said that I knew he was failing. And such a brilliant man poor man buried alive you might say" (62). The paucity of white people in the West Indies is also another point of contention for Hester: "And never seeing a white face from one week's end to the other and you growing up more like a nigger ever day. Enough to drive anybody mad" (62).

It is the letter-writer Bo who most strongly arouses Hester's anger over his social transgressions of the plantation political culture. Biologically white and a West Indian, Bo writes that he has "three children to support." Hester points to out-of-wedlock children, "all colours of the rainbow," whom he was not required to support:

> With illegitimate children wandering about all over the place called by his name—called by his name if you please. Sholto Costerus, Mildred Costerus, Dagmar. The Costeruses seem to have populated half the island in their time. . . . And you being told they were your cousins and giving them presents every Christmas. . . . But I gave Ramsay a piece of my mind. . . . I said, "My idea of a gentleman an English gentleman doesn't have illegitimate children and if he does he doesn't flaunt them." "No I bet he doesn't," he said, laughing in that greasy way—exactly the laugh of a negro he had—"I should think being flaunted is the last thing that happens to the poor little devils. Not much flaunting of that sort done in England.' " (64–65)

Hester's critique of Ramsay's "flaunting" of his illegitimate children demonstrates that the code of conduct decreed not sexual segregation of the races but legal and social prohibitions for breaching the cultural codes. (See Long, *History*, 2:333–43). Bo's misconduct derives from his "flaunting"—that is, acknowledging paternity by giving his name to his own flesh and blood by women of color. If Hester calls attention to the rule of conduct that does not require him to financially support these children, she upholds strenuously the rule that also requires him not to "flaunt" them.

Hester's discourse, as I mentioned before, is exemplary as a parody of metropolitan writing on the plantation societies of the West Indies. The concern with white men producing children by black and colored women and the anxieties about the blood connections between black and white people repeat themselves insistently. Maria Nugent, for example, observes in her journal: "A little mulatto girl was sent into the drawing-room to amuse me. . . . Mr. T appeared very anxious for me to dismiss her, and in the evening, the housekeeper told me she was his own daughter, and that he had a numerous family, some almost on every one of his estates. The housekeeper's name was Nelly Nugent. She told me that her father was a Mr. Nugent from Ireland, who had been some years ago upon that estate. She of course considers herself a connection of ours" (*Journal*, 93).

Hester then alludes to Anna's "unfortunate propensities"—that is, her sexual promiscuity—and observes that, "everything considered," Anna is much to be pitied. Anna understands the meaning of her innuendo: "You are trying to make out that my mother was coloured. And she wasn't" (*Voyage*, 65). The taken-for-granted and unspoken premise of their discussion is the sexual promiscuity of African-Caribbean women, by whom the white men fathered children. Her stepmother denies making such an insinuation about Anna, but she also notes that "I tried to teach you talk like a lady and behave like a lady and not like a nigger and of course I couldn't do it. . . . That awful sing-song voice you had! Exactly like a nigger you talked and still do" (65). Hester's assertion repeats another common concern of colonialist discourse on the West Indies. Maria Nugent observes: "The Creole language is not confined to the negroes. Many of the ladies, who have not been educated in England, speak a sort of broken English, with an indolent drawling out of their words, that is very tiresome if not disgusting" (*Journal*, 132). Edward Long also alludes to the "contamination" of Creole girls by their "Negroe domestics, whose drawling, dissonant gibberish they insensibly adopt, and with it no small tincture of their awkward carriage and vulgar manners; all of which they do not easily get rid of, even after an English education" (*History*, 2:279). Even as Anna asserts her biological whiteness, Hester swiftly counters by pointing to another example of her racial contamination—the language she speaks.

If "race," that is, blackness, is contagious and mobile, the borders must be firmly guarded. This is achieved through legal, social, and discursive institutions that indissolubly link property to propriety and preach a system of decorum inseparable from the ideological construction of "race" and class. For Hester, the Englishwoman, who received most of the money from her husband's West Indian estate, Anna is a nigger because of a wide and slippery range of attributes: her "unfortunate propensities" (which derive from her putative colored mother), her West Indian accent, her proximity to black people growing up in the West Indies, her colored relatives, and her lack of financial security. Hester's discourse incorporates the contamination of the West Indian Creoles due to their proximity and sexual interaction with black people, "miscegenation," the superiority of the English over the Creole, and the maintenance of discursive boundaries to counter or nullify biological connections. Anna's efforts at defending herself against these "charges" are rendered ineffective because Hester's authority, which depends on Anna's exclusion and degradation, is enabled by the social and political systems within the imperial context. This "history" of the relationship between West Indian Creoles and the English in the West Indies becomes Anna's present in England. Her relatives' disowning her because she has neither property nor money, her stepmother and others inventing her as "black," must be read as part of the historical processes that, in large measure, constitute her subjectivity. *Voyage in the Dark* proposes that sexual, gender, and nationalist ideologies are deeply implicated in racialized specificities. It acknowledges whiteness, not just blackness, as a racial category.

Through the use of reverse discourse, the Rhys text probes the mystification of class divisions, which is central to the imperializing project's construction of the English domestic subject over and against the peripheral Other. The narrator says: "The ones without any money, the ones with beastly lives. Perhaps I am going to be one of the ones with beastly lives. They swarm like woodlice when you push a stick into a woodlice-nest at home. And their faces are the colour of woodlice" (26). The narrative portrayal of poor white people as repulsive (but familiar) West Indian insects rewrites the textual production and containment of the black Other as animalistic and inhuman in precursory European texts. The exploration of the class anomalies is also suggested in the language of Anna's landlady, a poor Englishwoman, who attacks Anna's morals and her West Indian accent in ungrammatical English and a Cockney accent: "I won't 'ave you calling me a liar. . . . You and your drawly voice. And if you give me any of your lip I'll 'ave my 'usband up to you. . . . I don't want no tarts in my house, so now you know" (30). (Other references include fair versus dark baboons.) By troubling and displacing the discursive formation of racial and class hierarchies, the reverse discourse underscores the role and function of narrative in the formation of the imperial Self and its peripheral Others. It produces a knowledge of the dominant that was suppressed and shows that this suppression was one of the conditions of possibility for dominance.

The Creole woman, as the peripheral Other, recognizes that England as textual production clashes with the England that she actually "experiences": "This is England. . . . I had read about England ever since I could read—smaller meaner everything is never mind—this is London—hundreds thousands of white people white people rushing along and the dark houses all alike frowning down one after the other all alike all stuck together" (17). The shock of seeing so many white people in England derives from the experience of seeing mostly black people in the West Indies. The narrative also parodies the common representation of blacks as "hordes." The intensely negative reaction to England is being measured against the experiences and memories of the West Indies.

The Creole's antimetropolitan position represents "the other side" of the European writers on the West Indies. She insists upon the gap between the discourse and the "experience." (This is not to suggest that there can be unmediated readings or experiences.) European writers, for the most part, suppressed the "reality" of the West Indies and reproduced, even as they were empowered by, the discourses and ideologies of "race" and empire. Anna, who lacks authority, property, and propriety, cannot be made to overturn the power relations. Labeled by her peers as the Hottentot and "blackened" by her stepmother, Anna appears powerless. The textual strategy, however, constitutes the othered subjectivity as a discursive self possessing the textual (if not the social) authority to rewrite some of the dominant codes. The Other returns the gaze.

Anna's gender identity as a function of her sociohistorical location as a Creole is most clearly articulated in the ending of her relationship with Walter. Vincent, Walter's cousin and employee, does the "hard work" of extricating him from an untenable situation. In his letter terminating the relationship, Vincent advises Anna on love:

> Love is not everything—especially that sort of love—and the more people, especially girls, put it right out of their heads and do without it the better. . . . Life is chock-full of other things. . . . friends and just good times . . . and books. Do you remember when we talked about books? I was sorry when you told me that you never read because, believe me, a good book like that book I was talking about [The Rosary] can make a lot of difference to your point of view. It makes you see what is real and what is just imaginary. My dear Infant, I am writing this in the country, and I can assure you that when you get

into a garden and smell the flowers and all that all this rather beastly sort of love simply doesn't matter. (93)

Wealthy Vincent, in his beautiful garden, advises Anna to read in order to discover that what is real (what the books say) as opposed to what is imaginary (what she feels). Vincent demonstrates the power that resides in his and Walter's economic and social position by offering to take care of her financially, for a time, on the condition that she return Walter's letters.

After Anna reads the letter, her memory takes her back to the time when she saw Uncle Bo metamorphose into a frightening animal with "long yellow tusks like fangs [coming out] of his mouth" (92). What is conveyed is the image of a loved one becoming a source of terror. A chain of associations also recalls her father, who once told her, "I've met some Englishmen . . . who were monkeys too" (95). "Monkey," a common pejorative for African people, has a special historical resonance in this context. In nineteenth-century Dominica, members of the Mulatto Ascendancy were often referred to as "half-French monkeys." The symbolic affiliation of Uncle Bo as a terrifying animal and English men as monkeys with Walter's betrayal reflexively and ironically invokes dehumanizing racial myths secreted within the politics of empire and "race." Yet again the text collapses Anna's West Indian "past" into the present, her subjective suffering into the historical collectivity. The link between the Englishman and the West Indian woman is written by discourses that make a "personal" relationship well nigh impossible. Mary Louise Pratt observes in a different but related context:

> As an ideology, romantic love, like capitalist commerce, understands itself as reciprocal. Reciprocity, love requited between individuals worthy of each other, is its ideal state. The failure of reciprocity, or of equivalence between parties, is its central tragedy and scandal. . . . Such is the lesson to be learned from the colonial love stories, in whose dénouements the "cultural harmony through romance" always breaks down. Whether love turns out to be requited or not . . . outcomes seem to be roughly the same: the lovers are separated, the European is reabsorbed by Europe and the non-European dies an early death. (*Imperial Eyes*, 97)

When Anna tells Walter that if she doesn't see him she will die, she prefigures her own death through the memory of her mother's funeral:

The candles crying wax tears and the smell of stephanotis and I had to go to the funeral in a white dress and white gloves and a wreath round my head and the wreath in my hands made my gloves wet—they said so young to die. (*Voyage*, 97)

. . . and she was too young to die Meta said with tears running down her face but I was only thinking of my new white dress and the wreath I would carry. (original ending in Howells, "Jean Rhys," 382)

Anna also experiences her own "death" by drowning: "It was like letting go and falling back into water and seeing yourself grinning up through the water, your face like a mask, and seeing the bubbles coming up as if you were trying to speak from under water. And how do you know what it's like to try to speak from under water when you're drowned? 'And I've met a lot of them who were monkeys too,' he said . . ." (98; Rhys's ellipsis). The death by drowning of the narrative subject is written as an effect of Walter's rejection and his enabling contexts—imperial history and the interlocking formations of class, gender, and racial hierarchies.

Many years after Rhys had written *Voyage in the Dark*, in a letter to Selma Vaz Dias on 17 September 1963 Rhys reads Anna as a split subjectivity: "The girl is *divided*, two people really. Or at any rate one foot on sea and one on land girl. . . . Her dream must be so vivid that you are left in doubt as to which is dream and which is reality (And who knows?) In the end her dream takes her entirely so perhaps *that* is reality" (*Letters*, 241). If Anna is unable to fit her "dream" and "reality" together, the text makes clear that the one is mediated by the other. The vivid recall of the West Indies is triggered and mediated by her experiences in England, even as these experiences are apprehended in terms of her memory of the West Indies. Some examples of this are useful.

When Anna discovers she is pregnant, she says: "Everything was still heaving up and down. 'Connais-tu le pays où fleurit l'oranger?' [Do you know the country where the orange tree grows?]" (162). This triggers a recollection of music lessons in the Caribbean, the landscape and the mountains, the obeah woman, and words of censure from people who did not approve of Anna. She tells her dream of an island "which was home except that trees were all wrong. These were English trees" (164). Her dream shows her effort to get off the ship and to step ashore. "I took huge, climbing, flying strides among confused figures. I was powerless and very tired, but I had to go on" (165). Anna says that after this she kept dreaming about the sea. The dream figures the voyage in the dark of the divided protagonist, who remains caught between sea and land, trying, though tired and powerless, to get on an island that is her West Indian home but with English trees.

On another level the textual function undercuts the binary opposition of England and the West Indies, dream and reality; and it shows the interconnectedness and the inseparability of both. Additionally, the text insists upon England's political, economic, and discursive power over the colony, even as it underscores the racial and social hierarchies in the West Indies. Anna's own awareness of the social and political continuities between center and periphery undermines any reliance on the West Indies as a place of solace. If in England Anna becomes a woman used for sex, in the West Indies she was brought up to be a "lady": "Brown kid gloves straight from England, one size too small. . . . The thought of having a wet patch underneath your arms—a disgusting and a disgraceful thing to happen to a lady" (41–42). She understands, too, that her religious upbringing in the West Indies forms part of the system that legitimizes and naturalizes social hierarchies and racial separation. The church services "gave you a peaceful and melancholy feeling. The poor do this and the rich do that, the world is so-and-so and nothing can change it. For ever and for ever turning and nothing, nothing can change it" (43). Anna also remembers incidents from the West Indies that were traumatic and difficult.

The West Indies as an ever-present "past" is also constituted by her imagination and desire. Anna, the subject who relies on her feelings, imagination, and memory, as opposed to Anna, the object of discourse, is seeking to situate her subjectivity in the "imagined community" of the West Indies. It is imagined to the extent that it does not now exist for her, it cannot be politically or socially available, and, most important, her text stands for the community evoked. If Anna as a discursive object is a site traversed by dominant discourses and codes, Anna as resistant subject derives her status from her experience in another social space, organically linked to but not exclusively defined by the imperial text. The novel simultaneously historicizes the subjectivity of the white West Indian woman showing the effects of colonization even as it attempts to forge another subjectivity out of memory, senses, and the imagination. The "dream" of the West Indies stands for a refusal by the white Creole of absorption into the ideology that constitutes Englishness and an attempt to valorize what Raymond Williams has usefully termed a "structure of feeling" grounded in the West Indies. Within this space there is room to maneuver. It is in that perhaps very small margin that *possibility* may lie.

The major distinction between England and the West Indies is not cold England versus warm, safe West Indies. There may the possibility of forging something new in the West Indies, in which England is both present and not present. In England there is no way out. The repeated focus on the houses and inhabitants in England rewrites the precise botanical and ethnographic accounts of the West Indian islands in European travel writing even as it suggests the ways in which the peripheral Other is trapped within and between the "houses and streets" of the imperial space. (Even the painting *Cries of London* follows her wherever she goes. She smashes it in one apartment, but it turns up again in another [139, 179].) Anna notes:

> I got used to everything except the cold and that the towns we went to always looked so exactly alike. You were perpetually moving to another place which was perpetually the same. (8)

> I kept telling myself, "You've got to think of something. You can't stay here. You've got to make a plan." But instead I started counting all the towns I had been to, the first winter I was on tour—Wigan, Blackburn, Bury, Oldham, Leeds, Halifax, Huddersfield, Southport.... I counted up to fifteen and then slid off into thinking of all the bedrooms I had slept in and how exactly alike they were, bedrooms on tour. (150; Rhys's ellipsis)

> Everything was always so exactly alike—that was what I could never get used to. And the cold; and the houses all exactly alike, and the streets going north, south, east, west, all exactly alike. (179)

In Part Four of the original ending, Anna's abortion leads to complications and she is dying. In a letter to Evelyn Scott on 10 June 1934, Jean Rhys observes that "the worst is that it is precisely the last part which I am most certain of that will have to be mutilated.... [I]t is not a disgusting book—or even a very grey book. And I *know* the ending is the only possible ending" (*Letters*, 25). In "Leaving School" Rhys also says: "The last chapter is not confused. She is dying. So there is no time for her any more as we think of time" (Jean Rhys Collection).

The erasure of temporality allows for the dissolution of the boundaries of the chronological and the historical that constrain the Creole subjectivity. Yet, at the same time, the description of the carnival scene, linked to the intense discussion of postslavery politics among the whites who are peering through half-closed windows, marks the historical determination of Anna's memory and consciousness. Rhys, like many later writers and historians, understands West Indian carnivals as "rituals of power and rebellion" (Liverpool, "Rituals"). As the white people are debating whether or not the carnival should be "allowed," the child Anna recognizes that the talk about what should or should not be "allowed" is, in a sense, irrelevant because "I knew what they were singing they were singing defiance to I don't know what but singing it all the same I knew what they were singing" (original ending in Howells, "Jean Rhys," 386).

The debate among Anna's family members touches on the pressing concerns of the immediate postslavery era. The most intense discussion centers on the abolition of slavery:

> Without any compensation Hester said I don't know the figures but you were voted a large sum in compensation.
>
> Voted Uncle Bo said voted Oh yes it may have been voted all right but we never got it it all stayed in the good old home coop and if you like to come and have a look at things I can prove that to you easily enough if you'd like to come and have a look
>
> Slavery was a wicked thing Aunt Jane said and God Almighty frowned on it and so it had to stop you can't treat human beings as if they were bits of wood it had to stop
>
> English people don't think like that Uncle Bo said they may talk like but they don't think like it (386)

As the narrator listens to the discussion and watches the carnival scene, she understands the relationship between the two: "Their voices went up and down and I was looking out of the window and I knew why the masks were laughing" (386).

By abolishing "time" in the mind of a young white West Indian woman dying of an abortion gone wrong in England, the original ending of *Voyage in the Dark* writes the memory and imagination of the young woman as a "collective assemblage of enunciation" of the West Indies that she knows and remembers (*Kafka*, 18). The Creole subjectivity in *Voyage in the Dark*, as in *Wide Sargasso Sea*, dissolves into counterdiscursive and social "blackness": "And the concertina-music stopped and it was so still so still and lovely like just before you go to sleep and it stopped and there was the ray of light along the floor like the last thrust of remembering before everything is blotted out and blackness comes . . ." (389; Rhys's ellipsis). Done to death by "life" in England, the subjectivity sabotages recuperation in the English / European texts by evacuating itself into the collective enunciation of the West Indian social scene. The Rhys text appropriates the "blackness" of Zola's diseased heroine, recombines it with the subjugation and resistance embodied in the carnival of anonymous black bodies and voices, and rewrites it as potential for liberation, through death, of the white Creole woman. Apparently trapped within the conjuncture of English epistemology and ontology, the Creole self escapes / dies into the writing memories of the West Indies.

"Again the Antilles"

"Again the Antilles," first published in 1927, is also grounded in the specific political and historical context of postslavery Dominica. The short story covers the period from the 1830s to the 1900s. Dominican politics and culture provide the locus of an imaginative exploration of the interconnectedness of imperial / colonial politics, history, narrative, and the acts of reading and writing. For purposes of clarity and comparison, I shall first cite in chronological order some of the specific historical events of the period as recorded in accounts by historian Joseph Borome and the present-day Dominican writer Lenox Honychurch.

Borome notes that, by the late 1830s (the immediate postslavery period), the mulattoes comprised the majority in the Legislative Assembly in Dominica: "Two political parties, conservative and liberal, developed rapidly, supported by two newspapers, the *Colonist* (white) and the *Dominican* (colored) respectively. Acrimony and personal vituperation, which appeared to flow in the bloodstreams of Dominica politicians, continued to characterize deliberations, especially of the House." After several decades, he continues, the volatile political situation was accepted as the norm, as the excerpt quoted from the *Antigua Weekly Register* attests: "The political disputes, engendering social discord and strife, of our neighbours in Dominica, have for so long a period been a reproach to the legislation and government of that island, as to cease to attract even an ordinary degree of attention" ("Crown Colony," 120–21).

Lenox Honychurch highlights the "religious riots" of 1847:

> On 4th May, a staunch Catholic member of the House of Assembly, T. F. Lockhart, introduced a bill to provide incomes for the Roman Catholic clergy. Mr. Lockhart's emotional address in the House caused much agitation among Catholics and this was heightened by the strong opposition of Charles Falconer, a fiery Methodist. He objected to any religious denomination receiving money from the government, especially in a poor island such as Dominica. Because of this, Falconer and his fellow Methodists became the targets of insult. . . . On the evening of 18th October, 1847 . . . a general riot ensued. (*Dominica*, 106)

In the 1850s some leading whites sought to change the governmental structure in order to effectively remove the mulattoes. Their view is articulated by the printer of the *Colonist*, John Finlay, in the 1 July 1854 issue. He claimed that the government was

> mostly composed of men who are entirely ignorant of the first principles of government, and whose only reason for going there is to aggrandise themselves, and to bring ruin on the more respectable classes of society. They are uneducated, ignorant and revengeful; and most of them have neither status [n]or property in the Island. The majority of these would-be-legislators, is made up of Journey-men Printers and Tailors, Bankrupt Shopkeepers, a Blacksmith and a few fourth rate Planters. *Very few of them articulate English decently, and a still smaller number are able to write it with any degree of accuracy or propriety.* (qtd. Borome, "Crown Colony," 121; emphasis added)

In 1865, Borome continues, a bill to make Dominica a Crown Colony was introduced in the Legislative Assembly. Falconer was part of a group that sailed to England to put their case against Crown Colony government to the secretary for the colonies. Despite this move, the new act for a modified Crown Colony status was put into effect. In 1871 Dominica and the other Leeward Islands became a federal colony.

In the 1880s William Davies emerged as "the most skillful colored political leader after Falconer." He leased Falconer's old press and started the *Dial* in 1882. This newspaper folded for lack of funds in 1893. In that same year another newspaper, the *Dominican Guardian*, appeared. It was backed by Davies and other colored men. Adopting the motto "Fiat Justicia," the newspaper proposed "to *guard* and protect our country from the tyranny of those who believe it to be their duty to add oppression to our misfortunes." Like Falconer, Davies was fundamentally opposed to Crown Colony government. In 1898, when the resolution for Crown Colony government was passed, an editorial in the *Guardian* advocated civil disobedience. In 1905 another mulatto, A. R. C. Lockhart, started the *Leeward Islands Free Press*. The newspaper attacked Governor Hesketh Bell's "self-advertisement" and declared itself in favor of a federal union of all the West Indian colonies (122–39).

The narrator of Rhys's "Again the Antilles" is an unnamed West Indian living in a foreign country. She recalls the editor of the *Dominica Herald and Leeward Islands Gazette*—Papa Dom:

> A born rebel, this editor: a firebrand. He hated white people, not being quite white, and he despised the black ones, not being quite black. . . . "Coloured" we West Indians call the intermediate shades, and I used to think that being coloured embittered him.
>
> He was against the Government, against the English, against the Island's being a Crown Colony and the Town Board's new system of drainage. He was also against the Mob, against the gay and easy morality of the negroes and the "hordes of priests and nuns that overrun our unhappy Island," against the existence of the Anglican bishop and the Catholic bishop's new palace.
>
> He wrote seething articles against that palace which was then being built, partly by voluntary labour—until, one night his house was besieged by a large mob of the faithful, throwing stones and howling for his blood. . . . In the next issue of his paper he wrote a long account of the "riot": according to him it had been led by several well-known Magdalenes, then, as always, the most ardent supporters of Christianity. (*CS*, 39–40)

The collation of Papa Dom's grievances provides a "thick description" of the political and social issues of nineteenth-century Dominica. The Papa

Dom figure of Rhys's story strongly suggests Falconer. At the same time, this character and the story as a whole are constructed according to the recurrent Rhysian techniques of layering or eliding different time periods and the deliberate fictionalization of historical figures. The references to the "religious riot" suggest the 1840s, while the political concerns cited cover a period extending to the 1890s. The mulatto figure of Papa Dom may also suggest William Davies and A. R. C. Lockhart.

By placing "riot" in quotation marks, the Rhys narrative suggests that Papa Dom uses words (and his newspaper) as a means of inventing or distorting "real" situations and labeling or attacking those with whom he disagrees. Within the context of Rhys's writing, this is particularly ironic, since her own construction of the mulatto does precisely that. In addition, the mulatto does double duty for the Creole—the despised Other, patronized, belittled, labeled as hate-filled, *and* the oppositional figure whose very existence questions the premise of European racial and cultural supremacy.

These uses of the mulatto figure are clearly shown in the narrator's recall of a feud, carried out in the newspaper, between Papa Dom and the transplanted Englishman Hugh Musgrave, a member of the governing class. According to the narrator, Hugh Musgrave, who had been in Dominica for twenty years, "employed a great deal of labour, but he was certainly neither ferocious nor tyrannical" (40). Papa Dom, writing under such pseudonyms as Pro Patria, Indignant, Liberty, and Uncle Tom's Cabin, "let himself go," while Mr. Musgrave replied, "briefly and sternly." The exchange between the two increases publication of the newspaper and the feud intensifies. Papa Dom writes:

> "It is a saddening and a dismal sight . . . to contemplate the degeneracy of a stock. How far is such a man removed from the ideals of true gentility, from the beautiful description of a contemporary, possibly, though not certainly, the Marquis of Montrose, left us by Shakespeare, the divine poet and genius.
> *"He was a very gentle, perfect knight . . ."*
> Mr. Musgrave took his opportunity:
> Dear Sir: he wrote
> "I never read your abominable paper. But my attention has been called to a scurrilous letter about myself which you published last week.

The lines quoted were written, not by Shakespeare but by Chaucer, though you cannot of course be expected to know that, and run. . . .

"It is indeed a saddening and a dismal thing that the names of great Englishmen should be thus taken in vain by the ignorant of another race and colour."

Mr. Musgrave had really written "damn niggers."

Papa Dom was by no means crushed. Next week he replied with dignity as follows:

"My attention has been called to your characteristic letter. I accept your correction though I understand that in the mind of the best authorities there are grave doubts, very grave doubts indeed, as to the authorship of the lines, and indeed the other works of the immortal Swan of Avon. However, as I do not write with works of reference in front of me, as you most certainly do, I will not dispute the point.

"The conduct of an English gentleman who stoops to acts of tyranny and abuse cannot be described as gentle or perfect. I fail to see that it matters whether it is Shakespeare, Chaucer or the Marquis of Montrose who administers from down the ages the much needed reminder and rebuke."

I wonder if I shall ever again read the *Dominica Herald and Leeward Islands Gazette*. (41)

The Englishman's disavowal of Papa Dom's reading and his calling the mulatto a "nigger" derives from his recognition of the English Book as a signifier of authority and his Englishness as a sign of difference. It is useful and interesting to compare the fictional Englishman's contempt for the mulatto's inability to identify accurately an English text with the view of John Finlay, the printer of the *Colonist*, that the inability to speak and write English "with any degree of accuracy or propriety" ought to disqualify "ignorant" men from having a say in the government of Dominica and from becoming legal and political human beings.

As we have already seen, erroneous attribution, misreading, and imperfect recall in Rhys's writing are strategies that pry the text loose from its individual author(ship), disseminating or evacuating its material into a larger discursive matrix. Such a move calls attention to its indissoluble fusion with political and social authority. In Bakhtinian terms, Papa Dom, the West Indian mulatto who, lacking propriety and accuracy, takes the name of the Fathers in vain, deploys the "authoritative discourse" as "internally persuasive discourse" and adjusts it to the specific political and historical situation of British colonialism in the West Indies (*Dialogic*, 340–48). Papa Dom appropriates the properties of the highest echelons of the English literary tradition, invoking its claims of universal humanism and transcendental authority in order to expose and condemn the ethnocentrism of the English gentleman in the West Indies. By polemically drawing the privileged metropolitan literary language into the contact zone, the mulatto indicts the Englishman for his betrayal of the values embodied in the authority he espouses. This double inscription and repetition expose the flaws and contradictions embedded in the ideology of European supremacy. By laying claim to these texts, Papa Dom disarticulates given signs and rearticulates them so that they may mean differently. He deterritorializes the language and literature of Europe and uses them as a site for cultural intervention. Embedded in Papa Dom's rereading and rewriting is the figuration of the West Indian writer who uses "privileged texts as the object of conscious rather than reactive processes of cognition" (Wynter, "Beyond Miranda's Meanings," 365).

The narrator implicates herself in her own dramatization of the social, political, and cultural conflicts by wondering (an implicit longing) whether she will "ever again read the *Dominica Herald and Leeward Islands Gazette*." In one sense, in her account of the feud between Papa Dom and Mr. Musgrave, the narrator's sympathies clearly lie with the latter as she ridicules the former. Here again we see the Creole figure whose identity depends upon the simultaneous belittling and appropriation of the mulatto as an oppositional figure and as a means of expressing *ressentiment* toward the metropolitan subjectivity to whom she also feels some affinity.

"Fishy Waters"

Almost fifty years after "Again the Antilles," Rhys's work takes up the same preoccupation with newspapers and debates about race, history, and writing in the West Indies. These debates provide the context for a horrifying tale of alleged child abuse. Yet the struggle for legal and discursive representation among distinct social groups, which comprises the major part of the narrative, conceals or obliterates the event itself. The structure of the story analyzes the ways in which subjectivities are simultaneously constituted *and* canceled by discourses of race, gender, and history. The protagonists are absent and, except for a brief letter from Mr. Longa, voiceless; the little child whom he allegedly abused is unable to speak. Their story is told through indirection and innuendo, through gossip and silence, through juridical and other forms of official or public discourse. In a sense, then, it is the social text that is the protagonist. Given the structure of the short story, it will be necessary for me to paraphrase and quote at length.

The story opens with a month-long debate in the *Dominica Herald* centering on race, writing, and history. Under the pseudonym "Disgusted," someone who is not white asserts that Mr. Longa, an Englishman, was cruelly treated and ostracized because he was a socialist and that he was accused of child molestation on a "trumped-up charge": "In this way, they plan to be rid of a long-standing nuisance and to be able to boast about their even-handed justice. The hypocrisy of these people, who bitterly resent that they no longer have the power over the bodies and minds of the blacks they once had (the cruelty of West Indian planters was a by-word), making a scape-goat of an honest British workman is enough to make any decent person's gorge rise" (*CS*, 298).

The letter draws a sharp response from a named reader:

> Who is "Disgusted"? Who is this person (I believe people) who tries to stir up racial hatred whenever possible? Almost invariably, with gloating satisfaction, they will drag in the horrors of the slave trade. Who would think, to hear them talk, that slavery was abolished by the English nearly a hundred years ago? They are long on diatribes, but short on facts. The slave trade was an abominable one, but it could not have existed without the help and cooperation of African chiefs. Slavery still exists, and is taken for granted, in Africa, both among Negroes and Arabs. Are these facts ever mentioned? The bad is endlessly repeated and insisted upon; the good is ridiculed, forgotten or denied. Who does this, and why? (299)

The following week, "Disgusted" identifies himself as a store proprietor: "It is sometimes said that African chiefs probably had a good deal to do with the slave trade, but I never heard before that this was proven. In his typical letter I noticed that Mr. MacDonald places all the blame on these perhaps mythical Africans and says nothing about the greed of white merchants or the abominable cruelty and indifference of white planters. The treatment meted out to Mr. Longa shows that their heirs and successors have not changed all that much" (299).

Another pseudonymous writer, "Fiat Justicia," brings the debate to a close by invoking the power and authority of the British juridical system that governs the colony: "I hate to interfere with the amusement of your readers, but I must point out that according to English law it is highly improper to discuss a case that has not been tried (*sub judice*). In this country the custom seems to be more honoured in the breach than in the observance" (299). The letters to the newspaper are followed by a "personal" letter to Caroline, who, it is inferred, lives in England. It is written by an English expatriate, Maggie, whose husband, Matthew Penrice, is "main witness for the prosecution" in the case against Mr. Longa.

In the ensuing courtroom drama, the prosecution charges Mr. Longa with molesting the child and claims that Matthew Penrice rescued her and took her to a woman who was in his pay. The child herself is unable to talk. The doctor explains the child's silence as trauma, saying: "I have known cases when, after a frightening and harmful experience, the mind has protected itself by forgetting" (306). The lawyer for the defense refuses such an explanation on racial and social grounds: "Do you really think that this interesting but rather complicated theory could apply to a Negro child, completely illiterate, only eleven or twelve years of age? Is it not more likely that she remains silent because she has either been persuaded or threatened—probably a bit of both—not to talk?" (306). He also questions Mr. Penrice's decision to take the child to his former servant instead of to a doctor. In countering the lawyer's argument, the doctor insists that the result of illiteracy is not an uncomplicated mind.

Mr. Longa's lawyer reads a letter from the defendant saying that he saw the child crying and meant to frighten her because the children had been nuisances and he disliked them. He said he did not hurt her but did mean to frighten her. He also stated his decision to leave the island. In summing up, the judge observed that it was difficult to obtain direct evidence in the island because of the deep distrust of the police and the law. He settled the case by accepting Mr. Longa's decision to leave.

Matthew Penrice is attacked by a group of people outside the courthouse. When he goes home, he tells his wife that the little girl will be given an opportunity to "start again." Maggie later reads a letter from the Syrian woman who is taking care of the child: "Thank you for the money you sent. I will keep it faithfully and carefully for her when she grows up and thank you from my heart for giving her to me. You would be pleased to see her. She is getting quite fat and pretty and hardly ever wakes up screaming as she used to do. I now close and say no more from my over-flowing heart" (310).

When Maggie confronts her husband with the rumor that he was the one who abused the child and then blamed Longa because of his status as an outcast, Matthew Penrice dismisses it. However, he insists on leaving the island at all costs. He then considers the matter completely settled: "He . . . took up a book; but Maggie . . . saw that he never turned a page. . . . She was trying to fight the overwhelming certainty that the man she was looking at was a complete stranger" (311).

The letters to the editor, to Caroline, to Matt Penrice, Mr. Longa's letter to the court, the hearing, and the rumors—all form part of the competing discourses that stand in for and construct the "event." What, then, is the story? Is it that Matt Penrice abused the child and paid off her guardian, then became a witness for the prosecution, using as a scapegoat a supporter of the British working class? Why does he seem a stranger to his wife? The wealth of information conceals more than it reveals. The "people" whom the story is "about" are absent and enigmatic. What is not said and who does not speak are important—the white man of an "inferior" class, a carpenter and a socialist, the young girl who is illiterate. The sociopolitical realm of the postslavery West Indies of the late nineteenth century and the representational discourses are the substance that constitutes and disassembles individual subjectivities.

3 : The 1920s and 1930s
The Enigma of the Creole in Europe

Marya . . . looked for a long time at the blank sheet of writing paper in front of her, imagining it covered with words, black marks on the white paper. Words. To make somebody understand.
(*Quartet*)

By the early decades of the twentieth century, when Jean Rhys begins her writing career in Europe, the West Indian planter class has fallen, the forms of colonial domination have changed, and the region has been assigned to the "rubbish heap" of metropolitan history. It is V. S. Naipaul, one of the twentieth century's most articulate exponents of the colonialist discourse on the West Indies, who effectively elucidates the dilemma of the Creole in Europe at that time:

> Two hundred years . . . ago, when the sugar colonies of the Caribbean were valuable and important, the white West Indian in Europe was better known. . . . But by the 1920s, when Jean Rhys began to write, the Caribbean . . . belonged to antique romance; and the West Indian needed to explain [her]self.
>
> Jean Rhys didn't explain herself. She might have been a riddle to others, but she never sought to make her experience more accessible by making it what it was not. It would have been easy for someone of her gifts to have become a novelist of manners; but . . . she had . . . no home audience to play to; she was outside that tradition of imperial-expatriate writing in which the metropolitan outsider is thrown into relief against an alien background. ("Without a Dog's Chance," 54)

Although Rhys did not explain herself, the problematics of reading, writing, and the self are repeatedly confronted and examined from her earliest work. She recalls, "I used to write stories with very melodramatic endings. . . . Ford stopped that and told me to write about what I knew. So

I did" (Stevens, "Every Day," 6). Yet what Jean Rhys "knew" in Europe of the 1920s and 1930s was not part of the accepted literary or cultural discourse. The Creole mode of subjectivity and its complicated history, in terms of both Europe and the now "fishy waters" of the West Indies that underwrote her fiction, would have seemed enigmatic or would have been rendered invisible.[1]

Rhys's early writing often inscribes the self-reflexivity of an Outsider who is aware that tactically she is both constrained and marginalized by the discursive system within which she is caught. In "Hunger" the protagonist tells of being hungry. She details the emotions, contemplations, and reactions arising from her situation in an apparently straightforward manner. It is an opening up of the self, a baring of the soul, as it were. However, the last line, the *coup de canon*—"I have never gone without food for longer than five days, so I cannot amuse you any longer"—undermines the deceptive simplicity (*CS*, 44). It implicates the reader by calling attention to the assumptions that shape a reading of the text. The implied reader is someone who will not understand, who mocks her suffering and the expression of that suffering, someone whose system of values is opposed to that of the narrator. In the process of being read, the narrator is also reading the reader. The irony is twofold. The narrative strategy undermines even as it invites the gaze and the moral judgments implicit in the gaze. The same technique is repeated with startling effect, almost forty years later, in *Wide Sargasso Sea* when Antoinette, in the attic of her husband's house, directly addresses the reader.

This rhetorical strategy foregrounds an acute understanding of the dominant literary and social conventions that underwrite the production of a narrative voice, of a self. Rhys's writing recognizes these conventions as being antagonistic to certain kinds of selfhood that fall outside of the accepted protocols. Epistemological and moral value varies, depending on the social and historical position of the subjectivity. Certain categories of existence are worthy of reading, writing, and approval. Others are not. Rhys's narrative and textual strategies are not only concerned with telling a story but with telling the story behind the story—how a work is written and read/rewritten is based on prior assumptions about writing, writers, and identity. These assumptions are constituted by cultural, political, social, and historical praxes.

"In a Café," an early story that Rhys later suppressed, sketches no more than a few minutes in a cafe in which, to the discomfort of most people present, a *chansonnier* sings of the poor treatment meted out to a *grue* (prostitute). The story is narrated in the third person. After the song ends, the singer is selling copies of his song: "'Give me two,' she said with calm self-assurance'" (*CS*, 15). This sentence stands out. The "she" is not identified. She is not the narrator. Who is she? Why is she self-assured and calm? Why is she buying two copies of a song that made most other people uncomfortable? For whom? These unanswerable questions suggest an indeterminacy of status. She, who has no discursive authority as narrator or protagonist, nevertheless asserts her subjectivity and questions the social arrangement as represented in the text of the song. Her presence suggests an emergent consciousness, an oppositional voice not yet named, identified, or clearly articulated.

I shall focus on two of the novels of the early period, *After Leaving Mr. Mackenzie* and *Good Morning, Midnight*, to read the ways in which they inscribe the Creole's engagement with the problematics of reading, writing, the self, and the metropolitan Book.

After Leaving Mr. Mackenzie

In *After Leaving Mr. Mackenzie*, perhaps Rhys's most enigmatic work, the reading of the "life" of this "Rhys woman" (into Jean Rhys's own biographical life) is severely undercut by the narrative strategies, the problematics of style, and the many points of resistances produced by this text. The work is often taken to be a conventional novel and read as one. But if we begin at the beginning, we see that the text provides instructions as to how it should (and should not) be read. The Table of Contents shows a very careful division of the text into three parts, with titles, subdivisions, and page numbers—reminiscent perhaps of an Agatha Christie murder mystery. The "existential life" of Julia Martin is decomposed into episodic, almost picaresque segments, with enigmatic titles such as "The First Unknown" and "It Might Have Been Anywhere," juxtaposed with apparently straightforward ones such as "Change of Address" and "Death." The structure negates what the novel's title and "theme" seem to affirm—the life experiences of Julia Martin. Even the title of the novel is ironic since, after leaving Mr. Mackenzie, Julia meets up with him again at the novel's end.

Julia is an outsider, marginalized by "organized society, in which she had no place and against which she had not a "dog's chance" (*ALMM*, 17). If her "life" is overemplotted by the social text, her attempts to write her life are fractured by the weight of that text. An individual can only have a life and become a character in the Book, her story can only have cohesion, unity, and narrative authority to the extent that she is susceptible of inclusion within the social context. By placing the character within a diversity of familial and social situations from which she is then ostracized, the narrative demonstrates Julia's problems as an effect, not a cause. It articulates the process by which an individual becomes liminal, the institutionalized Other.

Julia first attempts to explain herself to the Englishman Mr. Mackenzie, of no given name: "His code was perfectly adapted to the social system and in any argument he could have defended it against any attack whatsoever. However, he never argued about it, because that was part of the code. You didn't argue about these things. Simply, under certain circumstances you did this, and under other circumstances you did that" (18). She confronts him about the brutal way in which he terminated their relationship, while arranging for his lawyer to send her money on a monthly basis. She begins "to talk volubly. . . . It was like a flood which has been long dammed up suddenly pouring forth." The exchange is made up of "She said that . . . ," followed by his interior monologue, which recodes her story and mockingly dismisses her point of view and her hurt feelings: "Surely even she must see that she was trying to make a tragedy out of a situation that was fundamentally comical. The discarded mistress—the faithful lawyer defending the honour of the client. . . . A situation consecrated as comical by ten thousand farces and a thousand comedies" (23–24; Rhys's ellipses).

Yet what Mr. Mackenzie reprocesses as comedy and farce is the very experience that is a turning point in Julia's life. By structurally laying out the exchange through a juxtaposition of Julia's words and Mr. Mackenzie's unspoken thoughts, the text also parodies and undercuts Mr. Mackenzie. His own thoughts expose his hypocrisy and unmask the horizon of his language and social formation. However, it also demonstrates that his ability to rewrite Julia's story and to legitimize his own point of view derives from the relations of power engendered by class and gender. Julia is defeated by Mr. Mackenzie. She can only use her glove to hit his cheek before she leaves him.

Mr. Horsfield, who observes the encounter through a looking glass, is the first person with whom Julia interacts after leaving Mr. Mackenzie. To him she has "the look in her eyes of someone who is longing to explain herself, to say: 'This is how I am. This is how I feel'" (37). Yet when she tries to tell the story of her life, she irritates him because "she spoke as if she were trying to recall a book she had read or a story she had heard." He feels that "'Your life is your life, and you must be pretty definite about it. Or if it's a story you are making up, you ought at least to have it pat'" (38–39). Mr. Horsfield, a young middle-class Englishman, assumes that an individual, as a unitary subject, possesses authority over her life or that, if she makes up a story, authority resides in the narrativization of that life.

Julia knows otherwise. She explains to Mr. Horsfield that she had tried to tell her life story to a woman sculptor who would not believe that anything outside of herself was true and who thought Julia stupid. As Julia talked to the woman, she was also looking at a painting by Modigliani. When she finished her story, it was clear that the sculptor had not believed a word of what she had said:

> ". . . I might have known she would be like that. It was a beastly feeling I got." . . .
>
> "Well, don't worry about it now," said Mr. Horsfield. "Have another whisky."
>
> "It was a beastly feeling I got—that I didn't quite believe myself, either. I thought: 'After all, is this true? Did I ever do this?' I felt as if the woman in the picture were laughing at me and saying: 'I am more real than you. But at the same time I *am* you. I'm all that matters of you.'
>
> "And I felt as if all my life and all myself were floating away from me like smoke and there was nothing to lay hold of—nothing.
>
> "And it was a beastly feeling, a foul feeling, like looking over the edge of the world. It was more frightening than I can ever tell you." (41)

The repetition of "beastly feeling" underscores Julia's inability to describe adequately with words, in human terms, what she had endured. She is reduced to inchoate animal status. A narrative is as much constructed by the hearer as it is by the speaker. A story is only a story if it is heard. As Bakhtin teaches us, "Responsive understanding is a fundamental force, one that participates in the formulation of discourse, and it is moreover an *active* understanding, one that discourse senses as resistance or support. . . . To some extent, primacy belongs to the response, as the activating principle" (*Dialogic*, 280–82). If epistemological and discursive value or legitimacy is withheld by the hearer, the ontological status of the speaker is thereby fractured or destroyed. Julia was marginalized—pushed to "the edge of the world," silenced—by not being heard or believed.

Julia's response is to pull out letters, photographs, her passport, her marriage book, and other social and legal documents that confirm her juridical status, her "reality." The documentary evidence records an apparent continuity and cohesiveness, but it also serves to emphasize loss and estrangement: " 'It had all gone, as if it had never been. And I was there, like a ghost. And then I was frightened, and yet I knew that if I could get to the end of what I was feeling it would be the truth about myself and about the world and about everything that one puzzles and pains about all the time' " (41). It is estrangement from the self that provides the possibility for a creation of personhood. The loss itself becomes the beginning of the "truth" of her existence. It is out of dispossession that the self and the text are engendered.

A central paradox remains. Mr. Horsfield fails to understand (to hear and to grasp) what Julia says. Others refuse her story too. Yet Julia keeps trying. She attempts to explain herself to almost everyone with whom she has a social relationship: the sculptor, Mr. Mackenzie, Neil James, her first lover, her sister, her dying mother. In each case she is refused or silenced. The consequence of their refusal is that she becomes a ghost who cannot recognize herself: "There was . . . the ghost of herself coming out of the fog to meet her. . . . And she had the feeling that . . . it looked at her coldly, without recognizing her" (49). The subject, stripped of textuality, "dies." But it is Julia's inability to be heard, to give testimony, and her death to the social and discursive text that keep her alive. If she had been allowed to "explain" herself, she would have become a fiction, banished from her own text, made into an image. Had she been allowed to speak herself, the materiality of the language would have effaced her and would have become more important than her "real" life. The woman in the Modigliani painting is a cautionary figure. The aesthetic object potentially effaces the historical woman and claims sovereignty: "I'm all that matters of you." The first condition for writing—that is, artistically creating the self—is death to the self. Inscription and erasure are complementary acts. If Julia "dies" because she has been denied language, she would also have died, been killed off, by her own text.

The fundamental image of *After Leaving Mr. Mackenzie* is death. It operates throughout the novel in the two diametrically opposed ways I have outlined—sociodiscursive marginalization as death and discursively inventing the self as death. These contradictory images of death and dying are used to explore a concern with the self-writing of the liminal subjectivity. Writing, de Certeau asserts,

> is born of and treats of admitted doubt, of explicit division; in sum, of the imposssiblity of its own place. It articulates the constantly initial fact that the subject is *never authorized* by a place, that he could never be founded on an inalterable *cogito*, that he is always foreign to himself and forever deprived of an ontological ground, and hence is always *left over, superfluous*, always the *debtor of death*, indebted in respect to the disappearance of a genealogical and territorial "substance," and bound to a name lacking in property.
>
> This loss and this obligation generate writing. (*Writing*, 320)

Images of death and ghostliness circulate throughout the text, but the central "act" around which the death image is organized is the funeral service for Julia's mother. This crucial scene suggests the many contradictions and possibilities relating to the self, reading, and writing. I shall attempt to unravel only some.

> She was obsessed with the feeling that she was so close to seeing the thing that was behind all this talking and posturing, and that the talking and the posturing were there to prevent her from seeing it. Now it's time to get up; now it's time to kneel down; now it's time to stand up.
>
> But all the time she stood, knelt, and listened she was tortured because her brain was making a huge effort to grapple with nothingness. And the effort hurt; yet it was almost successful. In another minute she would know. And then a dam inside her head burst. . . .
>
> They managed it all very well, very well indeed. The word slick came into her mind. Slick. (94)

If speech and signification ("talking and posturing") are based on mystification and deception ("slick"), the unyielding silence, or that which is hidden, must therefore be examined for answers. The use of the religious ceremony evokes Julia's search for the ultimate point of language, which Foucault describes as "the whole apparatus of Revelation . . . the Word of God, ever secret, every beyond itself" (*Birth*, xviii). Julia's efforts to challenge the silence inevitably fails: "She was great. She was a defiant flame shooting upwards not to plead but to threaten. Then the flame sank down again, useless, having reached nothing" (*ALMM*, 94–95). The attempts to challenge the void from which discourse is created are represented in parodic terms. She achieves nothing. And it is her failure that keeps her alive. It is the failure that *is* her life. If telling her story would have killed her off, if she endures social death, to have transgressed the boundaries of silence to obtain total knowledge and to discover the point where everything (and nothing) is readable would also have been a death. When Norah reluctantly offers her sympathy for Julia's sorrow at the funeral service, her sister tells her that it is rage, not sorrow—a refusal to go softly, a determination to rage at the dying, which has been simultaneously imposed and withheld.

As reader of the text that seeks to annul her existence, Julia's anxiety of interpretation is analogous to that of the reader / critic of the literary text, who approaches it in search of "meaning," seeking to decipher that which is not given. *After Leaving Mr. Mackenzie* is a self-reflexive text engaged as it is with analyzing the means and process of artistic production from a position of liminality in terms of the dominant metropolitan discourse. This critical dimension suggests possible ways of reading Jean Rhys's writing as a whole. The use of death as the space from which to measure the connections between artistic production and the social text that engenders it, as well as their homologous relationship, suggests that there is no space in the society and in the discourses that the writer knows to undertake this examination. A case could be made for a reading of the image of death as indicative of the writer's "rage" at being excluded (or included as an Other) from the historical and discursive texts by virtue of being a Creole woman. The text itself comes to represent a writing-into-being of that which was previously suppressed or denied. In articulating a critique of the lack of available space for a liminal woman / writer, the novel inscribes the negative construction of the Othered subjectivity and analyzes the consequences for the Other when the old / dominant discourse refuses to enter into a dialogical relationship.

The concern with writing is combined with a figuration of a stubborn, socially dead protagonist who refuses to allow herself to die or disappear: "Of course, you clung on because you were obstinate. You clung on because people tried to shove you off . . ." (130); "I haven't the slightest intention of committing suicide, I assure you" (132). In the end, Julia remains suspended at the hour "between dog and wolf" — in the twilight zone, caught between the "impossible" tasks of narrating her life and remaining the object of the dominant discourse, caught between symbol and sign. She remains suspended between speech and silence, between "art" and "life." Yet perhaps her achievement is that she breaks the closure of the dominant texts by remaining in a state of suspension, by refusing to "die."

However, Julia's doppelgänger, the haunting figure of the "mad" woman in the upper room, suggests her possible "end." Throughout the text, Julia uses makeup elaborately and is concerned with her appearance. The gesture of checking her face in the mirror and powdering it is repeated several times. Her made-up face, the text suggests, is a kind of mask. Not to wear the mask / makeup, she believes, would be "the first step on the road that ended in looking like that woman on the floor above. . . . The woman had a humble, cringing manner. . . . But her eyes were malevolent. . . . She was a shadow, kept alive by a flame of hatred for somebody who had long ago forgotten all about her" (11–12). After Julia returns to Paris, she goes back to the same hotel where the woman lives. She later tells Mr. Mackenzie that the woman makes her uncomfortable. Instead of responding, he looks at Julia and decides that her badly applied makeup suggests that women suddenly "go phut." The juxtaposition of Julia's recall of her neighbor, the woman in the upper room, and Mr. Mackenzie's comment is the final irony. The textual strategy suggests that these women do not suddenly degenerate but are done in by a long process of rejection and mistreatment by powerful, individual members of organized society such as Mr. Mackenzie. His last word is undermined by the image of the woman in the attic.

If Julia's life is death, the position of those who conform to the social system and help to reproduce its codes is a kind of slavery: "Norah . . . was labelled for all to see. She was labelled 'Middle class, no money.' . . . Everything about her betrayed the woman who has been brought up to certain tastes, then left without the money to gratify them; trained to certain opinions which forbid her even the relief of rebellion against her lot; yet holding desperately to both her tastes and her opinions" (53). Seeing Julia arouses anger and deep "rebellion to tear her to bits." The book that is at hand for Norah and from which she reads is Joseph Conrad's *Almayer's Folly*. The quotation on slavery ("The slave had no hope . . . after the day's labour") leads Norah to look at herself in the mirror and to conclude: "My life's like death. It's like being buried alive" (75). However, Norah's existence is validated by the support she receives from the social network: "Everybody always said to her: 'You're wonderful . . . .' It was a sort of drug . . . the feeling that one was doing what one ought to do, the approval of God and man. It made you feel protected and safe, as if something very powerful were fighting on your side" (75). Her conformity ensures her place within organized society, even as it ensures her own form of slavery, which is a kind of death.

Neil James, who is a wealthy man and a privileged member of society, is also a slave. He is dismissive of Julia, refuses to hear her story, sees gender inequalities as biologically determined, and believes that everything is for the best. Yet in the presence of paintings he has collected, he becomes modest and unsure of his opinion. He is anxious, the narrator observes, because he does not want to love the wrong thing. Desire, love, emotional valences are seen to be not natural or free, but culturally determined. Mr. Horsfield, who, in some respects, is a rebel, weakly attempts to break away but ultimately fails. When he bids Julia good-bye, "the atmosphere of his house enveloped him . . . part of a world of lowered voices, and of passions, like Japanese dwarf trees, suppressed for many generations. A familiar world" (127).

The diversity of people demonstrates that it is not only the "Rhys woman" who is a victim. Jean Rhys observes that, in the organization of society as she sees it, everyone is a victim: "Everyone sees the characters [protagonists] in my books as victims, and I don't like that. Everyone's a victim in a way, aren't they?" (Stevens, "Every Day," 6).

Good Morning, Midnight

The Other's Text: Sasha as Reader and Writer

Several critics, Judith Kegan Gardiner most effectively, point to the obvious literariness of *Good Morning, Midnight*, with its critique of the politics of High Modernism and its use of intertextuality and allusions ("Good Night, Modernism"). A complementary reading would allow us to examine the "main character" as an oppositional speaking subject as she recollects and orders her "life" during a ten-day period in Paris. Her style is sardonic, off-handed, self-deprecatory, inflected by intensely remembered hurts. Sasha constructs herself as constitutive Otherness, especially with respect to name and nationality. She refuses her given name, Sophia, and names herself Sasha. Although she is considered English by some, her nationality is undecided and problematic, though never given: "Name So-and-so, nationality So-and-so. . . . Nationality—that's what has puzzled him. I ought to have put nationality by marriage" (14); "I have no pride . . . no name, no face, no country" (44); "We stop . . . to guess nationalities. . . . They tactfully don't guess mine" (46).

An artist manqué, Sasha interprets her "life" through language, books, music, painting, writing, and memory. She notes the trivialization of writers and their production under the guise of celebrating art: "We waited for a couple of hours to see Anatole France's funeral pass, because . . . we mustn't let such a great literary figure disappear without paying him the tribute of a last salute. There we were, chatting away affably, paying Anatole France the tribute of a last salute, and most of the people who passed in the procession were chatting away affably too . . . and we were all paying Anatole France the tribute of a last salute" (16–17). In her hotel, where the *Times Literary Supplement* "peeps coyly from the letter-rack," Sasha overhears two American tourists observe that Rimbaud and Verlaine had both lived there (38–39).

Sasha, the outsider, is also on the other side of the privileged classes and the language they speak. One of her earliest recollections is of being dismissed from a job because the English manager of a Parisian store mispronounced a French word. The irony is that, unlike Sasha, who understands and can manipulate the language of the masters, Mr. Blank cannot communicate effectively in French. His pronunciation of the word for cashier—"kise" instead of *"caisse"*—sends Sasha on an impossible and tortured journey in search of the "kise" and leads to her dismissal. If Mr. Blank is unable to connect signifier and signified, his economic power ensures that it is Sasha who pays for his misarticulation. In recalling and reconstructing the event, Sasha connects the laws of capitalism to a system of social dominance built on exclusion and subordination: "Well, let's argue this out, Mr. Blank. You, who represent Society, have the right to pay me four hundred francs a month. That's my market value, for I am an inefficient member of Society. . . . We can't all be happy, we can't all be rich, we can't all be lucky—and it would be so much less fun if we were. . . . There must be the dark background to show up the bright colours. Some must cry so that the others may be able to laugh the more heartily. Sacrifices are necessary" (29).

Sasha also criticizes the individuals who are inside privileged groups as lacking imagination and originality, another form of commodification: "They think in terms of a sentimental ballad. And that's what terrifies you about them. . . . Everything in their whole bloody world is a cliché. Everything is born out of a cliché, rests on a cliché, survives by a cliché. And they believe in the clichés—there's no hope" (42). When Sasha is insulted by a young Englishwoman, she mocks, "What language, what language! What would Debenham & Freebody say, and what Harvey Nichols?" (51). The Englishwoman is represented as nothing more than a product, a commodified object of leading department stores.

Yet Sasha, too, tries to fit in. When she goes to the hairdresser to obtain "educated hair," a *blonde cendré*, she avoids looking in the mirror but reads the women's magazines—which purport to be a social mirror of women's lives: "*Féminas, Illustrations, Eves,* the *Hairdresser,* the *Art of Hairdressing,* the *Hairdresser's Weekly* and a curious journal with answers to correspondents. . . . 'No, mademoiselle, no, madame, life is not easy. Do not delude yourselves. Nothing is easy. But there is hope (turn to page 5), and yet more hope (turn to page 9). . . .'" (61–62; Rhys's ellipses). Parody and self-parody go hand in hand. If Sasha mocks the suggestion that life can be lived by turning the pages of a magazine for advice, she is still trying very hard to look like the average woman—middle-class and made (up) by hairdressers, milliners, department stores, and certain kinds of employment opportunities. She is trying to fit in, to be accepted, if only on the surface, even though or because she knows that she is imprisoned by the Book: "Every word I say has chains round its ankles; every thought I think is weighted with heavy weights. Since I was born, hasn't every word I've said, every thought I've thought, everything I've done, been tied up, weighted, chained? And, mind you, I know that with all this I don't succeed. Or I succeed in flashes only too damned well. . . . But think how hard I try and how seldom I dare. Think and have a bit of pity. That is, if you ever think, you apes, which I doubt" (106; Rhys's ellipsis).

Sasha recalls being a ghostwriter for the wife of an extremely wealthy man in the south of France and being reprimanded for not writing in a style that reflected the amount of money she was being paid and the financial status of her employers: "'Considering the cost of these stories, he [the husband] thinks it strange that you should write them in words of one syllable. He says it gets monotonous, and don't you know any long words, and if you do, would you please use them? . . . Madame Holmberg is most anxious to collaborate with me. And she's a real writer—she's just finished the third volume of her Life of Napoleon'" (166–67). Here, as in the essay "The Bible Is Modern," the literary and sociopolitical realms are shown to be mutually constituting. The wealthy woman in the south of France wants her ghostwriter to use complex syntax and sophisticated language as a mark of High Culture, which is in keeping with her status as a member of the Haute Bourgeoise. She knows too that "real writers" are concerned with the biographies of great men and great nations. Rhys's writing insists upon the permeability of the boundaries—social, ideological, literary— that construct the fiction of the individual self: "They explain people like that by saying that their minds are in water-tight compartments, but it never seemed so to me. It's all washing about, like the bilge in the hold of a ship, all washing around in the same hold" (168).

Sasha recalls the episode with the rich woman in the south of France when she is talking to the man she says is a gigolo, René, who had also lived in the same house at a different time. The thematics of sex, which are present from the first paragraph of the novel with the image of the two beds for monsieur and madame, are intricately structured around images of mirrors, doubles, and artistic production. In what follows, I shall discuss some of the linkages and interconnections. Shortly after meeting René, Sasha observes: "You imagine the carefully pruned, shaped thing that is presented to you is truth. That is just what it isn't. The truth is improbable, the truth is fantastic; it's in what you think is a distorting mirror that you see the truth" (74). Sasha's insights can be made to apply to her own text. Within her own necessarily selective narrative, there are gaps, exclusions, and distortions. In telling her own story in which yesterday, today, and tomorrow are sometimes confused in her mind, she articulates her insights and experiences of others and their impact on her life. She recalls her humiliations, her rejections, and her sense of being excluded. Yet Sasha practices this very exclusion against her neighbor, the man in the dressing gown—the man she says may be a *commis voyageur*. This man is a distorted mirror image of the man she says is a gigolo. It is through this analysis of sex that the novel inscribes questions about the sources of creativity and the social responsibility and function of art and artists. It is possible to read in Sasha's story the traces of another—a morality fable about the dangers of constructing the self and self-writing on the basis of exclusion.

The Mephistopheles figure of the man in the dressing gown is a shadow, in the Conradian sense, a misshapen Other, of René, the handsome young man who Sasha says is a gigolo. Sasha tells of her antipathy toward her neighbor, but for the most part she ignores him. He is antagonistic, enraged by her indifference and abusive, on one occasion calling her a cow (*vache*). Sasha does not answer him but listens to his abuse while she is in her room. When she hears a knock on her door, "I march to the door and fling it open. The gigolo is outside, looking excited and pleased with himself" (149). The textual strategy makes a connection between the gigolo and the man in the dressing gown and adumbrates ironically the end of the novel. Sasha is certain that it is the hostile, abusive neighbor who has knocked on her door, but it turns out to be the smiling gigolo. At the end, when Sasha wills the gigolo to come back to her, it is the man in the dressing gown who enters. This technique suggests that both men are alter egos, distorted shadows, one of the other. The one is extremely handsome and engaging, the other is decrepit and repulsive. Sasha's final embrace of the man in the dressing gown can be read as her accepting her responsibility to the reviled Other, getting rid of her scorn, of that which is considered repulsive and less than human.

In this way Sasha, the writer, does what Serge, the Jewish painter, was unable to do in his meeting with the mulatto woman in London. Before Serge is introduced, he is described by an admirer as an artist who possesses empathy for all: " 'He's a painter.... Yes, Serge understands everybody— it's extraordinary.' (And, whether prince or prostitute, he always did his best....) (67; Rhys's ellipses). Serge, like Sasha, plays with notions of identity and otherness. Africa, the West Indies, and the black Other punctuate their discussion. When Sasha asks whether Serge's masks are West African, he responds, straightfaced: "Straight from the Congo.... I made them" (91; Rhys's ellipsis). (This is perhaps an ironic allusion to the widespread use of the "primitive" in the plastic arts of modernist Europe at this time.)

He plays beguine music, a musical form that originated on the slave plantations of Martinique and became very popular in Europe of the 1930s. The music takes Sasha back to an unnamed place: "I am lying in a hammock looking up into the branches of a tree. The sound of the sea advances and retreats as if a door were being opened and shut. All day there has been a fierce wind blowing, but at sunset it drops. The hills look like clouds and the clouds like fantastic hills" (92). They also talk about "negro music" and the Cuban cabin.

Good Morning, Midnight positions Serge as the Othered European artist who appropriates the cultural production of Africa and the West Indies as a mark of apparent oppositionality, but who is unable to touch a flesh-and-blood West Indian colored woman in a human way. Serge's story recounts his encounter in London with a Martinican woman who had been verbally and psychologically abused to the point of appearing dehumanized: "She was like something that has been turned into stone. . . . [S]he . . . was on . . . the top floor. . . . [I]t was difficult to speak to her reasonably, because I had all the time this feeling that I was talking to something that was no longer quite human, no longer quite alive" (96–97). (Once again the figure of the dehumanized West Indian woman, abandoned on the upper floor of a house in England, reappears.) Serge says that he knew that what she wanted was that "I should make love to her and that it was the only thing that would do her any good. But alas, I couldn't" (97). Despite his interest in Martinican music and "African" masks and his status as Other, despite his revulsion against the racism of the English, Serge was unable to embrace a Martinican person because of her difference. When Sasha empathizes with the Martinican woman's story, saying she was just like her, Serge rejects this identification on the basis of race—Sasha is white and the Martinican woman was not. The use of the cultural practices of the Other, side by side with the personal and physical recoil from an othered individual, is a gesture that simultaneously objectifies and appropriates.

If Serge is unable to embrace the dark Other, it is his painting that gives Sasha the knowledge and the courage to understand her own responsibility. The pervasive irony in which *Good Morning, Midnight* is engendered demonstrates that Sasha, like Serge, embodies a contradictory and disabling duality. When René attempts to make love to her, she brutally accuses him of wanting her money. Even as one Sasha carries out a verbal attack, the other Sasha silently pleads, "Don't listen, that's not me speaking. . . . Nothing to do with me—I swear it" (183). At René's departure Sasha cries, "Who is this crying? The same one who laughed on the landing, kissed him and was happy. This is me, this is myself, who is crying. The other—how do I know who the other is? She isn't me" (184).

As Sasha thinks about her ten days in Paris, she recalls Serge's painting: "'Don't forget the picture, to remind you . . . of human misery. . . .' He'll stare at me, gentle, humble, resigned, mocking, a little mad. Standing in the gutter playing his banjo. . . . I'll look back at him and I'll say: 'I know the words to . . . every tune you've ever played on your bloody banjo'" (186).

The figure in the painting is also linked to Venus and Apollo: "Madame Venus is angry and Phoebus Apollo is walking away from me down the boulevard to hide himself in la crasse [grime]. Only address: Mons P. Apollo, La Crasse" (187). Apollo, the patron of beauty, poetry, thought, and self-discipline, is walking away to live in the filth and grime (like the banjo player in the gutter). This suggests that the cerebral, the artistic, and the "pure" must merge with the "sordid" reality of the sensual and the discarded. Implicit in this is the view espoused by medieval alchemists and Nietzsche that the "rubbish heap" must be worked through and embraced in order to gain access to the beautiful, pure, and creative impulse. The artistic logos is often engendered in the detritus of existence. Yet Sasha concludes that the gods are dead—Apollo, Venus, and Jesus Christ. All that remains is a mechanized world emblematized by the Exhibition.

When Sasha wills René to return, she uses the same words that Serge used when talking about Van Gogh: "Le peintre, it seems cries about Van Gogh. He speechifies about 'the terrible effort, the sustained effort—something beyond the human brain, what he did' Etcetera, etcetera" (94). Sasha's sardonic mockery and skepticism toward the painter's emotions disappears when, in her bid to have René return, she repeats the same words, with slight variation, with the same intensity of effort: "Come back, come back, come back. . . . This is the effort, the enormous effort, under which the human brain cracks. But not before the thing is done, not before the mountain moves" (188; Rhys's ellipsis).

When the man in the dressing gown, the dark, reviled Other of the desired "gigolo" enters, Sasha embraces him. Through an ironic redoubling, Sasha's embrace of the Mephistopheles figure becomes a distorted mirror image of Serge's inability to "make love" to the mulatto woman in London. The woman turned to stone by the racism of the occupants of the house in London mirrors the despised, nameless, "paper man" on the upper floor of the seedy hotel in Paris. The man in the dressing gown is a man *in extremis*, a ghost, a repugnant Other, "cringing, ingratiating, knowing" (14), whom Sasha barely sees as human when she first encounters him:

> He doesn't answer or move. He stands in the doorway, smiling. (Now then, you and I understand each other, don't we? Let's stop pretending.)
>
> I put my hand on his chest, push him backwards and bang the door. It's quite easy. It's like pushing a paper man, a ghost, something that doesn't exist.
>
> And there I am in this dim room with the bed for madame and the bed for monsieur and the narrow street outside (what they call an impasse). (35)

The impasse, a trap, a closing off of escape, can only be negotiated by embracing the repugnant Other, the personal stranger who is right next door. Sasha's challenge is to embrace him without denying his otherness, his strangeness, without remaking him according to her desires. He remains an unpleasant person, but Sasha can "look straight into his eyes and despise another poor devil of a human being for the last time. For the last time . . ." (190; Rhys's ellipsis).

For the artist/Sasha, embracing the repugnant Other, through empathy and an opening up of the self, is the only means by which she can cease to be herself while trying hard to remain so. It is the only way out of a destructive binarism. *Good Morning, Midnight* deliberately invokes and transgresses dominant ontological and ethical domains. Notions of self, sexuality, and morality are called into question. By disturbing notions of good and bad in terms of sexual and moral choices and behavior, the novel asks us to question whether "sensibility" and "morality" are not, in fact, deeply rooted prejudices, a function of socially constructed divisions that dehumanize ourselves and others.

If the subtext of Sasha's story is a morality tale about the responsibility of the artist, it is also a cautionary tale for those who call themselves, and are, Others. It demonstrates that the production of othering is often carried out even by those who are othered. The detachment that Serge tried to feel toward the mulatto woman still haunts him; but his painting helps Sasha to understand her own responsibility to her Other. In a sense, Sasha and Serge share an identity. René is also a mirror image of Sasha.

Their relationship turns on ambiguous images. It is never clearly established that he is a gigolo. He is a parodic reflection of Sasha's past, symbolized by the fact that they both lived in the same house in the south of France. If René is part of her past, like her, he is also going on to London.

It is the moral responsibility of the Other to forge a practice of the self that is inclusive rather than exclusionary. The "I" is not only the Other but all the Others. The novel constructs a hall of mirrors with Sasha-as-the-mulatto-woman-as-Serge, René as Sasha's double, and René-as-the-man-in-the-dressing-gown. The use of mirroring, linked to a concern with sexuality and artistic production, dismantles the I/Not I. The pathos and "depressing" quality that is often ascribed to Jean Rhys's writing may sometimes serve to deflect her insistent inscription of personal pain and alienation as, in large measure, a social event and, inescapably, a social and moral responsibility. As Rilke advises a young artist: "We must accept our reality as *vastly* as we possibly can; everything, even the unprecedented, must be possible within it. This is in the end the only kind of courage that is required of us: the courage to face the strangest, most unusual, most inexplicable experiences that can meet us. . . . [T]he fear of the inexplicable has not only impoverished the reality of the individual; it has also narrowed the relationship between one human being and another" (*Young Poet,* 88–89). To turn away from that which appears horrible or repugnant, to discriminate, is to betray the artistic responsibility.

4 : The 1940s to the 1970s
The Creole's Uses of "Race"

The Creole's English Subject

The short stories which I examine in this section were written during the late 1930s and the 1940s and were published in the 1960s and 1970s. Although Jean Rhys, like other British and colonial women authors, articulates a concern with war, feminism, exclusion, and writing, the construction of the metropolitan subjectivity, in terms of "race," nationalism, and the imperialist project, is one of the major preoccupations of this period of her writing. In this regard, Rhys understands the sociopolitical conflicts within Europe of the 1930s and 1940s historically. As Aimé Césaire and others would argue, Hitler's attempts to reduce other Europeans to the status of "natives" meant doing unto Europeans what Europe had done to its Others. One of the pretexts for much of Rhys's writing of this period is the "programme for empire," the massive volume of writing of the late nineteenth and early twentieth centuries that celebrated British imperial might. I have in mind such texts as Edmond Demolins, *Anglo-Saxon Superiority: To What Is It Due?* (1898); Benjamin Kidd, *Social Evolution* (1894) and *The Control of the Tropics* (1898); John Seeley, *The Expansion of England* (1909); and Emil Reich, *Success among Nations* (1904), to cite just a few.

The writing of Reich, who dedicated one of his books "To the British Nation, A Grateful Hungarian," is symptomatic of the discourse invoked and examined in Rhys's short story "Kikimora," which is named after Rhys's cat and set in the interregnum period. It focuses on a concern with Englishness and the denigration of women. A cat-and-mouse game ensues between Elsa, the female protagonist, and her dinner guest, Baron Mumtael:

"Charming," said Baron Mumtael watching her maliciously. . . . "The spoilt female is invariably a menace."

"And what about the spoilt male?"

"Oh the spoilt male can be charming. No spoiling, no charm."

"That's what I always say," said Elsa eagerly. "No spoiling, no charm." . . .

After Stephen came in the tension lessened. Baron Mumtael stopped fidgeting and settled down to a serious discussion of the politics of his native land, his love of England and his joy at having at last become a naturalized Englishman. (*CS*, 322)

The verbal war game between Elsa and Baron Mumtael links misogyny to the construction of the "Englishman" through an examination of the processes of role playing and exclusion: Elsa plays the role of the nervous, gauche housewife who takes comfort in her good cooking. However, when Baron Mumtael praises her, she lies, saying that she purchased the meal in various shops in Soho. When he asks her for the names of the shops, Elsa pleads forgetfulness but tells him how to prepare the dishes (332–33). Here Elsa destabilizes the stereotype of the domesticated wife by simultaneously playing and undercutting the role.

If her guest likes the food, he is also fascinated by a picture that he sees in Elsa's home. The painting alluded to is based on an actual work. In a letter to Peggy Kirkcaldy on 11 February 1946, Rhys refers to it: "Talking of blue seas I have such a comic picture near my bed—Patrick Trench did it for me—I think he was pulling my leg as so many English people do. I asked him to paint me something to remind me of my native land and my God, he's got *everything* into that picture—from a whale to a butterfly" (*Letters*, 43–44).

In "Kikimora" Baron Mumtael says:

"That picture fascinates me. What is it supposed to be?"

"Paradise."

A naked man was riding into a dark blue sea. There was a sky to match, palm trees, a whale in one corner, and a butterfly in the other. "Don't you like it?" she asked.

"Well . . . I think it's colourful. It was painted by a woman, I feel sure."

"No, it was painted by a man. . . . He said he put in the whale and the butterfly because everything has its place in Paradise."

"Really," said Baron Mumtael, "I shouldn't have thought so. One can only hope not." (332)

The opposing viewpoints on "Paradise" rest on Baron Mumtael's belief in exclusivity and exclusion in contrast to the artist's and Elsa's perception of inclusiveness. For the naturalized Englishman, who feels joy at his newfound status, England is "Paradise," and the individuality and special character of the English race depends on separation and exclusion.

After his departure, both Elsa and her English husband express contradictory feelings toward their guest. Stephen observes:

"It's a relief to meet somebody who doesn't abuse the English."
"Abuse the English?" said Elsa. "He'd never abuse the English. It must be comforting to be able to take out naturalization papers when you find your spiritual home." (CS, 334)

The differing points of view of the couple on the European man are connected to questions of identity, nationality, "race," and gender as these are constructed through acts of discursive violence, denigration, and exclusion.

Metropolitan social arrangements are informed by imperialist aggression and denigration. Class distinctions, which may be strategically blurred in relation to the peripheral Others, are nevertheless ruthlessly maintained. These class differentiations assign a place and a role to the individual metropolitan subject. In "Outside the Machine" the narrator notes: "An English person? English, what sort of English? To which of the seven divisions, sixty-nine subdivisions, and thousand-and-three sub-subdivisions do you belong? . . . My world is a stable, decent world. If you withhold information, or if you confuse me by jumping from one category to another, I can be extremely disagreeable. . . . Don't underrate me. I have set the machine in motion and crushed many like you. Many like you . . ." (192; Rhys's ellipses). Individuals are subject to this system, whose working has become naturalized and transcendent: "[The nurses] were like parts of a machine . . . that was working smoothly. The women . . . too were parts of a machine. They had a strength, a certainty, because all their lives they had belonged to the machine and worked smoothly, in and out, just as they were told. Even if the machine got out of control, even if it went mad, they would still work in and out, just as they were told, whirling smoothly, faster and faster, to destruction" (193).

"Race," gender, and Englishness as signifiers of difference are textually inscribed in overt and covert ways in "A Solid House." Teresa, the protagonist, observes that the tobacconist "always refused women customers when there was shortage—and very pleased he was to be able to do it. . . . His open hatred and contempt were a relief from the secret hatreds that hissed between the lines of newspapers or the covers of books, or peeped from sly smiling eyes. A woman? Yes, a woman. A woman must, a woman shall or a woman will" (221).

Teresa envies Miss Spearman as an example of a woman who has conformed to the social system. Miss Spearman looks like a housekeeper, maid, poor relation, or half-acknowledged relation: "There must be some half-acknowledged relations knocking around, even in this holy and blessed isle" (223). The allusion to half-acknowledged relations evokes, as in *Wide Sargasso Sea* and *Voyage in the Dark*, the racial and familial relations of West Indian slave society. (Some relations, usually of mixed race, were only half-acknowledged, and sometimes, during slavery and after, they were "privileged" as house servants.) The embedded reference to the racialized system of oppression in the West Indies, based on denial and denigration, is connected to the explicit reference to the construction of hierarchies within the metropolitan social and cultural system of values. Miss Spearman advises Teresa that in order to fit in she should avoid hysteria, socialize, and cultivate humor. Teresa considers and rejects this advice: "See people. Write letters. Join the noble and gallant army of witch-hunters—both sexes, all ages eligible—so eagerly tracking down some poor devil, snouts to the ground. Watch the witch-hunting, witch-pricking ancestor peeping out of those close-set Nordic baby-blues" (231). It perhaps requires restating that the strident antagonism toward the manifestations of "whiteness" revealed in Rhys's writing of this period is based on an ideological postulate and is not an attempt to demonize people of European ancestry, of whom she was one. Interviewers and commentators spoke admiringly of Rhys's own "Nordic" features—beautiful blue eyes and pale white skin.[1]

Conforming to the social system, for Teresa, means confirming a system of values she does not wish to uphold. It also means denying her own perceptions. Despite her opposition, however, her liminal position causes unbearable terror: "But are you telling me the real secret, how to be exactly like everybody else? Tell me, for I am sure you know. If it means being deaf, then I'll be deaf. And if it means being blind, then I'll be blind. I'm afraid of that road, Miss Spearman—the one that leads to madness and to death, they say. That's not true. It's longer than that. But it's a terrible road to put your feet on, and I'm not strong enough; let somebody else try it. I want to go back. Tell me how to get back; tell me what to do and I'll do it" (231). This points to the agony of the outsider who cannot fit in because she is not ideologically "white" and because she is a woman. She wants to avoid the pain of isolation, liminality, and the price of knowing. Fragments from Rhys's journal, *The Black Exercise Book*, contain similar sentiments about the road that leads to madness, death, and worse. To interpret the utterance as pathetic or pathological limits our understanding. Within the text, in the context of the surrounding words, it is the enclosure of the "solid house," its inhabitants and contents and what they emblematize, that endow Teresa's words with significance. The context of the utterances makes it public. The "solid house" marks off a terrain that the protagonist cannot enter or of which she cannot be a part because she has been constructed as an outsider.

The major characters of "I Spy a Stranger," also set during the Second World War, are Englishwomen. The text anchors its concerns implicitly and explicitly to the writings of Dorothy Richardson and Virginia Woolf. The sophisticated narrative technique relates the destruction of a woman considered different, hence threatening. When the story begins, her ignominious end is already established. She has been taken away. We later learn that she has been committed to an unnamed place described in the following manner: "[It was] a large, ugly house with small windows, those on the top two floors barred. The grounds were as forbidding as the house and surrounded by a high wall" (255). The figure of the madwoman confined to the attic is again suggested.

The protagonist/subject is absent from the action of the story. She has been made to disappear, or, more precisely, she is present as an absence, a discursive construct removed from the here and now. By refracting Laura's story through the words of Mrs. Trant and Mrs. Hudson, whose Christian names are never given, the text shows the common if unacknowledged dispossession that women share within and without the inner circle of respectability and marriage. Laura, who is from another place, is a fiction, the story of other women's lives. It is her absence that constructs their presence. Her "voice," that which is unspeakable and unspoken, is the enabling signifier of the women's story. She is the Other whose experiences are considered inauthentic, so her story must be told through the discourse of the Englishwomen. Her story is mediated by the Englishwomen's words, and the possibility of hearing her own is endlessly deferred. The power of representation has been wrested from Laura. The ontological and epistemological ramifications of such a silencing are clear: no language, no self.

Nevertheless, there exists a gap or slippage in the women's discourse, emblematized by Laura's book, which had been confiscated by the police and later returned with a torn page. Laura's writing is made up of her reading and rereading. She composed her book by cutting and pasting paragraphs from the newspapers into an exercise book. Mrs. Trant and Mrs. Hudson look at a page from which the top part has been torn. Mrs. Trant wonders, "A forlorn hope? What forlorn hope?" Laura's text begins ". . . a forlorn hope. First impressions—and second?" (247). The enigmatic allusion to forlorn hope is not explained. There are intriguing questions, too, about what is torn off—what is missing and why. Mrs. Trant observes that Laura seems to be writing to someone in particular, but Mrs. Hudson says she has no idea who it could possibly be. Laura's text shows that her writing is directed to a reader projected into the future: "You will never read this, I shall not escape" (249). The sentence makes clear that liberation for Laura depends upon an ideal reader who will spring her from the "prisonhouse of language" and the Englishwomen's discourse.

Despite affinities with British and colonial women writers of her generation, especially with respect to her critique of ideologies of gender, Rhys's writing still seems to place her more radically on the outside. Writers like Virginia Woolf attacked nationalism and linked fascism and patriarchy; but Laura's book also connects fascism and gender inequalities to "race": "The world dominated by Nordics, German version—what a catastrophe. But if it were dominated by Anglo-Saxons, wouldn't that be a catastrophe too?" (248). Traces of differences cluster around the signifiers of "race" and nationality and mark a vision not contained by (though connected to) the English episteme. As I noted earlier, this suggests Rhys's own awareness of the parallels between European colonialism and German fascism.

If Laura was punished because she was different and threatening, she was punished most of all because she was a "writer" and did not hide that fact: "Careless! leaving the wretched book lying about . . ." (250). She got on the "wrong side of everybody." One of the people she got on the wrong side of was a neighbor who christened his dog "Emily Brontë" and abused it. Laura also incurred the enduring hatred of the army officer, Fluting. (It is he, the story implies, who was responsible for her having been taken away.) When he complains, in Laura's presence, about the body odor of the "Waafs," she replies heatedly: "Sir, they smell; you stink" (245). The echo of Dr. Johnson's remark links the short story to Woolf's *A Room of One's Own*, in which the narrator remarks that Dr. Johnson, unlike Napoleon, thought that women were capable of education (*Room*, 28).

When Laura, a woman writer who seeks to protect "Emily Brontë" from denigration, verbally attacks a military man engaged in warfare, through the use of literary allusion, the text makes explicit connections between misogyny and the war: "There is something strange about the attitude to women as women. Not the dislike (or fear). That isn't strange of course. But it's all so completely taken for granted, and surely that is strange. It has settled down and become an atmosphere, or, if you like, a climate, and no one questions it, least of all the women themselves. There is *no* opposition" (248). Laura proposes titles of possible books to be written anywhere between ten and a hundred years hence: *Woman an Obstacle to the Insect Civilization?*, *The Standardization of Woman*, *The Mechanization of Woman*, *Misogyny and British Humour*, *The Misery of Woman and the Evil in Men or the Great Revenge That Makes All Other Revenges Look Silly*, *Misogyny and War*. Significantly it is the last title that most upsets Mrs. Trant: "Couldn't she find something else to occupy her mind—now, of all times?" (249).

Hermione Lee notes that when Virginia Woolf first published *Three Guineas*, "the most common response to the essay . . . was . . . a condescending resistance to its arguments, expressed in the form of anxiety about the author's coherence and mental stability. . . . The idea that the position of women in England, rather than the threat of Fascism in Europe, could be a major topic in 1938 was considered frivolous; the connection was not willingly perceived. . . . Such critiques looked very much like refusals to admit to the essay's most challenging assertion—that patriarchy and Fascism are akin" (Introduction, xix).

The structure of "I Spy a Stranger" is made up of dialogue interpolated by unspoken observations and the use of vivid imagery. The roses and light are metonyms for the absent Laura, and they help to construct her story. The "fierce, defiant . . . dazzling colour" of the roses and their fragile strength and permanence imprint themselves on Mrs. Trant and the reader in a way in which the absent Laura will do as the story unfolds (242). While listening to Mrs. Hudson's account of Laura's experiences, Mrs. Trant "glanced at the roses again and decided that their colour was trying. The brilliant, cloudless sky did that. It made them unfamiliar, therefore menacing, therefore, of course, unreal" (250). The roses were the last thing Laura spoke about before being taken off to what she was led to believe was a sanatorium: "Let them live. . . . One forgets the roses—always a mistake" (254). The pretext under which Laura was removed from the community was that she had put on "*the merest glimmer*" of light during the blackout, legally enforced because of the war (253). But in a place where enforced blackouts symbolize the brutal darkness of war, bigotry, and fear, the glimmer was enough of a reproach to have her silenced. As Mrs. Trant reads Laura's book, she becomes increasingly annoyed and closes it, commenting, "Too much light, don't you think?" (249). The word "light" is deliberately placed. Faced with the terrible lucidity of Laura's perceptions, Mrs. Trant cannot bear to acknowledge what they reveal. The light and flower imagery is foregrounded while in the background the untold story, Laura's story, has to be constructed within the interstices of the two women's discourse. It is one of horror, repression, and dehumanization based on difference.

The reiterative character of Rhys's portrayal of the outsider is underwritten by the writer's insistence on a stubborn, unassimilable otherness. This recalcitrance also directs attention to the weight of the literary tradition and the ideological constraints of the dominant discourse on the writer who is aware that there are those whose worlds are not acceptable subjects of discourse. They include those of othered races, sexualities, and genders. A writer who is part of the Others is faced with a formidable task. The responsibility is to write an/other way. She who is different must write differently. The experience of being Other is the beginning of writing, and it pressures the writer to produce distinctive modes and procedures. There is no choice. Conformity to the dominant models would be the same as silence: nonwriting. While the impulse to write an/other way is true of modernism in general, Jean Rhys's writing gives it a "particularly historicized inflexion."[2]

In "Tigers Are Better-Looking, Aren't They?" Mr. Severn is a colonial journalist and an oppositional thinker. (This is seen in his attitude to the monarchy and the jubilee celebrations.) He is also bisexual.[3] His lover, Hans, brings their relationship to an abrupt if expected end by means of a playful and painful letter. In his letter Hans is deliberately reticent about the "personal" reasons for leaving, but he attacks the social system and the political views of both Right and Left, insisting that both groups are primarily concerned with constructing Others whom they can look down on or abuse. In this regard, "tigers are better-looking, aren't they?" (176). The animal world is superior to the human one. Animals are not as cruel or inhumane. *Homo lupus homini* is one of the recurrent topoi in Rhys's writing. Animal imagery is written as an intense critique of a social organization based on epistemic and discursive violence done to those who are forced into the position of underdogs. Throughout Rhys's writing the use of animal imagery, particularly allusions to and rewritings of the fables of La Fontaine and Aeschylus, construct analogues of relationships of dominance within the sociopolitical realm. Hans also suggests that within this system Severn is a tame gray mare, someone who is trying to conform.

Attempting to write his regular column on the Royal Jubilee celebrations for the Australian newspaper, Mr. Severn begins: "*The figure in the carriages bowed from right to left—victims bowed to victimized. The bloodless sacrifice was being exhibited, the reminder that somewhere the sun was shining, even if it doesn't shine on everybody. 'E looked just like a waxwork, didn't e?' a woman said with satisfaction*" (177). The journalist's text constructs British Royalty as effigies of the political system, which fetishizes aristocracy (sacrificing their humanity), victimizes its nonelite domestic subjects (personified by the unidentified Cockney speaker), and colonizes large portions of the globe—"The sun . . . everybody" is a parody of the proud boast that the sun never sets on the British Empire. Yet, as a writer, Mr. Severn's political antagonism to the oppressive order is not enough to produce an effective story. He discards this piece of writing, considering it unacceptable. He is experiencing "writer's block": "He couldn't get the swing of it. The swing's the thing, as everybody knows —otherwise the cadence of the sentence. Once into it, and he could go ahead like an old horse trotting, saying anything that anybody liked" (177).

Unable to find his form, Mr. Severn idly looks through a mainstream newspaper. He is drawn to the personals and the advertisements, one of which reads "'I will slay in the day of My wrath and spare not, saith the Lord God.' Who pays to put these things in anyway, who pays? 'This perpetual covert threat. . . . Everything's based on it'" (177–78). The personals, anonymous, unattributed, and unattributable, are part of the fabric of discourse, whose origins and sources have been suppressed, whose authority is invisible and therefore invincible. The Old Testament idea of a vengeful God is invoked to punish those who do not conform. Mr. Severn's only comfort is the thought of a drink and "the jubilee laughter afterwards. Jubilant—Jubilee—Joy . . . Words whirled round in his head, but he could not make them take shape" (178; Rhys's ellipsis).

One of the two women he picks up is Maidie, who is poor and unsophisticated. She understands that for women to survive in the society, as she perceives it, conformity is an absolute requirement: "It isn't being pretty and it isn't being sophisticated. It's being—adapted, that's what it is. And it isn't any good *wanting* to be adapted, you've got to be born adapted" (187). Mr. Severn agrees with her and pinpoints exactly what the women have to be born adapted to: "the livid sky, the ugly houses, the grinning policemen, the placards in shop windows" (188)—the entire apparatus of the social formation and even the climate.

The other woman is a mixed-race woman who looks almost white and is very concerned with getting ahead. Her West Indian background is suggested by the confusion over the pronunciation of her name. Her name is Heather, a very British name. Mr. Severn hears Hedda. To his ear, Hedda sounds like a Continental-European name. She is offended at his ascribing such a non-English-sounding name to her and observes that she wouldn't be seen dead with a name like that (178). She wants the British-sounding Heather. In West Indian Creoles, the Received Standard English sound *th* is often changed to *d*. The suggestion is that Heather did in fact pronounce her name with the *d* sound. Despite her claims to Britishness, her language/enunciation defines her as Other. Her language also "exposes" her later when, in a moment of surprise and annoyance, she cries, "My Lawd . . . My Lawd" (182). The code-switching, unconsciously impelled by stress and embarrassment, identifies her "place." It unmasks her effort, even as it underscores her inability, to "pass."

The protagonist's response to her and his attitudes to race are suggestive. He finds Heather/Hedda "admirable. Disdainful, debonair and with a touch of the tarbrush too. . . . Just my type. One of my types. Why is it that she isn't white?" (181). He finds her attractive but is ambivalent about her not being white. His thoughts about Hedda/Heather are followed by other observations on "race":

"London is getting very odd, isn't it?" Mr. Severn said in a thick voice. "Do you see that tall female over there, the one in the backless evening gown? . . . Well, that sweetiepie's got to be at Brixton tomorrow morning at a quarter past nine to give a music lesson. And her greatest ambition is to get a job as stewardess on a line running to South Africa."

"Well, what's wrong with that?" Maidie said.

"Nothing—I just thought it was a bit mixed. Never mind. And do you see that couple over there at the bar? The lovely dark brown couple. . . . When I gave them my address the girl said at once, 'Is that in Mayfair?' 'Good Lord, no; it's in the darkest, dingiest Bloomsbury.' 'I didn't come to London to go to the slums,' she said with the most perfect British accent, high, sharp, clear and shattering. Then she turned her back on me and hauled the man off to the other end of the room." (181–82)

The young woman is going to Brixton, the area in London with the largest concentration of West Indian people of African ancestry, to "help." Yet her greatest aspiration is to work on a ship that goes to South Africa, a country whose system of government (at the time of the story) is legally based on white supremacy and the systematic oppression of African and African-derived people. Mr. Severn's reticence and his use of the word "mixed" invite the reader to think about the implications of the woman's actions and desires. The other side is that phenotypically "dark brown" people uphold the system of class and racial hierarchies. The woman, in a flawless British accent, refuses the slums of Bloomsbury for Mayfair, with its sophistication, wealth, and whiteness. If he is personally ambivalent about the mixed-race woman, Mr. Severn is politically astute and understands the constructed nature of "race."

Mr. Severn is kicked out of the nightclub and put in jail because of his loud insistence that the band play "Dinah," a "black" song familiar only to the mulatto in the orchestra. In his jail cell, the journalist reads a different kind of writing, the inscription of former inmates: "Lord save me; I perish" and underneath it "SOS, SOS, SOS (signed) G.R." He also sees at eye level the words "I died waiting." On his way to court to pay the fine, Mr. Severn observes, "What is wanted . . . is a brand-new lot of words that will mean something. The only word that means anything now is death— and then it has to be my death. Your death doesn't mean much" (184–85).

His experiences teach him that the words that he knows are not adequate or relevant. The dominant language in which he tries to function kills him off. His experiences require and therefore must give birth to a new language.

When Mr. Severn is released from jail and returns home, the disparate elements of his room form themselves into a coherent pattern. Things have acquired a certain lucidity. He can see. His ability to "see" prefigures the way his words will come together in a writerly way: "Other phrases, suave and slick, took their place. The swing's the thing, the cadence of the sentence. He had got it. He looked at his eyes in the mirror, then sat down at the typewriter and with great assurance tapped out 'JUBILEE' " (188).

If Mr. Severn's assignment is to write an article on the anniversary of royalty, the word "jubilee" has other meanings he needed to "experience." "Jubilee" means an anniversary celebration, a period of remission from penal consequences, granted under certain conditions, and in Jewish history the year of Emancipation. The root of the word is in jubilation and joy. Mr. Severn's writing is *shaped* by his experiences of and insights into being on the outside, being the Other. It is out of his experiences of otherness, imprisonment, and "death" that his writing emerges. It is these experiences and insights that allow him to deploy strategies of writing that produce "new" forms and structures. The practice of oppositional writing does not consist in challenging the dominant material and discursive practices in the established forms of the language. Neither does it consist in inventing a totally new language. It requires a reworking of the master narrative, the pushing of language, as Deleuze and Guattari insist, to its limits. If the writer's experiences provide procedures for the practice of writing, the paradox remains — writing dissolves the experiences *into the text, into the book.* Writing is also a source of joy and jubilee.

The genre of travel writing forms one of the pretexts for another short story of the period. In "The Insect World" the split self, the ontological disjunction, derives from the protagonist's inability to erase from her consciousness her Other knowledge, which is not sanctioned by the social and discursive framework in which she is located.[4] " 'It's as if I'm twins,' [Audrey] said . . . in an attempt to explain herself. . . . Only one of the twins accepted. The other felt lost, betrayed, forsaken, a wanderer in a very dark wood. The other told her that all she accepted so meekly was quite mad, potty. And here even books let her down, for no book — at least no book that Audrey had ever read—even hinted at this essential wrongness or pottiness" (351).

One example of such a book is *Nothing So Blue*. Audrey's story is told through her reading of and response to this text. *Nothing So Blue* is the title of a work written by Elma Napier, the daughter of Sir William Gordon Cumming, who settled in Dominica during the 1930s. She was later to become the first woman to be elected to government office in the British colony. Elaine Campbell argues for a place for the writer and politician in the archives of West Indian literary production, pointing to Napier's contribution to West Indian literature and to the region's political evolution. She observes that *Nothing So Blue* "belongs to a genre of English literature that is long historied, widely represented. . . . [I]t is in the tradition of Robert Louis Stevenson's *Travels with a Donkey*, William Henry Hudson's *Idle Days in Patagonia*, and Alec Waugh's *Hot Countries*. . . . [The book that Audrey reads] *does not sound at all like Elma Napier's book. Perhaps Rhys used only Napier's title and invented her own details*" ("Expatriate," 86–87; emphasis added).

"The Insect World" erases the "content" and "themes" of *Nothing So Blue* in an attempt to excavate and foreground the enabling conditions of the text and the genre of travel writing to which it belongs. Such a textual strategy is a critique of the cultural and political contexts that enable the textual production of the West Indies and the colonized world. Rhys's theoretical stance is similar to that which Fredric Jameson articulates as the "demystifying vocation to unmask and to demonstrate the ways in which a cultural artifact fulfills a specific ideological mission, in legitimating a given power structure, in perpetuating and reproducing the latter, and in generating specific forms of false consciousness" (*Political Unconscious*, 291). The relationship of "The Insect World" to *Nothing So Blue* is palimpsestic. Rhys's techniques erase the surfaces of Napier's text to expose its subtextual dependence upon Eurocentric colonialist discourse. At the same time, the Rhys short story writes the other side, which was silenced. As we have seen so far, the "other side" includes a concern with the *interconnectedness* of patriarchy, women's degradation, Europe's obsession with the production of othering, and the crucial role of writing. In the latter text, the author of *Nothing So Blue* is referred to as "the man" or "he." The Creole misreading and misrepresentation of the colonialist text becomes a form of defensive warfare.

Audrey had bought a second-hand copy of the book, and despite her strong desire to blot out signs of previous ownership, she finds it difficult to erase the name of Charles Edwin Roofe, who previously read the work. Mr. Roofe had written not only his name but such comments as " 'Women are an unspeakable abomination' with such force that the pencil had driven through the paper" (352). Audrey observes this before she even starts reading the text. She thinks, too, that the man's handwriting suggests that he was a very ordinary person: "It was always the most ordinary things that suddenly turned round and showed you another face, a terrifying face. That was the hidden horror, the horror everybody pretended did not exist, the horror that was responsible for all the other horrors" (352). The man's words and reactions to the book are inserted between Audrey and the text. Her reading of the literary text is overdetermined by the social context and its assumptions about women. The second-hand book from which the denigrating inscription about woman cannot be erased calls attention to the second-hand "reality" of woman, who is always already read and inscribed. The destructive and dangerous complicity of social and discursive practices in colonizing a woman's existence is foregrounded and placed within a consideration of imperialism.

The interdependency of racial, national, and gender divisions is also examined. Audrey observes, once she starts reading, that the book itself is not so cheering, either: "The natives were surly. They always seemed to be jeering behind your back. And they were stupid. They believed everything they were told, so that they could be easily worked up against somebody. Then they became cruel—so horribly cruel, you wouldn't believe . . . . Finally, there were the minute crawling unseen things that got at you as you walked along harmlessly. Most horrible of all these was the jigger" (352–53). Stereotypical, clichéd description of the "natives" and a juxtaposition of the "natives" with the flora and fauna are standard conventions of travel writing on the Caribbean.

Audrey, who is English and has never traveled, discusses the work with her friend Roberta, who has been to New York, Miami, Trinidad, and Bermuda. Roberta observes that English people are often unaware of geography. She notes, " 'I think it's dangerous to be as ignorant as that, don't you?' " (355). Roberta also explains that jiggers are in fact quite nasty but warns Audrey against believing everything she reads. Audrey understands, though, that the author's rendering of the tropics is not based on a reality that is out there but on his perceptual framework: "It all depends on how people see things. If someone wanted to write a horrible book about London, couldn't he write a horrible book? I wish somebody would. I'd buy it" (355).

In order to demonstrate the implicit and unspoken politics of narrative and structure in the prior text, "The Insect World" suggests that core assumptions can be changed if the teller of the story is changed. The description of the jiggers is what Audrey remembers most vividly in the book's account of the tropics. As she travels in the London subway, the people not only look like insects but, under her gaze, they metamorphose into large insects. While on the escalator "she pressed her arm against her side and felt the book. That started her thinking about jiggers again. Jiggers got in under your skin when you didn't know it and laid eggs inside you. Just walking along, as you might be walking along the street to a Tube station, you caught a jigger as easily as you bought a newspaper or turned on the radio. And there you were—infected—and not knowing a thing about it" (356). Audrey appropriates the jiggers motif, a synecdoche of the reification of Others, and uses it to lay bare the pernicious effects of institutionalized forms of differentiation. Through the reference to the major forms of dissemination within the metropolitan center, Audrey grasps that the construction of England's Others as insects (not-human) is continuous with the "insect world" that exists within the center itself. And the poison of the metropolitan "jiggers" is all the more insidious because it remains hidden.

After she "sleeps on it," Audrey articulates her position even more clearly, pointing out that the people themselves become the "jiggers," dehumanized by the same systems that reify the non-European Others: "And there's another sort of tropical insect that lives in enormous cities. They have railways, Tubes, bridges, soldiers, wars, everything we have. And they have big cities, and smaller cities with roads going from one to another. Most of them are what they call workers. They never fly because they've lost their wings and never make love either. They're just workers. Nobody quite knows how this is done, but they think it's the food. Other people say it's segregation" (359). The deliberate misreading demonstrates that the text, *Nothing So Blue*, can be made to say other than it intends. The reverse discourse demonstrates the ways in which construction of the Other becomes a mirror of the dominant. And the mirror returns the gaze.

However, the power of the text, discursive and social, over the reader's mind cannot be so easily displaced or overthrown. Despite resistances and articulation of Other knowledge, what is powerful remains powerful. If Audrey is able to understand the mechanisms of power and the "false consciousness" of the dominant discourses, she remains trapped within the constraints of gender. Despite her efforts, she cannot "blot out" what has been written upon the text of woman, the man's inscription that had been pressed into the page. She cannot erase the traces of history and politics. At twenty-nine, she fears growing old. Her fear of aging derives from her perception that the value of woman as a commodified object diminishes sharply with age. Her fear reveals itself most fully in an intense hatred of most women, especially women who are older and unattractive. An incident on the Tube in which an old woman is shoved violently by a younger one leaves her shaken. When Monica, her roommate, affectionately calls her "old girl," Audrey goes berserk, "Damn you, don't call me that. Damn your soul to everlasting hell *don't call me that*" (360).

Draft manuscripts of the short story published as "Pioneers, Oh, Pioneers" reveal other interesting uses of the construction of "race" in terms of the English and the West Indian—both Creoles and people of color. The early undated drafts were titled "The Price of Peace" and "A Candle in the Sun." In a letter to Francis Wyndham on 31 May 1960, Rhys says, "I found a long short story about the West Indies as I knew the West Indies, but the final version seems to have got lost. So I fixed up the two first versions . . . title 'The Same Sun'? Price of Peace? I've wanted for a long time to do a series of short stories—all about that period and setting" (*Letters*, 186).

In these drafts, Rhys returns to the postslavery period. The European, Dr. Cox, thinks of his life in the West Indies in the late nineteenth century: "Above all, there was his place in the hills. . . . 'Before beauty,' he said, 'you can only fall down and worship.' At first there was the worry about trying to make the place pay. And that was good too, that put an edge to it. When you plant a thing yourself and watch it grow—that's the life, that's the only life. When, on . . . top of that, you had dark-skinned people to do the dirty work, then it was heaven. Not that he minded doing the dirty work, oh no" (Jean Rhys Papers, Add. MS 57859, 4–5). The aestheticization of the West Indian landscape, the desire to exploit the land for financial gain, and the dark-skinned people doing the dirty work construct a subjectivity whose "private" thoughts deploy the rhetoric of the economy of imperialism: profit, self-help, hard work, rugged individualism, and aesthetic appreciation of the colonized land, all of which are dependent on the racialization of labor and the dehumanization of people of darker skin.

The third-person narrator also tells the story of the West Indian woman Miss Shew, who had a "slight misfortune":

> The Anglican curate had proposed to her and the engagement was announced. Then he had had an anonymous letter saying that she was not really quite white. "Look out what your are doing," the letter said. "None of these creoles is white. Not English white, not chalk white. Before you know where you are you'll have a nice little black baby. How would you like that? You think twice about what you are doing and when you have thought twice think three times. There is a skeleton in the cupboard." Well, it was like a horse shying—as everybody said. . . . Miss Shew had been very dignified about it, and never said a hard word. . . . One day they found a photograph of Queen Victoria in pieces on the floor, trampled on and spat on, but nobody ever spoke about that. (8–9)

The curate's hasty departure from Miss Shew's life underscores the complicity of established religion in the maintenance of racial and social hierarchies. The "personal" cost of the political is also being exposed. As in *Voyage in the Dark* and *Wide Sargasso Sea*, the story underscores the concern with the Creole as racially contaminated.

When an Englishman, Mr. Ramage, marries the colored woman with whom he had been living, "it was like tearing up the map of England, as somebody said" (11). The narrator says that the marriage aroused intense responses among the black, colored, and white people:

> Well, after that they were off and there was no stopping them. The white people were worse than the black. Why did they make such a dead-set against the man, Dr. Cox thought. It wasn't as if he were the only hermit in the island. As a matter of fact, the place was noted for hermits. . . . They had made a dead-set at Ramage because he was young, because he was handsome, because they were afraid he would break out of the net and be happy with his black girl. . . . The whole place was buzzing with rumours about Ramage. . . . The black people said he was a zombie, what the white people said was unrepeatable. And it was the white women who had been worst. (59)

"Breaking out of the net" of social control and "tearing up the map of England" suggest a betrayal of imperialist doctrine that is even worse than treason. England depends for its superior status on the acquiescence of individual subjects to institutionalized forms of racial and "national" separation. The English curate flees from the Creole woman after receiving word that she is not "English white"; the English hermit who marries the colored woman is ostracized and becomes socially and politically dead.

These stories written during the 1940s examine the claims of Englishness as being dependent upon the dehumanization of both the metropolitan Self and its peripheral Others. The English race, in its insistence on exclusivity, depends for its existence upon a recuperation of its colonial Others into its self-engendering.

The Creole's Mulatto

It is the mulatto figure, more than any other, that the Creole deploys insistently both as a container for the self and the hateful Other. In this section I shall analyze its construction in some detail.

"Let Them Call It Jazz" was conceived in the 1940s and published in 1962. The biographical information that provided, in part, the material for the writing of the story was Jean Rhys's own experience in the hospital at Holloway, a women's prison, where she spent five days after being found guilty of assault on 6 May 1949. Rhys's letters show that this happened at a time when her second husband was facing serious financial and legal difficulties. Rhys wrote to Selma Vaz Dias on 9 December 1949 to say that she was working on "Black Castle" but doubted "whether it will be suitable for broadcasting" (*Letters*, 66). This story was published later as "Let Them Call It Jazz." Yet the journey from "event" to story was to take many turns. In a 1950 letter to Peggy Kirkcaldy, Rhys says in her usual elliptical, ironic style, "One day the man in the flat upstairs was rude to me. I slapped his face. He had me up for assault. I had no witnesses. He had his wife and umpteen others. I began to cry in the witness box and the magistrate sent me to Holloway to find out if I was crazy" (76). When Kirkcaldy suggested that she start writing again, Rhys responds, "I couldn't . . . write much about Holloway because I wasn't there long enough. . . . I saw enough to be quite sure it's an evil and useless place—it does nothing but harm to everybody—but that's not enough to write a true book. . . . I'm seething to write an article . . . but it would not be published. . . . The English clamp down on unpleasant facts and some of the facts they clamp down on are very unpleasant indeed, believe me" (*Letters*, 56).

In a letter to her daughter on 15 February 1960, Rhys says, "The other day I wrote a short story as a holiday. It's called 'They thought it was jazz' and it is not typed. A bit of a crazy story" (184). She writes to Francis Wyndham on 12 April 1960 that the short story is " 'not serious' " (185). On 31 May 1960 she again writes to Wyndham: "The story I wrote called 'They Thought it was Jazz' is about Holloway Prison—So, all things considered, must not be taken too seriously. It is supposed to be a Creole girl talking but still—" (186).

When the story does appear, we see that Jean Rhys's "personal" difficulties are processed into a fiction about the victimized West Indian mulatto woman in England. The concerns with self and other, "race" and difference, art and life are underwritten by a historical subtext that draws on specific events in England, the Caribbean, and the Americas of the late nineteenth and early twentieth centuries. Selina's mother is a "fair-coloured woman, fairer than I am." Her father is a white man who has disappeared: "I wish I could see my father. I have his name—Davis. But my grandmother tell me, 'Every word that comes out of that man's mouth a damn lie. He is certainly first class liar, though no class otherwise.' " So perhaps I have not even his real name" (164). Selina is reared by her dark-skinned grandmother because her mother has left for Venezuela in search of work.

The careful detailing of the phenotypical, racial, geographical, and socioeconomic background of the protagonist writes the subjectivity as an effect of the historical conditions of the slavery and postslavery periods of the West Indies. According to historical documents, an estimated seven thousand Dominicans migrated to Venezuela in 1893 in search of employment opportunities. The opening up of the oil fields in Venezuela in 1916 also provided employment opportunities for many West Indians, mainly from the eastern Caribbean (Trouillot, *Peasants*, 113). Another important historical referent is the building of the Panama Canal in the 1880s, for which West Indians formed the bulk of the labor force. In this century, another wave of migration to Panama from the West Indies occurred between 1904 and 1914. These historical referents, in large measure, constitute the subjective and locational identity of the West Indian mulatto woman in England in the 1940s. With the money sent by her mother from Venezuela, Selina gained a skill as a seamstress and migrated to England in search of better economic opportunities.

She is now in a precarious situation because she has been turned out of her rented rooms and has no recourse to the law because she can't "prove" her mistreatment. Selina, in England, draws emotional sustenance and support from singing and from songs learned in the West Indies: "I can sing and when I sing all the misery goes from my heart. Sometimes I make up songs but next morning I forget them so other times I sing the old ones like 'Tantalizin'' or 'Don't Trouble Me Now'" (160). When she is offered a place by a man she hardly knows and moves in, she incurs the wrath of the neighbors. Selina says that two days after she moves, she is verbally abused by her neighbor "in very sweet quiet voice" and she responds by singing loudly. They call the police and she is taken to court and is ordered to pay a fine of five pounds. Selina later sings and dances as a form of resistance to the abuse and injustice she faces: "A song comes in my head, I sing it and I dance it, and more I sing, more I sure this is the best tune that has ever come to me in all my life" (167). The song that is her "best tune" comes after her legal defeat. Her artistic expression comes out of her outcast status. Later, however, Selina responds to racist innuendo—"At least the other tarts . . . were *white* girls" (167)—by hurling a stone and breaking the window of the neighbor's house. When she tries to sing "Don't Trouble Me Now," her voice fails her and she thinks of her grandmother and the historical context of the song:

Don't trouble me now
You without honour
Don't walk in my footstep
You without shame. . . .

It's about a man whose doudou give him the go-by when she find somebody rich and he sail away to Panama. Plenty people die there of fever when they make that Panama canal so long ago. But he don't die. He come back with dollars and the girl meet him on the jetty, all dressed up and smiling. Then he sing to her, "You without honour, you without shame." It sound good in Martinique patois too: "*Sans honte.*" (168)

Even as Selina recalls the history behind her grandmother's songs and uses the song about shameless behavior to mock the Englishwoman, Selina's own song disappears: "As to my own song it go *right* away and never come back. A pity" (168). By responding violently to the abuse of the neighbor, the artist temporarily loses her art.

Taken to court, Selina cannot effectively present herself, her point of view, within institutional systems that designate her as poor and despised, a racial and sexual outcast, and therefore illegitimate: "Too besides it's no use, they won't believe me, so I don't finish. I stop, and I feel the tears on my face. 'Prove it.' That's all they say. They whisper, they whisper. They nod, they nod" (170). Sentenced and imprisoned, Selina, the singer, hears the melody of a song that gives her the will to live and to escape: "It's a smoky kind of voice, and a bit rough sometimes, as if those old dark walls theyselves are complaining because they see too much misery — too much. . . . [S]eems to me it could jump the gates of the jail easy and travel far, and nobody could stop it. I don't hear the words — only the music" (173). Selina believes in the power of the musical melody to help her triumph over social injustice and imagine a different kind of future: "One day I hear that song on trumpets and these walls will fall and rest. I want to get out so bad . . . for I know now that anything can happen, and I don't want to stay lock up here and miss it" (173). The song inspires Selina to change her behavior, to "play the game," and to be released from prison.

Out of prison and employed, she whistles the Holloway Song at a party, and an unknown man plays the tune, "jazzing it up." She objects to the change, but she is told that it is "first class." He later sends her a letter, telling her he has sold the song, "and as I was quite a help he encloses five pounds with thanks" (175). The mulatto woman's experience of social oppression and imprisonment provides her with a beautiful tune, which an unknown man "rewrites" as jazz and sells as his commodity.

The figure of the victimized mulatto woman singer, like the bisexual, colonial journalist Mr. Severn in "Tigers Are Better-Looking," articulates the dilemma of the liminal artist whose experience of oppression, imprisonment, and resistance provides a new form and a new structure of expression. Selina is initially devastated by the man's letter since the song was "all I had. I don't belong nowhere really, and I haven't money to buy my way to belonging. I don't want to either. . . . But when that girl sing, she sing to me and she sing for me. I was there because I was *meant* to be there. It was *meant* I should hear it—this I *know*. Now I've let them play it wrong, and it will go from me like all the other songs—like everything. Nothing left for me at all" (175).

Yet she later dismisses this: "But then I tell myself all this is foolishness. Even if they played it on trumpets, even if they played it just right . . . no walls would fall so soon. 'So let them call it jazz,' I think, and let them play it wrong. That won't make no difference to the song I heard" (175). If Joshua and his people could tear down the walls of Jericho with their music, the individual artist, who has nothing and is now from nowhere, cannot. Selina derives consolation from keeping intact her memory of the song she had heard and what she knows.

As first reader and critic of this story, Jean Rhys has two major concerns. She writes to Francis Wyndham on 6 December 1960 that she is unsure about the language because she had "not read any of the 'West Indian' people. It's by ear and memory" (*Letters*, 197). She also says on 23 May 1961 that it is a sentimental story and "I don't feel quite like that about the black, coloured, white question either. It's more complicated don't you think?" (202). If, as a reader, Rhys disagrees with her short story's portrayal of the racial and sexual politics of familial and blood ties in the postslavery West Indies, her body of work shows that she insistently returns to this concern. As we've seen, it is an important part of the structure and characterization of *Voyage in the Dark* (1934) and *Wide Sargasso Sea* (1966). It reappears in the draft manuscript of "Pioneers, Oh, Pioneers," written in the 1940s: "The girl, whose name was Mildred Watts (though what right she had to the name of Watts few people knew), was an orphan. Her father was in Venezuela, her mother was dead. She had been brought up by her old godmother—her old Nounounne" (Jean Rhys Papers, Add. MS 57859, 57).

Referring to "The Day They Burned the Books," written in the 1950s, Rhys says in a letter to Selma Vaz Dias on 6 April 1953, "One would have to explain that it is about the West Indies a good while ago when the colour bar was more or less rigid. More or less . . . I like it because it's about what used to be my home. I've never had another anyway" (*Letters*, 105). In its ironic engagement with identity, self and other, "home," and its use of a child narrator, perhaps more than any other piece of Jean Rhys's fiction, this short story shows striking affinities with other West Indian writers. The idea of England as "home," experienced through the Book and the weight of British literary tradition on the imagination, is ceaselessly written as a "beginning" by many West Indian writers. "Beginning" is used here in the sense that John Frow defines it — "as a more or less differential repetition of a series of other texts, that is structured by its inscription within limits and within textual chains" (*Marxism*, 1). (Interestingly, William Wordsworth's "The Daffodils," perhaps more than any other text, has been attacked, parodied, ironized, and thereby privileged as a symbol of the discursive and historical limits against, within, through, and out of which they write.)[5] The deployment of the child narrator in the Rhys story focuses the charged issue of reading and writing in the specific context of colonial history. The child narrator emblematizes the dilemma of the reader/writer who must draw on the myth of the "mother country" (which is supposedly "akin to the nutritive function of milk") and its implicit denigration of the local (Lamming, *Pleasures*, 26). Yet the child narrator also demonstrates the fertile possibility that lies in that dilemma.

In the Rhys story contradiction structures the narrative movements and the characterization. "Meanings" move in several directions at once. The characters' words and actions often undercut and contradict themselves. The unnamed narrator tells of her friend Eddie, the son of an uneducated and "lower-class" Englishman. Mr. Sawyer is constructed by means of what he is not: "Nobody could make out what he was doing in our part of the world at all. He was not a planter or a doctor or a lawyer or a banker. He didn't keep a store. He wasn't a schoolmaster or a government official. He wasn't — that was the point — a gentleman. We had several resident romantics who had fallen in love with the moon on the Caribees — they were all gentlemen and quite unlike Mr. Sawyer who hadn't an 'h' in his composition. Besides, he detested the moon and everything else about the Caribbean and he didn't mind telling you so" (*CS*, 151).

He marries a "decent, respectable, nicely educated coloured woman," who often remains silent while he verbally abuses her as a "nigger" and praises her "beautiful" hair (151–52). Their son Eddie personifies the contradictions of their relationship:

It was Eddie with the pale blue eyes and straw-coloured hair — the living image of his father, though often as silent as this mother — who first infected me with doubts about "home," meaning England. He would be so quiet when others who had never seen it — none of us had ever seen it—were talking about its delights, gesticulating freely as we talked—London, the beautiful, rosy-cheeked ladies, the theatres, the shops, the fog, the blazing coal fires in winter, the exotic food (whitebait eaten to the sound of violins), strawberries and cream—the word "strawberries" always spoken with a guttural and throaty sound which we imagined to be the proper English pronunciation.

"I don't like strawberries," Eddie said. . . . "I don't like daffodils either. Dad's always going on about them. He says they lick the flowers here into a cocked hat and I bet that's a lie." . . .

We were so shocked that nobody spoke to him for the rest of the day. But I for one admired him. (152–53)

Eddie looks like his father but refuses the assumptions of imperial superiority and England as "home." At the same time, he values and claims his father's library, the very symbol and embodiment of the assumptions he refuses: " 'My books,' he would say, 'my books' " (154).

Like her husband and son, Mrs. Sawyer reveals a deep ambivalence when she decides to destroy the library after her husband's death: *The Encyclopaedia Britannica, British Flowers, Birds and Beasts*, various histories, books with maps, Froude's *English in the West Indies* . . . are going to be sold. The unimportant books, with paper covers or damaged covers or torn pages, lie in another heap. They are going to be burnt—yes, burnt" (154). The "good-looking" books, bound in leather, which Mrs. Sawyer decides to sell, represent the very texts that circulate ideologies of English cultural dominance and superiority. These texts are part of the cultural substance that produced her husband's contradictory attitude toward Mrs. Sawyer. In her decision to save and sell these books, she is instrumental in perpetuating the same discursive systems that construct her as Other. At the same time, she demonstrates almost vicious hostility toward a woman writer: "The flicker in her eyes" toward Christina Rosetti's book is interpreted by the narrator as a desire to torture women who write. The dismantling of the library provides a catharsis for Mrs. Sawyer, who regains her lost beauty.

The three Sawyers all demonstrate contradictory positions toward the discourses of domination: Mr. Sawyer, who "hadn't an 'h' in his composition" maintained a library with many "great books," as totem and fetish of English cultural superiority. Eddie refuses the veneration of England but loves the books and angrily hates his mother for burning the one he was reading. Mrs. Sawyer despises the library but ensures the perpetuation of the values that its symbolizes.

The contradictory and slippery positions occupied by the English and the West Indian, the male and the female in the colonized space over the questions of books, self, and other, are articulated in the engagement with "race." When Eddie grabs a book from his mother's hand, and the narrator one from the "condemned pile," she worries about the consequences of their actions:

> "What will she do?" I said.
> "Nothing," Eddie said. "Not to me."
> He was white as a ghost in his sailor suit, a blue-white even in the setting sun, and his father's sneer was clamped on his face.
> "But she'll tell your mother all sorts of lies about you," he said. "She's an awful liar. She can't make up a story to save her life, but makes up lies about people all right." (156)

In his contempt for his mother and her inability to speak for herself, Eddie mirrors his white father. Yet when the white narrator counters, uncertainly, that Mrs. Sawyer won't be believed, Eddie understands the narrator's assertion as racially coded—since Mrs. Sawyer is not white, the narrator's white parents would not believe her. He rushes to his mother's defense and asserts her beauty (by white standards), compared with the narrator's own mother. Like his father, Eddie is contemptuous of Mrs. Sawyer, yet proud of her white features. In their mutual insecurity, dependency, and confusion, the children cry. To the narrator, caught in the web of confusion and intimately connected to the other by self-contradictory systems of belief concerning race and gender, self and other, they reenact the adult cathexes they have known and therefore are "married": "Then I began to cry too and when I felt my own tears on my hand I thought, 'Now perhaps we're married' " (156).

The Creole's Natives and Black People

"Temps Perdi," set in Europe, England, and the West Indies, inscribes time, place, and history as subjective space, even as it acknowledges the powerful weight of European history and its handmaidens: the paradigm of progress and the discursive invention of Others. The story's formal structures enact the problematic of rewriting as a form of simultaneous complicity and resistance.

The "I" of the short story understands the function of texts and textuality in self-fashioning and repudiates those that "lie": "Now I am almost as wary of books as I am of people. They also are capable of hurting you, pushing you into the limbo of the forgotten. They can tell lies—and vulgar, trivial lies—and when there are so many all saying the same thing they can shout you down and make you doubt, not only your memory, but your senses" (*CS*, 257). In *Wide Sargasso Sea* the topos of the sudden, fortuitous discovery of the book is repeated and undermined. In this short story, the book found by the othered subjectivity is an oppositional text, which reassures: "However, I have discovered one or two of the opposition. Listen: '. . . to conduct the transposition of the souls of the dead to the White Island, in the manner just described. The White Island is occasionally also called Brea, or Britannia. . . . It would be a very humorous idea if England was designated as the land of the dead . . . as hell. In such a form, in truth, England has appeared to many a stranger" (257; Rhys's ellipses).

In addition to discovering an oppositional text, the narrator has learned how to keep warm in a cold English house—by rearranging the furniture and keeping out the draft. She concludes: "I am learning how to make use of you, my enemy" (258). To rearrange the furniture in a borrowed house, to learn how to keep out the cold, and to make use of the enemy can be read metaphorically to suggest the rewriting of the master narrative, borrowing and appropriating to write an/other story.

The title of the short story and its privileging of the memory and senses through an effacement of temporal distances clearly allude to Marcel Proust's *À la recherche du temps perdu*. Like the canonical work to which it intertextually and ironically refers, the short story insists upon the primacy of self-consciousness and a concern with the luminous and that which lies beyond chronological time and visible reality: "Yes, I can remember all my dresses, except the one on the chair beside me, the one I wore when I was walking on the cliffs yesterday. Yesterday,—when was yesterday? . . . And thinking [of a yellow and blue dress] . . . I am free again, knowing that nobody can stop me thinking, thinking of my dresses, or mirrors and pictures, of stones and clouds and mountains and the days that wait for you round the corner to be lived again" (266–67).

The third section, which gives the story its title, will be the focus of my analysis. It moves the reader from the east coast of England to the West Indies. The narrator states that the Creole term *temps perdi* is not a bastardization or imitation of the European term (*temps perdu*) but that it has a special meaning in terms of the West Indian landscape, which repudiates an imposed chronological time: "Temps Perdi is Creole patois and does not mean, poetically, lost or forgotten time, but, matter-of-factly, wasted time, lost labour. There are places which are supposed to be hostile to human beings and to know how to defend themselves. When I was a child it used to be said that this island was one of them. You are getting along fine and then a hurricane comes, or a disease of the crops that nobody can cure, and there you are—more West Indian ruins and labour lost. It has been going on for more than three hundred years—yes, it's more than three hundred years ago that somebody carved 'Temps Perdi' on a tree nearby, they say" (267–68). ("More than three hundred years" suggests the period of colonization and chattel slavery in the West Indies.) The words carved on the tree prior to the European presence in the Caribbean constitute an awareness of the impossibility of controlling the land. It is more than geopolitical space and source of wealth; it resists the imposition of imperial economic politics, labor, and history and remains itself.

If the Caribbean land resists control, the discursive invention of the pre-Columbian, aboriginal people is also called into question. In the Creole's representation of the original West Indians, the ambiguity of her position is foregrounded—the simultaneous complicity with and resistance to Eurocentric discourse in the textualization of the Other: "All my life I had been curious about these people because of a book I once read, pictures I once saw." The next sentence, however, emphasizes the impossibility of authentic "knowledge" based on discursive representation: "Whenever the Caribs are talked about, which is not often, the adjective is 'decadent,' though nobody knows much about them, one way or the other or ever will know" (268–69).

This ambiguity is further dramatized through the reference to an actual painting that appeared in the 23 November 1935 issue of *L'Illustration* and in the narrator's retelling of "history."[6] The unnamed companion's statement that his family had a print of the same picture suggests the replication and circulation of commodified images of the aboriginals. The narrator's description of the Carib as "more frightened than frightening" implicitly critiques the colonialist invention of the Caribs as fearsome and monstrous. At the same time, the narrator retells the "history" of the aboriginal peoples from a more or less metropolitan English perspective: "The original West Indians were killed by the Spaniards or deported to Hispaniola—Haiti. Well, most of the men were. The Spaniards told them they were going to Heaven. So they went. Weren't they suckers? Then the Caribs, the cannibals, came from the mainland of South America and killed off the few men who were left" (270). This account is specifically English, not European.

If she retells the "history" from an English perspective, the narrator immediately takes issue with a nineteenth-century "Englishman's" ethnographic account:

> But that book, written by an Englishman in the 1880s, said that some of the women, who had survived both Spaniards and Caribs . . . had carried on the old language and traditions, handing them down from mother to daughter. *This language was kept a secret from their conquerors, but the writer of the book claimed to have learned it.* He said that it was Mongolian in origin, not South American. He said that it definitely established the fact that there was communication between China and what is now known as the New World. But he had a lot of imagination, that man. Wasn't there a chapter about the buried Carib treasure in La Soufrière, St. Lucia . . . and another about the snake god, and another about Atlantis? *Oh yes, he had a lot of imagination.* (270; emphasis added)

The intertexts being invoked suggest James Anthony Froude's *The English in the West Indies* (1888) and the American ethnographer Frederick Ober's *Camps in the Caribbees* (1880). Ober's discussion of the Caribs is representative of the kind of discourse that is being satirized: "The true Carib type is likely soon to be lost. . . . [T]hey have acquired the name of *Yellow* Indians. From my photographs it will be seen that the type is more of the Mongol than of any other. A peculiar instance came under my observation . . . where a Chinaman—pure Mongolian—had married a yellow Carib. Their progeny, a numerous family of children, could not be distinguished from the Indian children around them" (92). On the question of the languages, Ober observes: "I found . . . that this people spoke *two* dialects, in confirmation of which my vocabulary, from which I can quote but briefly, will testify. For certain things they had two words entirely different. . . . In the following, for instance . . . the woman expresses a wish for a fish for dinner: 'Noó-iz, há-ma-gah, oó-do.' And the man: 'U-I-DI, há-ma-ga, oó-do'" (100).

The narrator of "Temps Perdi" calls attention to the problem of which the prior text is apparently unaware—an Englishman's access to and mastery of the language of the conquered, which he says is supposed to be secret. If it is secret, how does he gain access to it? By what rules of orthography and translation does he render it? The narrator mocks the "imagination" of the Englishman and points to his other inventions, thereby exposing the fantasy of an "English" text that believes itself to be an accurate eyewitness account based on factual data and observation of the "natives." By blurring the lines between fiction ("imagination") and historical accounts, Rhys insists upon the textuality—the narrative and ideological functions—of both forms of writing. Eurocentric "knowledge" is constituted by imperial control and the imperial gaze and is predicated on myths of "race" and otherness. This re-presentation of European history and discourse foregrounds its incongruities and distortions (what the narrator calls "vulgar, trivial lies").

Despite her awareness of the incongruity of attempting to "know" the aboriginal people, the narrator decides to go to Salybia, the Carib Quarter, to see for herself. She suggests that at the time of her visit, the Caribs, now constructed as mere remnants of a dying breed, were "nothing": "Nobody seemed at all anxious to take a long ride in the sun with nothing much to see at the end" (269). Here the Creole's desire to see for herself is shown to be not altogether different from what she dismisses as a fantasy (imagination) of Europe.

"Temps Perdi" includes a recollection of what is called the "Carib Uprising," which took place in September 1930. According to newspaper reports and historical accounts of the period, Dominican police entered the Carib Reserve at Salybia and in the ensuing battle two Caribs were killed and others injured. A commission of enquiry, set up to investigate the matter, forbade the Carib chief, known as the "king," to use his title (Honychurch, *Dominica*, 121).

The Rhys narrative incorporates the black Other in the form of Charlie, who guides them to Salybia, operating a common trope in colonial eye-witness and travel accounts—the "native" who is responsible for the physical safety of the white observer/explorer. Like many of these precursory texts, the narrator—the imperial I/eye—comments upon and ridicules the black Other. She points to Charlie's shoes to which, she suggests, he is not accustomed: "Negroes like to be in the movement and hate anything old-fashioned" (271). The narrator also comments on Charlie's inhuman attitude toward the Caribs. In answer to her concern about anyone being hurt in the uprising, Charlie responds, " 'Oh no, only two or three Caribs' he said. 'Two-three Caribs were killed.' " The narrator then observes, "It might have been an Englishman talking" (272). The "Negro" is also made to voice attitudes of racism and condescension toward the Carib, which are overheard by the narrator and her European companion: "We heard [Charlie's] condescending voice: 'Will you turn your side face? Will you please turn your full face? *Don't* smile for this one.' ('These people are quite savage people—quite uncivilized')" (273). It is worth noting that the sympathetic attitude toward the Caribbean aboriginal (*le bon sauvage*), recruited into contempt for the "Negro," faithfully follows many European ethnographic texts and represents an ideological survival of the West Indian planter classes, notably Thomas Atwood's *The History of the Island of Dominica.*

The West Indies, to which the subjectivity returns for a visit, is a place where the hierarchies are firmly in place. This is seen not only in the contempt for the "Negro" but also in the estrangement of the Creole "I" from the Caribs, whom she fetishizes: "When you went in it was like all their houses" (272). This estrangement exists side by side with the usurpation of the identity of the aboriginal. She takes pictures of a beautiful, physically disabled Carib girl whose eyes and hair are, to the narrator's eyes, not Carib but Creole; and she feels empathy for her. In much of Rhys's writing, the Creole's ability to feel empathy with the female West Indian Other depends on a sufficient admixture of white "blood."

Despising the "imagination" of the Englishman, the narrator is entrapped in the same assumptions that she critiques. In terms of the metropolitan discourse, the Creole subjectivity is engaged in a dual relation of participation and opposition, collaboration and appropriation. The major distinction between the narrative of "Temps Perdi" and the precursory imperial texts is that the "I" foregrounds the connections and contradictions that structure her own subjectivity. The writing out of the prejudices that help to shape the identity of the Creole represents a form of self-consciousness and a measure of critical awareness. If the white West Indian is estranged from and connected to the "Negro" and the Carib in the West Indies, she knows she does not belong in England. Unable to sleep, the narrator thinks of "time," the old songs, the Caribs, and the "up-to-the-minute Negroes," and aches at the prospect of returning to the metropole.

In 1973 Rhys wrote "The Imperial Road," whose working titles were "Return of the Native" and "Mother Mont Calvary." The Imperial Road refers to a road built by Hesketh Bell, governor of Dominica during Rhys's childhood. In the second and final draft manuscript of this story, the white Dominican woman returns with her English husband and recounts her experiences of the hostility and hatred of the black and colored people even as they remain servants, guides, protectors, and laborers in the service of the Creole.

In the opening scene, the narrator is on deck admiring the landscape and talking to a West Indian colored man: " 'You have visited Dominica before?' he said politely. 'I was born in Roseau. I was just about sixteen when I left.' His expression changed at once. He gave me a strange look, contemptuous, hostile then walked away" (Jean Rhys Collection, MS 2, 1). The beginning of this story is reminiscent of James Anthony Froude's *The English in the West Indies* and Lafcadio Hearn's *Two Years in the French West Indies*, with an important difference.[7] While the white narrator of the nineteenth-century metropolitan texts observes and depicts the West Indian Other as object, in Rhys's text the Creole speaks to the colored man. Written in this way, the story calls attention to the undeserved cruelty exhibited by the colored man toward the friendly Creole.

The cast of characters depicted by the narrator includes Violet of the Paz bar, who had been written about in several American novels: "and there she was—a very black girl with bright eyes and a very white smile" (2). The narrator emphasizes the difference, according to her knowledge, between the black and the colored:

> I must explain that for me coloured people were half white or quarter white. Black people were negroes. It seemed that the English way of labelling all races except their own coloured led to a lot of misunderstanding and confusion, for I'd always understood that negroes and

coloured people were very different indeed. Coloured people, I'd been brought up to think, were of all shades and all sorts; some were beautiful and very intelligent; some had the worst qualities of both races—they were often troublemakers and often treacherous. They *hated*. Negroes though often . . . prejudiced were more honest. (2–4)

Like Christophine in *Wide Sargasso Sea*, the "very black" Violet protects the Creole and her husband from insults by colored men. The narrator, who had "heard so many stories of West Indian rudeness to strangers," assures her husband that "They aren't all like that" (4). But she is delighted at Violet's intervention on their behalf. Word of the incident at the bar spreads quickly: "As soon as it was known that Violet of the Paz was defending us, there was no more rudeness, but there wasn't either any great kindness— not to me at any rate" (8).

Their colored driver, who arouses wariness in the Creole, talks of the imminent departure of the Belgian nuns from the school she attended as a child. For the Creole it seems "a shame . . . to force them away when they've worked so hard here all their lives. They'll probably be cold and miserable in England." The Creole reminds herself that the colored man "like most people now [was] . . . hostile" (6). On the estate where she stays for weeks, she grows fond of the kind-faced black overseer, Theodore, but his daughter, "smirking Dora," she "liked less. . . . [T]he spirit of rebellion had obviously started in her" (10). The narrator says in retrospect: "Whenever I think of Theodore or Jimmy [a black 'boy'] I can't help hoping they weren't called Uncle Toms for being so sweet to us" (12). When she insists, against all advice, that she wants to return to the capital via the Imperial Road, kindly Theodore says that she must have two guides. One "was the grimmest-looking negro I had ever seen. He came, I think, from Martinique. The other was a Dominican and seemed quite pleasant but . . . a bit weak-willed" (11–12).

As she travels along the Imperial Road, a symbol of the past that the Creole narrator is determined to recuperate, "everything went splendidly at first. I felt as if I were back in my girlhood, setting out on some wonderful adventure which would certainly end happily and remembered all the old names, Malgré tout, Sweet River, Castle Comfort. On this side the names were Portsmouth, Hampstead and so on, the people Protestants of various sects, the language a sort of English" (12). The reverie and reconstitution of the past ends abruptly when the Imperial Road itself comes to an end and turns into a steep, uphill, very stony track on which the Creole damages her foot. The sharp, painful reminder that the imperial road has indeed ended and cannot be retraced seems to be an undercutting of the Creole's desire for the past.

Yet once again the Creole is rescued by unnamed black people after some "jabbering." The house to which she is taken looks almost like the ones she "remembered so well."

> Just as I was thinking that perhaps the "Jesus, Mary, Joseph, grant me the grace of a happy death" which was a favourite expression, wasn't up anywhere now, she reappeared with a large basin of cold water. She knelt down and eased off my shoe and sock then took hold of my foot and plunged it into the cold water. I wasn't feeling at all happy. She seemed to me to look decidedly unfriendly and unsmiling and I didn't like her touching me. I liked it less when she straightened up and said "I don't do this for *you*, for I know who you are and for one of your family I would do *nothing*. I do it for your husband for I hear that he's a good man and kind to all. I pulled my foot out of the water and without looking at her put on my sock and shoe again and limped out. (13–14)

When she climbs the mule to depart from the "woman's extreme rudeness," it throws her the first time. As they continue on their journey through pouring rain, the guides cut a path through the forest. She realizes: "There wasn't a vestige left of the Imperial Road" (15). She begins to fear that the knowledgeable guide will leave them behind and she will be lost in the forest. They finally emerge from the forest into "a very civilized scene"—a house rented by an American couple. The colored driver takes them back to Roseau. The narrator insists that she remembers the Imperial Road, the engineers coming from England to build it, the ceremony with which it was declared open by the governor: "I couldn't have imagined it and the Imperial Road couldn't have disappeared without a trace, it just wasn't possible. No Imperial Road or a trace of it. Just darkness, cut trees, creepers and it just wasn't possible" (17–18).

The familiar theme of the "natives" reverting to the jungle after the civilizing influence of the European has been removed takes on particular relevance because of the time in which this short story was written. When Jean Rhys, in the 1970s, writes about the disappearance of the Imperial

Road, built in 1902, and fetishizes black people as sullen, hostile servants and laborers, this inscription is in direct response to the political changes that are sweeping the Caribbean in the 1960s and 1970s, especially the Black Power movement and the rise in Dominica of the Rastafarian movement (Dreads). Rhys speaks about this explicitly: "And what is Dominica like now? They say there are no roses in Dominica now. There were, I remember them. . . . "Lies! Lies! . . . A pack of lies. And who cares? Who does anything? . . . No roses in Dominica. Who got rid of them? I know. I know. Up the Dreads. Yeah, the dreads. They're in London, too, and they wear dark glasses. In Dominica they live in the forests. They're taking over" (qtd. Plante, "A Remembrance," 274). What may read like the ramblings of a senile and incoherent old woman, placed in a historical context, can be seen as part of the Creole's own hostility to the political and cultural assertion of independence by those whom she could only perceive as servants, caretakers, and props.

The rhetorical and ideological strategies of "The Imperial Road" allow the Creole to hegemonically reinvent West Indian "black people" as laborers, responsible for the physical care of the white subject, and as hostile menace. Once again the set piece of Rhys's inscription of "black people" in the West Indies is the black mammy and hostile nigger. The guide to the Jean Rhys Collection notes that Rhys "has stated that her publishers declined to include this story in *Sleep It Off Lady*, considering it to be too anti-Negro in tone" (n.p.).

Conclusion
Death: The Creole's Return to the West Indies

Death was . . . her allegiance to . . . the West Indies.
(*Kamau Brathwaite*)

Only writing takes you out of yourself. Only writing is important.
(*Jean Rhys*)

Jean Rhys's writing has sometimes been criticized as being too self-absorbed and solipsistic. Yet the intense focus on the self in her long writing career proves to be more than a narcissitic concern with her individual psychology. As Gordon Rohlehr asserts, "Truly creative writing about the West Indian past and present whether it has been accomplished by poets . . . novelists . . . or historians . . . has always been a question of trying to understand [the] self, of self-knowledge. Ultimate deficiency in the historiography of the West Indies, has for both colonizer and colonized, almost invariably implied a failure in self-knowledge" (*Strangled City*, 29).

Within her examination of self, it is possible to discern certain distinctive tropes and topoi that recur in Rhys's writing. These strategies help to define the subjectivity in terms of its historical and discursive locations. As I have argued throughout this study, intertextuality provides the underpinning of Rhys's fiction. Her writing draws on high culture and popular culture, music, film, painting, but most of all on other books. Books can provide a means of helping the individual, but they are also a part of the mechanism of control. They can harm and they can heal. Works of art are mysterious and numinous and yet are deeply rooted in the social world and its historical contexts. In her work the textual modalities of imitation and translation, parody and pastiche seek to effect a transgression by intervening in dominative systems of knowledge, to open up for examination their ground of possibility. Rhys elaborates a fictional practice that effaces the distinction between literature and criticism, between historical and fictional narratives. She demonstrates the ways in which reading has shaped writing, especially with respect to the West Indies.

The double is perhaps the most recurrent topos, and certainly the most complicated. There are not many Rhys texts from which this figure is excluded. The use of the double suggests a subjectivity split by the pressure of difference and exclusion based on binary oppositions: black and white; the West Indies and England; insider and outsider; sanity and insanity; resistance and conformity to the dominant social codes. The figure of the madwoman consigned to the upper room, another recurrent image, is tied to the concern with the doppelgänger. *Good Morning, Midnight,* as I suggested earlier, seems to offer a way out of the inherently destructive paradigm, through the constitution of a self based on a practice of inclusion instead of exclusionary practices.

It is the trope of death that most clearly reveals an ambivalence in Rhys's writing toward the Creole's place in the West Indies and her relationship with "black people." It is significant that death is the only means by which the Creole protagonist can return to the West Indies. The protagonists who endure in the metropolis do so in the face of daunting odds, but they remain alive. In "La Grosse Fifi" (1927), Roseau, the protagonist, named after the Dominican capital, survives in Paris. In *After Leaving Mr. Mackenzie,* although Julia is "socially dead," she refuses to go under; she endures, suspended between "dog and wolf." In *Good Morning, Midnight,* Sasha embraces the reviled Other as a means of ensuring her own survival.

In both *Voyage in the Dark* and *Wide Sargasso Sea,* the protagonists return to the West Indies through death. In their dying, the Creole self is evacuated into a black collectivity in the form of a carnival of rebellion or the black Other (Tia). In the original ending of *Voyage in the Dark,* blackness is simultaneously figured as collective enunciation and as a rewriting/recuperation of Zola's diseased heroine. In *Wide Sargasso Sea,* it is Tia whom Antoinette sees reflected in the pool at Coulibri. When she jumps to Tia, she jumps to her mirror image, her death, the ultimate cathexis. The Creole's return to the West Indies can only be imagined through writing as a form of discursive self-destruction, as death.

This may indicate Rhys's awareness that the logic of the Creole mode of subjectivity, dependent as it is upon the structures and ideology of European colonialism and imperialism, becomes unraveled in a postcolonial Caribbean. Such a subject *cannot* any longer exist. The white West Indian, to remain alive, must negotiate a new relationship in terms of the sociopolitical structures in place in the West Indies. A lived return to the West Indies would require an end to the Creole's parasitism on the black / mulatto Other as container for the self and a recognition of the ontological and sociopolitical autonomy of West Indians of other races. Perhaps this was, for Jean Rhys, unimaginable.

Yet, as always, in Jean Rhys's writing there is the other side. In one of the last short stories written before her death in 1979, "I Used to Live Here Once," she paints a tableau of the Creole's return to the land of her birth. Significantly, she encounters not black but young white West Indians. Even then, though, the ultimate return is via death:

> She was standing by the river looking at the stepping stones and remembering each one. There was the round unsteady stone, the pointed one, the flat one in the middle—the safe stone where you could stand and look round. The next wasn't so safe for when the river was full the water flowed over it and even when it showed dry it was slippery. But after that it was easy and soon she was standing on the other side.
>
> The road was much wider than it used to be but the work had been done carelessly. The felled trees had not been cleared away and the bushes looked trampled. Yet it was the same road and she walked along feeling extraordinarly happy.
>
> It was fine day, a blue day. The only thing was that the sky had a glassy look that she didn't remember. That was the only word she could think of. Glassy. She turned the corner, saw that what had been the old *pavé* had been taken up, and there too the road was much wider, but it had the same unfinished look.
>
> She came to the worn stone steps that led up to the house and her heart began to beat. The screw pine was gone, so was the mock summer house called the *ajoupa*, but the clove tree was still there and at the top of the steps the rough lawn stretched away, just as she remembered it. She stopped and looked towards the house that had been added to and painted white. It was strange to see a car standing in front of it.
>
> There were two children under the big mango tree, a boy and a little girl, and she waved to them and called "Hello" but they didn't answer her or turn their heads. Very fair children, as Europeans born in the

West Indies so often are: as if the white blood is asserting itself against all odds.

The grass was yellow in the hot sunlight as she walked towards them. When she was quite close she called again shyly: "Hello." Then, "I used to live here once," she said.

Still they didn't answer. When she said for the third time "Hello" she was quite near them. Her arms went out instinctively with the longing to touch them.

It was the boy who turned. His grey eyes looked straight into hers. His expression didn't change. He said: "Hasn't it gone cold all of a sudden. D'you notice? Let's go in." "Yes let's," said the girl.

Her arms fell to her sides as she watched them running across the grass to the house. That was the first time she knew. (*CS*, 387–88)

Notes

INTRODUCTION

1. "She . . . apparently engaged in a more literal kind of prostitution" (O'Connor, *Jean Rhys*, 47); "Jean Rhys's truth was that of a woman who was no good at managing life . . . and who suffered from a tendency to be paranoid" (Athill, Introduction, viii); "The life of the British writer Jean Rhys . . . included demoralizing love affairs, divorce, the death of two husbands, the death of an infant son from negligence, estrangement from an entire large family, near madness, poverty and alcoholism" (Berne, Review, 20).

2. See also Fromm, "Making Up Jean Rhys."

CHAPTER ONE

1. See Williams, *British Historians*; Cudjoe, *Resistance and Carribbean Literature*; and Hall, *White, Male, and Middle-Class*.

2. Green's argument is best understood in terms of the debate between himself and Caribbean historian Nigel Bolland, in particular. The texts that form part of this debate are listed in the bibliography.

3. The literature on the Morant Bay uprising is extensive. See, for example, Beckles and Shepherd, eds., *Caribbean Freedom*, 577.

4. Although Mill is critical of Carlyle, in other contexts, as Edward Said points out, he shares the latter's imperialist posture: "Our West Indian colonies, for example, cannot be regarded as countries with a productive capital of their own . . . [but are rather] the place where England finds it convenient to carry on the production of sugar, coffee and a few other tropical commodities" (qtd. Said, *Culture*, 59).

5. A few examples are instructive:

A world is at last revealed to us that we can transpose backward, with some hesitation, but with some meaning, to the books as a whole. . . . And that is the world of magic—the West Indian staples of Voudoo, witchcraft, and possession. (Moss, "Going," 162)

[*Wide Sargasso Sea* is] a triumph of atmosphere—of what one is tempted to call Caribbean Gothic atmosphere—brooding, sinister, compounded of heat and rain and intensely colored flowers, of racial antagonisms and all-pervasive superstition. (Allen, "Bertha," 5)

Jean Rhys . . . identifies with the people of her island—whose capacity for pleasure, whose belief in and dependence upon luck, and whose oppression all her women share. (Thurman, "Mistress," 51)

The colonial world that Miss Rhys treats is more than white and genteel, for the white West Indian on a black island is close to the black in temperament. . . . These blacks are steeped in obeah, West Indian voodoo. (Fulton, "Exterminating," 344)

The strikingly combined intensity and apathy of Miss Rhys's world view have their seeds in the black/white, fear-riddled atmosphere of Dominica. She was infected by the something macabre in the Caribbean, these threadbare economies perched on a sea of plangently lovely days. (Updike, "Dark Smile," 85)

Black people express their fear in *obeah*, the black magic of the islands. White people, at least the English people of Jean's time, had their own magic, which was to pretend they were not afraid. . . . There they were, marooned on a tiny hostile island, its total population 30,000 souls, and only 300 of them white. It was too frightening to think of. (Angier, *Jean Rhys*, 5)

The black community seemed to be laughter, singing; it had its folk-tales and masquerades; it accepted life including sex, with a freedom foreign to the whites. Modern stereotypes of West Indian societies tend to present a simple over-dramatic picture of white against black. Particularly on smaller islands such as Dominica, this is a myth. (James, *Jean Rhys*, 5)

The critical deployment of the stereotyped emblematic images of the black Other is what Toni Morrison defines as an "Africanist discourse": a term for "the denotative and connotative blackness that African peoples have come to signify, as well as the entire range of views, assumptions, readings and misreadings that accompany Eurocentric learning about these people. As a trope, little restraint has been attached to its uses" (*Playing*, 7).

6. For an analysis of Asian indentureship in the West Indies, including an extensive bibliography on the literature, see Look Lai, *Indentured Labor, Caribbean Sugar*.

7. As Anne Walmsley notes, "Honours and awards given to these writers during the 1950s and 1960s indicate something of their critical standing in Britain. Lam-

ming won the Somerset Maugham Award (1957); Selvon, a travelling scholarship from the Society of Authors (1958); Salkey, the Thomas Helmore Prize for Poetry (1955); and Naipaul, the John Llewellyn Rhys Memorial Prize (1958), the Somerset Maugham Award (1961), the Phoenix Trust Award (1962), the Hawthornden Prize (1964), and the W. H. Smith Prize (1968)" (*Caribbean Artists Movement*, 30).

8. The leading theorists include Smith, *The Plural Society in the British West Indies*; Patterson, *The Sociology of Slavery*; and Brathwaite, *The Development of Creole Society in Jamaica*.

9. For another reading that challenges Brathwaite's argument from a different perspective, see O'Callaghan, "The Outsider's Voice."

10. In the 1960s Rhys shared an editor, Diana Athill, with at least one other West Indian writer, V. S. Naipaul (Walmsley, *Caribbean Artists Movement*, 44).

11. Rhys's observation is similar to that of Thomas Atwood, who notes: "The Creole negro[e]s, that is to say, those who are born in the West Indies, having been brought up among white people, and paid some attention to from their infancy, lose much of that uncommon stupidity so conspicuous in their new negro parents; and are in general tolerably sensible, sharp, and sagacious" (*History*, 267).

12. The quotation that Rhys includes in her letter reads: "*Il faudrait parler de soi avec une rigeur inflexible. Et au premier effort pour se saisir, d'où vinennent cette pitié, ce relâchement de toutes les fibres de l'âme et cette envie de pleurer?*" (*Letters*, 103).

13. An example of Rhys's knowledge of and intervention in the work of the psychoanalysts named, especially with respect to gender, appears in an unpublished fragment in *The Black Exercise Book*:

> Once I went to Sylvia Beach's bookshop. . . . I wanted a book on psychoanalysis. I found one opened it [and] read something like this not the words but the sense
>
> "Women of this type will invariably say that they were seduced when very young by an elderly man. In *every* case the story is [fictitious]. They will relate a detailed story which in every case is entirely [fictitious]."
>
> No honey I thought it is *not* [fictitious] in every case. By no means, anyhow how do you know.
>
> A few pages further the gent again laying down the law about the female attitude and reaction to sex. . . .
>
> I was confirmed [and] established in this opinion by what Case no 934 told me . . . and by what Case no 796 told me. . . . Both it seeemed were potty.
>
> Then I put the book down. No dear no you don't play fair. If you're going [to] reject the evidence of one lot who contradict you you ought certainly to

reject the evidence of the other who agree with you [and] form your opinions along different lines and for different reasons. I wish that somewhere sometime some[one] . . . would [write] about women fairly. I suppose . . . [it is] impossible to ask. Some Frenchmen almost do it though. (Jean Rhys Collection, 58–60)

There is also an ironic allusion to Freud, by name, in "Tigers Are Better-Looking" (*CS*, 176).

14. There is a rewriting of Proust's *Remembrance of Things Past* in "Temps Perdi" (1930s; published 1969); quotations from Conrad's *Almayer's Folly* in *After Leaving Mr. Mackenzie* (1930); and an intertextual reworking of James Joyce's *Ulysses* in *Good Morning, Midnight* (1939).

15. For another reading in this vein, see O'Callaghan, "The Outsider's Voice."

16. Rhys's use of photography is similar to that of Roland Barthes. Linda Hutcheon observes that Barthes's

self-consciousness about the act of representing in both writing and photography undoes the mimetic assumptions of transparency that underpin the realist project. . . . *Roland Barthes by Roland Barthes* manages to de-naturalize both the "copying" apparatus of photography and the realist reflecting mirror of narrative while still acknowledging—and exploiting—their shared power of inscription and construction. . . . Both forms have traditionally been assumed to be transparent media which paradoxically could master/capture/fix the real. Yet the . . . photography and fiction [are revealed] to be, in fact, highly coded forms of representation. (*Postmodernism*, 41)

CHAPTER TWO

1. Elaine Campbell, in her introduction to Phyllis Allfrey's *The Orchid House*, also points to important intertextual references to this text in *Wide Sargasso Sea*.

2. The stereotype of the Creole woman in the West Indies as decoration for the Great House is reproduced insistently in colonialist discourse. For example, Edward Long constructs white West Indian women as "those who are born, not only to inherit, but to adorn a fortune" (*History*, 2:280). Thomas Atwood argues: "The generality of the English white women in the West Indies are as lovely as in any part of the world besides, make as good wives, tender mothers, and as agreeable companions" (*History*, 211).

3. See Edward Said, *Orientalism*, 99.

4. See Brathwaite's *Development of Creole Society in Jamaica*.

5. One notable exception is Lee Erwin, whose reading of the importance of

Daniel's name is similar in some respects to my own. See " 'Like in a Looking Glass.' "

CHAPTER THREE

1. Thomas Staley puts it well: "Of vital importance to an understanding and appreciation of Rhys's contribution to the modern novel is the recognition of the striking way in which her fiction reflects a complex of values and an attitude toward life which both undercuts and opposes so many of the most cherished values, both public and private, of the bourgeois world. There is an implicit challenge in all of her work to the entire fabric of social and moral order which governs so much of society. To recognise this challenge is to begin to understand the nature of her achievement" (*Jean Rhys*, 1). Critics of the 1920s and 1930s also focused on Rhys's difference. In her review of *After Leaving Mr. Mackenzie*, Gladys Graham concludes: "It is a book that does not invite comparisons. It does not appeal as being as-good-as or better-than. Its excellence is individual, intrinsic; it measures itself against itself" (Review, 8).

CHAPTER FOUR

1. Some of the many examples include "Miss Rhys's eyes are sapphire, wide-set, and long-lashed against a pale English skin: one cannot help thinking that had she stayed in Dominica she would not have that skin" (Vreeland, "Jean Rhys," 220); and "She is a beauty . . . [with] eyes that are an enormous blue-gray" (Cantwell, "A Conversation," 171).

2. I owe this formulation to Ross Chambers.

3. The use of a bisexual man as the protagonist of the story also mocks Freudian views of sexuality. In his letter Hans says, "I've drunk the milk. . . . I know how you dislike the stuff (Freud! Bow-wow-wow!!)" (*CS*, 176). The deprecating reference to milk and Freud suggests the psychoanalyst's theory of the pre-Oedipal stage and undifferentiated sexuality.

4. The date of writing is uncertain. But in 1959 Rhys sent it, along with *The Sound of the River* (which had been rejected in the 1940s) to Francis Wyndham. At that time she observed that the story was not finished. It was finished in 1973 and published in the *Sunday Times Magazine*; it was later included in *Sleep It Off Lady* (1976) and in *The Collected Short Stories* (1987), from which I have quoted.

5. Some writers whose work intertextually invokes "The Daffodils" include

V. S. Naipaul, *Miguel Street* (1959); Michelle Cliff, *Abeng* (1984); Jamaica Kincaid, *Lucy* (1990); and Merle Hodge, *Crick Crack Monkey* (1970).

6. This painting is reproduced in Hulme and Whitehead, eds., *Wild Majesty*, 302.

7. "A young man, awaking as I pass to my cabin, turns upon me a pair of peculiarly luminous black eyes,—creole eyes. Evidently a West Indian" (Hearn, *Two Years*, 13).

Works Cited

PRIMARY SOURCES

Rhys, Jean. *After Leaving Mr. Mackenzie.* 1930. Reprint. Harmondsworth: Penguin, 1973.

———. *The Collected Short Stories.* Introduction by Diana Athill. New York: W. W. Norton, 1987.

———. "A Conversation with Jean Rhys, 'The Best Living English Novelist.' " Interview with Mary Cantwell. *Mademoiselle,* October 1974, 170–71, 206, 208, 210, 213.

———. "Fated to Be Sad." Interview with Hannah Carter. *(London) Guardian,* 8 August 1968, 5.

———. *Good Morning, Midnight.* New York: W. W. Norton, 1986.

———. "Interviewed by Peter Burton." *Transatlantic Review* 36 (Summer 1970): 105–9.

———. Jean Rhys Collection. McFarlin Library, University of Tulsa.

———. Jean Rhys Papers. British Library.

———. *The Left Bank and Other Stories.* New York: Harper and Brothers, 1927.

———. *The Letters of Jean Rhys.* Edited by Francis Wyndham and Diana Melly; introduction by Francis Wyndham. New York: Viking, 1984.

———. "Making Bricks without Straws." *Harper's,* 16 March 1978, 12–14.

———. *My Day.* New York: Frank Hallman, 1975.

———. *Smile Please: An Unfinished Autobiography.* Harmondsworth: Penguin, 1981.

———. *Tales of the Wide Caribbean.* Edited with an introduction by Kenneth Ramchand. London: Heinemann, 1986.

———. *Voyage in the Dark.* New York: W. W. Norton, 1982.

———. *Voyage in the Dark: Part Four.* Original Version. Reprinted in Carol Ann Howells, "Jean Rhys (1890–1979)." In *The Gender of Modernism: A Critical Anthology,* edited by Bonnie Kime Scott, 381–89. Bloomington: Indiana University Press, 1990. Also reprinted in Nancy Hemond Brown, "Jean Rhys and *Voyage in the Dark.*" *London Magazine,* 25 April 1985, 40–59.

———. *Wide Sargasso Sea.* New York: W. W. Norton, 1982.

Adams, Percy G. *Travel Literature and the Evolution of the Novel.* Lexington: University Press of Kentucky, 1983.

Allen, Walter. "Bertha the Doomed." *New York Times Book Review,* 18 June 1967, 5.

Anderson, Paula Grace. "Jean Rhys's *Wide Sargasso Sea:* The Other Side / Both Sides Now." *Caribbean Quarterly* 28, nos. 1–2 (1982): 57–65.

Angier, Carole. *Jean Rhys.* Harmondsworth: Penguin, 1985.

Asein, Samuel. "The 'Protest' Tradition in West Indian Poetry from George Campbell to Martin Carter." *Jamaica Journal* 6, no. 2 (1972): 40–45.

Athill, Diana. Introduction to *Jean Rhys: The Collected Short Stories.* New York: W. W. Norton, 1987.

Atwood, Thomas. *The History of the Island of Dominica. Containing a Description of Its Situation, Extent, Climate, Mountains, Rivers, Natural Productions, &c. &c.* London: Frank Cass, 1971.

August, Eugene R., ed. *Thomas Carlyle, The Nigger Question; John Stuart Mill, The Negro Question.* New York: Appleton Century Crofts, 1971.

Bakhtin, M. M. *The Dialogic Imagination.* Austin: University of Texas Press, 1981.

Baugh, Edward, ed. *Critics on Caribbean Literature: Readings in Literary Criticism.* London: George Allen and Unwin, 1978.

———. "Edward Brathwaite as Critic: Some Preliminary Observations." *Caribbean Quarterly* 28, nos. 1–2 (1982): 66–75.

———. "Tribute to Vic Reid by Edward Baugh." *Journal of West Indian Literature* 2, no. 1 (1987): 1–3.

The Beacon. New York: Kraus Reprint Co., 1970.

Beaujour, Michel. *Poetics of the Literary Self-Portrait.* Translated by Yara Milos. New York: New York University Press, 1991.

Beckles, Hilary, and Verene Shepherd, eds. *Caribbean Freedom: Economy and Society from Emancipation to the Present.* Kingston, Jamaica: Ian Randle Publishers, 1993.

Bell, Hesketh. *Glimpses of a Governor's Life from Diaries, Letters, and Memoranda.* London: Sampson Marston, 1946.

Bender, Todd K. "Jean Rhys." *Contemporary Criticism* 22 (1981): 248–52.

Benveniste, Emile. *Problems in General Linguistics.* Miami: University of Miami Press, 1971.

Berne, Suzanne. Review of *Jean Rhys' Life and Work,* by Carole Angier. *New York Times Book Review,* 30 June 1991, 20.

Bhabha, Homi K. "Interrogating Identity: The Postcolonial Prerogative." In *Anatomy of Racism,* edited by David Theo Goldberg, 183–209. Minneapolis: University of Minnesota Press, 1990.

———. "The Other Question: Difference, Discrimination, and the Discourse of Colonialism." In *Literature, Politics, and Theory: Papers from the Essex Conference 1976–84*, edited by Francis Barker et al., 148–72. London: Methuen, 1986.

———. "Signs Taken for Wonders: Questions of Ambivalence and Authority under a Tree Outside Delhi, May 1817." In *"Race," Writing, and Difference*, edited by Henry Louis Gates Jr., 163–84. Chicago: University of Chicago Press, 1985.

Bolland, O. Nigel. "Creolization and Creole Societies: A Cultural Nationalist View of Caribbean Social History." In *Intellectuals in the Twentieth-Century Caribbean*, edited by Alistair Hennessey, 1:50–79. London: Macmillan Education, 1992.

———. "Reply to William Green's 'The Perils of Comparative History.'" *Comparative Studies in Society and History* 26, no. 1 (1984): 120–25.

———. "Systems of Domination after Slavery: The Control of Land and Labor in the British West Indies." In *Caribbean Freedom: Economy and Society from Emancipation to the Present*, edited by Hilary Beckles and Verene Shepherd, 107–23. Kingston, Jamaica: Ian Randle Publishers, 1993.

Borome, Joseph. "The French and Dominica, 1699–1763." In *Aspects of Dominican History*, 80–102. Dominica: Government Printing Office, 1972.

———. "George Charles Falconer." *Caribbean Quarterly* 6, no. 1 (1959): 11–17.

———. "How Crown Colony Government Came to Dominica by 1898." *Aspects of Dominican History*, 120–56. Dominica: Government Printing Office, 1972.

Bowen, Stella. *Drawn from Life*. London: Virago, 1984.

Brathwaite, Kamau [Edward]. "Caribbean Critics." *New World Quarterly* 5, nos. 1–2 (1969): 5–12.

———. *Contradictory Omens: Cultural Diversity and Integration in the Caribbean*. Kingston, Jamaica: University of the West Indies, 1974.

———. *The Development of Creole Society in Jamaica, 1770–1820*. Oxford: Clarendon Press, 1971.

———. "The Love Axe/1: Developing a Caribbean Aesthetic, 1962–1974." In *Reading Black: Essays in the Criticism of African, Caribbean, and Black American Literature*, edited by Houston Baker, 20–34. New York: Africana Studies and Research Center, Cornell University, 1976.

———. *Roots*. Ann Arbor: University of Michigan Press, 1993.

Brown, Laura. "The Romance of Empire: Oroonoko and the Trade in Slaves." In *The New Eighteenth Century: Theory, Politics, English Literature*, edited by Felicity Nussbaum and Laura Brown, 41–62. New York: Routledge, 1991.

Butler, Mary. "Fair and Equitable Consideration: The Distribution of Slave Compensation in Jamaica and Barbados." *Journal of Caribbean History* 22, nos. 1–2 (1988): 138–52.

Campbell, Elaine. "An Expatriate at Home: Dominica's Elma Napier." *Kunapipi* 4, no. 1 (1982): 82–93.

———. Introduction to *The Orchid House*, by Phyllis Allfrey. London: Virago, 1982.

———. "A Report from Dominica, B.W.I." *World Literature Written in English* 17 (1978): 305–16.

Cantwell, Mary. "A Conversation with Jean Rhys, 'The Best Living English Novelist.'" *Mademoiselle*, October 1974, 170–71, 206, 208, 210, 213.

Carew, Jan. Interview. *Journal of West Indian Literature* 2, no. 1 (1987): 37–40.

Certeau, Michel de. *The Writing of History*. Translated by Tom Conley. New York: Columbia University Press, 1988.

Chace, Russell, Jr. "Protest in Post-Emancipation Dominica: The Guerre Negre of 1844." *Journal of Caribbean History* 23, no. 2 (1989): 118–41.

Chambers, Ross. *Room for Maneuver: Reading (the) Oppositional (in) Narrative*. Chicago: University of Chicago Press, 1991.

Cliff, Michelle. "Caliban's Daughter: The Tempest and the Teapot." *Frontiers: A Journal of Women's Studies* 12, no. 2 (1991): 36–51.

Coulthard, G. R. *Race and Colour in Caribbean Literature*. London: Oxford University Press, 1962.

Cudjoe, Selwyn, ed. *Caribbean Women Writers: Essays from the First International Conference*. Wellesley: Calaloux Publications, 1990.

———. *Resistance and Caribbean Literature*. Athens: Ohio University Press, 1980.

D'Costa, Jean. "Bra Rabbit Meets Peter Rabbit: Genre, Audience, and the Artistic Imagination: Problems in Writing Children's Fiction." In *Caribbean Women Writers: Essays from the First International Conference*, edited by Selwyn Cudjoe, 254–62. Wellesley: Calaloux Publications, 1990.

———. "Jean Rhys 1890–1979." In *Fifty Caribbean Writers*, edited by Daryl Dance, 390–404. New York: Greenwood Press, 1986.

Dance, Daryl Cumber, ed. *Fifty Caribbean Writers*. New York: Greenwood Press, 1986.

———. *New World Adams: Conversations with Contemporary West Indian Writers*. Leeds: Peepal Tree Books, 1992.

Dash, J. Michael. *Literature and Ideology in Haiti, 1915–1961*. London: Macmillan, 1981.

Deleuze, Gilles, and Felix Guattari. *Kafka: Toward a Minor Literature*. Translated by Dana Polan. Theory and History of Literature, vol. 30. Minneapolis: University of Minnesota Press, 1986.

Eagleton, Terry, Fredric Jameson, and Edward Said. *Nationalism, Colonialism, and Literature*. Minneapolis: University of Minnesota Press, 1990.

Emery, Mary Lou. *Jean Rhys at "World's End": Novels of Sexual and Colonial Exile.* Austin: University of Texas Press, 1990.

Erwin, Lee. "'Like in a Looking-Glass': History and Narrative in *Wide Sargasso Sea*." *Novel: A Forum on Fiction* 22, no. 2 (1989): 143–58.

Fanon, Frantz. *The Wretched of the Earth.* Preface by Jean-Paul Sartre. Translated by Constance Farrington. New York: Grove Weidenfeld, 1963.

Field, H. John. *Toward a Programme of Imperial Life: The British Empire at the Turn of the Century.* Contributions in Comparative Colonial Studies, no. 9. Westport, Conn.: Greenwood Press, 1982.

Ford, Ford Madox. Preface to *The Left Bank and Other Stories*, by Jean Rhys. New York: Harper and Brothers, 1927.

Foucault, Michel. *The Birth of the Clinic: An Archaeology of Medical Perception.* Translated by A. M. Sheridan Smith. New York: Vintage Books, 1975.

Frickey, Pierrette, ed. *Critical Perspectives on Jean Rhys.* Washington, D.C.: Three Continents, 1990.

Fromm, Gloria. "Making Up Jean Rhys." *New Criterion* 4, no. 4 (1985): 47–50.

Froude, James Anthony. *The English in the West Indies: The Bow of Ulysses.* London: Longmans, Green, 1888.

Frow, John. *Marxism and Literary History.* Cambridge: Harvard University Press, 1986.

Fulton, Nancy J. Casey. "Jean Rhys's *Wide Sargasso Sea*: Exterminating the White Cockroach." *Revista Iberoamericana* 8 (1974): 340–49.

Gadamer, Hans-Georg. *Truth and Method.* Translated and revised by Joel Weisheimer and Donald G. Marshall. New York: Crossroad, 1990.

Gardiner, Judith Kegan. "Good Morning, Midnight, Good Night, Modernism." *Boundary 2* 11, no. 2 (1982): 233–52.

————. *Rhys, Stead, Lessing, and the Politics of Empathy.* Bloomington: Indiana University Press, 1989.

Gilman, Sander. "Black Bodies, White Bodies: Toward an Iconography of Female Sexuality in Late Nineteenth-Century Art, Medicine, and Literature." In *"Race," Writing, and Difference*, edited by Henry Louis Gates Jr., 223–61. Chicago: University of Chicago Press, 1985.

Gomes, Albert. "Periodicals." *Beacon* 1, no. 10 (1932): 24–25.

Goveia, Elsa. *Historiography of the British West Indies to the End of the Nineteenth Century.* Washington D.C.: Howard University Press, 1980.

Graham, Gladys. Review of *After Leaving Mr. Mackenzie*, by Jean Rhys. *Saturday Review of Literature*, 25 July 1931, 8.

Green, W. A. *British Slave Emancipation: The Sugar Colonies and the Great Experiment, 1830–1865.* Oxford: Clarendon Press, 1976.

————. "The Creolization of Caribbean History: The Emancipation Era and a Critique of Dialectical Analysis." In *Caribbean Freedom: Economy and Society from Emancipation to the Present*, edited by Hilary Beckles and Verene Shepherd, 28–40. Kingston, Jamaica: Ian Randle Publishers, 1993.

————. "The Perils of Comparative History: Belize and the Sugar Colonies after Slavery." *Comparative Studies in Society and History* 26, no. 1 (1984): 112–19.

Gregg, Veronica Marie. "Ideology and Autobiography in Jean Rhys' *oeuvre*." In *From Commonwealth to Post-Colonial*, edited by Anna Rutherford, 407–19. Mundelstrup, Denmark: Dangaroo Press, 1992.

————. "Jean Rhys on Herself as a Writer." In *Caribbean Women Writers: Essays from the First International Conference*, edited by Selwyn Cudjoe, 109–15. Wellesley: Calaloux Publications, 1990.

Hall, Catherine. *White, Male, and Middle-Class: Explorations in Feminism and History.* Cambridge: Polity Press, 1992.

Hall, Douglas. "The Flight from the Estates Reconsidered: The British West Indies, 1834–1842." In *Caribbean Freedom: Economy and Society from Emancipation to the Present*, edited by Hilary Beckles and Verene Shepherd, 55–63. Kingston, Jamaica: Ian Randle Publishers, 1993.

Hall, John. "Jean Rhys." *London Guardian*, 10 January 1972: 8.

Harris, Wilson. "Carnival of Psyche: Jean Rhys's *Wide Sargasso Sea*." *Kunapipi* 2, no. 2 (1980): 142–50.

————. "Jean Rhys's Tree of Life." *Review of Contemporary Fiction* 5, no. 2 (1985): 114–17.

————. *Tradition, the Writer, and Society: Critical Essays.* London: New Beacon, 1967.

————. "The Unresolved Constitution." *Caribbean Quarterly* 14, nos. 1–2 (1968): 43–47.

Hearn, Lafcadio. *Two Years in the French West Indies.* New York: Harper and Brothers, 1890.

Hearne, John. "The Wide Sargasso Sea: A West Indian Reflection." *Cornhill Magazine* 1080 (Summer 1974): 323–33.

————, ed. *Carifesta Forum: An Anthology of Twenty Caribbean Voices.* Kingston, Jamaica: Institute of Jamaica, 1976.

Holt, Thomas. *The Problem of Freedom: Race, Labor, and Politics in Jamaica and Britain, 1831–1938.* Baltimore: Johns Hopkins University Press, 1992.

Honychurch, Lenox. *The Dominica Story: A History of the Island.* Roseau, Dominica: Dominica Institute, 1975.

Hulme, Peter, and Neil L. Whitehead, eds. *Wild Majesty: Encounters with Caribs from Columbus to the Present Day. An Anthology.* Oxford: Clarendon Press, 1992.

Hutcheon, Linda. *The Politics of Postmodernism.* New York: Routledge, 1989.

James, Louis. *Jean Rhys*. London: Longmans, 1978.

Jameson, Fredric. *The Political Unconscious: Narative as a Socially Symbolic Act*. New York: Cornell University Press, 1981.

Jonson, Bari. "The Entertainers —1973." *Jamaica Journal* 7, no. 4 (1973): 38–46.

Kestleloot, Lilyan. *Black Writers in French: A Literary History of Negritude*. Translated by Ellen Conroy Kennedy. Washington, D.C.: Howard University Press, 1991.

Knorr, Klaus E. *British Colonial Theories 1570–1850*. Toronto: University of Toronto Press, 1944.

Kristeva, Julia. *Desire in Language: A Semiotic Approach to Literature and Art*. Edited by Leon S. Roudiez; translated by Thomas Gora, Alice Jardine, and Leon S. Roudiez. New York: Columbia University Press, 1980.

Labat, Jean-Baptiste. *The Memoirs of Père Labat 1693–1705*. Translated and abridged by John Eaden; introduction by Philip Gosse. London: Frank Cass, 1970.

Lamming, George. *The Pleasures of Exile*. Foreword by Sandra Pouchet Paquet. Ann Arbor: University of Michigan Press, 1992.

———. "The West Indian People." *New World Quarterly* 2, no. 2 (Croptime 1966): 63–74.

Lee, Hermione. Introduction to *A Room of One's Own and Three Guineas*, by Virginia Woolf. London: Hogarth Press, 1984.

Lewis, Arthur. *Labour in the West Indies: The Birth of a Workers' Movement*. 1938. Reprint. London: New Beacon, 1977.

Lewis, Gordon K. *Main Currents in Caribbean Thought: The Historical Evolution of Caribbean Society in Its Ideological Aspects, 1492–1900*. Baltimore: Johns Hopkins University Press, 1983.

Liverpool, Hollis. "Rituals of Power and Rebellion: The Carnival Tradition in Trinidad and Tobago." Ph.D. diss., University of Michigan, 1993.

Long, Edward. *The History of Jamaica or General Survey of the Antient and Modern State of That Island: With Reflections on Its Situations, Settlements, Inhabitants, Climate, Products, Commerce, Laws and Government*. 3 books. London: Frank Cass, 1970.

Look Lai, Walton. *Indentured Labor, Caribbean Sugar*. Baltimore: Johns Hopkins University Press, 1993.

———. "The Road to Thornfield Hall: *Wide Sargasso Sea*." *New World Quarterly* 4 (Croptime 1968): 17–27.

McFarlane, Basil. "On Jamaican Poetry." *Kyk-over-al* 3, no. 13 (1975): 207–9.

MacKenzie, John M. *Propaganda and Empire: The Manipulation of British Public Opinion, 1880–1960*. Manchester: Manchester University Press, 1984.

McWatt, Mark. "The Preoccupation with the Past in West Indian Literature." *Caribbean Quarterly* 28, nos. 1–2 (1985): 12–19.

Marshall, Woodville. *The 1990 Elsa Goveia Memorial Lecture: The Post-Slavery Labour Problem Revisited.* Kingston, Jamaica: University of the West Indies, 1990.

———. Preface to *Sealy's Caribbean Leaders*, by Theodore Sealy. Kingston, Jamaica: Kingston Publishers, 1991.

———. " 'We Be Wise to Many More Tings': Blacks' Hopes and Expectations of Emancipation." In *Caribbean Freedom: Economy and Society from Emancipation to the Present*, edited by Hilary Beckles and Verene Shepherd, 12–20. Kingston, Jamaica: Ian Randle Publishers, 1993.

Martin, Tony. "Marcus Garvey, the Caribbean, and the Struggle for Black Jamaican Nationhood." In *Caribbean Freedom: Economy and Society from Emancipation to Present*, edited by Hilary Beckles and Verene Shepherd, 359–69. Kingston, Jamaica: Ian Randle Publishers, 1993.

Marx, Karl. *Grundrisse: Foundations of the Critique of Political Economy.* Translated with an introduction by Martin Nicolaus. New York: Vintage Books, 1973.

Mendes, Alfred. "Talking about the Thirties: Interview with Alfred Mendes." By Clifford Sealy. *Voices* 1, no. 5 (December 1965): 3–7.

Miller, Jane. *Women Writing about Men.* London: Virago, 1986.

Molloy, Sylvia. "The Unquiet Self: Spanish American Autobiography and the Question of National Identity." In *Comparative American Identities: Race, Sex, and Nationality in the Modern Text*, edited by Hortense Spillers, 26–39. New York: Routledge, 1991.

Morrison, Toni. *Playing in the Dark: Whiteness and the Literary Imagination.* Cambridge: Harvard University Press, 1992.

Moss, Howard. "Going to Pieces." *New Yorker*, 16 December 1974, 61–68.

Munroe, Trevor. *The Politics of Constitutional Decolonization: Jamaica 1944–62.* Mona, Jamaica: Institute of Social and Economic Research, University of the West Indies, 1972.

Naipaul, V. S. "Without a Dog's Chance." In *Critical Perspectives on Jean Rhys*, edited by Pierrette Frickey, 54–66. Washington, D.C.: Three Continents, 1990.

Nettleford, Rex. *Identity, Race, and Protest in Jamaica.* New York: Morrow, 1972. Also published as *Mirror, Mirror: Identity, Race, and Protest in Jamaica.* Kingston, Jamaica: Collins and Sangster, 1970.

de Nève, Edouard. "Jean Rhys, Romancière Inconnue." *Les Nouvelles Littéraire*, no. 880 (26 August 1939): 8.

Nugent, Maria. *Lady Nugent's Journal: Jamaica One Hundred Years Ago. Reprinted from a Journal Kept by Maria, Lady Nugent, from 1801 to 1815, Issued for Private Circulation in 1839.* Edited by Frank Cundall. London: Adam and Charles Black, 1907.

Oakley, Leo. "Patriotism in Jamaican Writing." *Jamaica Journal* 4, no. 3 (1970): 16–21.

Ober, Frederick. *Camps in the Caribbees: The Adventures of a Naturalist in the Lesser Antilles.* Boston: Lee and Shepard, 1880.

O'Callaghan, Evelyn. "The Outsider's Voice: White Creole Women in the Caribbean Literary Tradition." *Journal of West Indian Literature* 1, no. 1 (1986): 74–88.

O'Connor, Teresa. *Jean Rhys: The West Indian Novels.* New York: New York University Press, 1986.

Parry, Benita. "The Contradictions of Cultural Studies." *Transition* 53 (1991): 37–45.

———. "Problems in Current Theories of Colonial Discourse." *Oxford Literary Review* 9 (1987): 27–58.

Patterson, Orlando. *The Sociology of Slavery: An Analysis of the Origins, Development, and Structure of Negro Slave Society in Jamaica.* Rutherford, N.J.: Fairleigh Dickinson University Press, 1967.

Plante, David. *Difficult Women: A Memoir of Three.* London: Victor Gollancz, 1983.

———. "Jean Rhys: A Remembrance." *Paris Review* 76 (1979): 238–84.

Pool, Gail. "Life's Unfinished Form." *Chicago Review* 32, no. 4 (1981): 68–74.

Pratt, Mary Louise. *Imperial Eyes: Travel Writing and Transculturation.* London: Routledge, 1992.

Ragatz, Lowell Joseph. *The Fall of the Planter Class in the British Caribbean, 1763–1833: A Study in Social and Economic History.* New York: Century, 1928.

Ramchand, Kenneth. *The West Indian Novel and Its Background.* London: Faber and Faber, 1970.

Reid, V. S. *A New Day.* New York: Knopf, 1949.

———. "The Writer and Work: V. S. Reid." *Journal of West Indian Literature* 2, no. 1 (1987): 4–10.

Review of *The Left Bank and Other Stories*, by Jean Rhys. *New York Times Book Review,* 11 December 1927, 28.

Rilke, Rainer Maria. *Letters to a Young Poet.* Translated with a foreword by Stephen Mitchell. New York: Random House, 1984.

Robbins, Bruce. *The Servant's Hand: English Fiction from Below.* New York: Columbia University Press, 1986.

Roberts, W. Adolphe. *The French in the West Indies.* New York: Cooper Square Publishers, 1971.

Rohlehr, Gordon. *My Strangled City and Other Essays.* Port of Spain: Longman's, 1992.

Said, Edward. *Culture and Imperialism.* New York: Alfred A. Knopf, 1993.

———. *Orientalism.* New York: Random House, 1978.

Samaroo, Brinsley. Introduction to *The Beacon*. New York: Kraus Reprint Co., 1970.

Sander, Reinhard. *The Trinidad Awakening: West Indian Literature of the Nineteen-Thirties*. New York: Greenwood Press, 1988.

———. "The Turbulent Thirties in Trinidad: An Interview with Alfred H. Mendes." *World Literature Written in English* 12, no. 1 (1973): 66–79.

Sander, Reinhard, and Ian Munro, eds. *Kas-kas: Interviews with Three Caribbean Writers in Texas: George Lamming, C. L. R. James, Wilson Harris.* Austin: African and Afro-American Research Institute, University of Texas, 1972.

Sartre, Jean-Paul. Preface to *The Wretched of the Earth*, by Frantz Fanon. New York: Grove Weidenfeld, 1963.

Sellers, Susan, ed. *Writing Differences: Readings from the Seminars of Hélène Cixous.* New York: St. Martin's Press, 1988.

Sewell, William. *The Ordeal of Free Labor in the British West Indies.* New York: Harper, 1861.

Spivak, Gayatri Chakravorty. "Can the Subaltern Speak?" In *Marxism and the Interpretation of Culture*, edited by Cary Nelson and Lawrence Grossberg, 271–313. Urbana: University of Illinois Press, 1988.

———. "Three Women's Texts as Critiques of Imperialism." In *"Race," Writing, and Difference*, edited by Henry Louis Gates Jr., 243–61. Chicago: University of Chicago Press, 1985.

Staley, Thomas. *Jean Rhys: A Critical Study.* London: Macmillan, 1979.

Steins, Martin. "Black Migrants in Paris." In *European-Language Writing in Sub-Saharan Africa*, edited by Albert S. Gerard, 354–78. Budapest: Akademiai Kiado, 1986.

Stevens, Gini. "Every Day Is a New Day." *BBC Radio Times*, 21 November 1974, 6.

Thomas, Ned. "Meeting Jean Rhys." *Planet* (Wales) 33 (August 1976): 29–31.

Thorpe, Michael. "The Other Side: *Wide Sargasso Sea* and *Jane Eyre*." *Ariel* 3 (1977): 99–100.

Thurman, Judith. "The Mistress and the Mask: Jean Rhys's Fiction." *Ms.* 4 (January 1974): 50–52, 81.

Trollope, Anthony. *The West Indies and the Spanish Main.* New York: Harper & Brothers, 1860.

Trouillot, Michel-Rolph. "Labour and Emancipation in Dominica: Contribution to a Debate." *Caribbean Quarterly* 30, nos. 3–4 (1984): 73–84.

———. *Peasants and Capital: Dominica in the World Economy.* Baltimore: Johns Hopkins University Press, 1988.

Updike, John. "Dark Smile, Devilish Saints." *New Yorker*, 11 August 1980, 82–89.

Visel, Robin. "A Half-Colonization: The Problem of the White Colonial Woman Writer." *Kunapipi* 10, no. 3 (1988): 39–45.

Vreeland, Elizabeth. "Jean Rhys: The Art of Fiction LXIV." *Paris Review* 76 (1979): 218–34.

Walcott, Derek. "The Caribbean: Culture or Mimicry?" *Journal of Interamerican Studies and World Affairs* 16, no. 1 (February 1974): 3–13.

————. "The Muse of History." In *Is Massa Day Dead?: Black Moods in the Caribbean*, edited by Orde Coombs, 1–27. New York: Anchor Press / Doubleday, 1974.

Walmsley, Anne. *The Caribbean Artists Movement 1966–1972*. London: New Beacon, 1992.

Ward, J. R. "Emancipation and the Planters." *Journal of Caribbean History* 22, nos. 1–2 (1988): 116–37.

Waugh, Alec. *The Sugar Islands: A Caribbean Travelogue*. New York: Farrar, Straus, 1949.

White, Hayden. *Metahistory: The Historical Imagination in Nineteenth-Century Europe*. Baltimore: Johns Hopkins University Press, 1973.

Williams, Eric. *British Historians and the West Indies*. London: Deutsch, 1966.

————. *Capitalism and Slavery*. Chapel Hill: University of North Carolina Press, 1944.

Woolf, Virginia. *Common Reader*. New York: Harcourt Brace Jovanovich, 1984.

————. *A Room of One's Own and Three Guineas*. London: Hogarth Press, 1984.

Wordsworth, William. *Poetical Works of William Wordsworth*. Cambridge Edition. Boston: Houghton Mifflin, 1982.

Wyndham, Francis. "An Inconvenient Novelist." *Tribune*, 15 December 1950, 16–18.

————. Introduction to *The Letters of Jean Rhys*, edited by Francis Wyndham and Diana Melly. New York: Viking, 1984.

Wynter, Sylvia. "Beyond Miranda's Meanings: Un/silencing the 'Demonic Ground' of Caliban's 'Woman.'" In *Out of the Kumbla: Caribbean Women and Literature*, edited by Carole Boyce Davies and Elaine Savory Fido, 355–75. Trenton, N.J.: Africa World Press, 1990.

————. "Creole Criticism—A Critique." *New World Quarterly* 5, no. 4 (1972): 12–36.

————. "Novel and History, Plot and Plantation." *Savacou* 5 (June 1971): 95–102.

————. "We Must Learn to Sit Down Together and Talk about a Little Culture: Reflections on West Indian Writing and Criticism." Parts 1 and 2. *Jamaica Journal* 2, no. 4 (1968): 23–32; 3, no. 1 (1969): 27–42.

Index

Bliss, Eliot, 41

Blyden, Edward Wilmot, 75

Bogle, Paul, 16

Bolland, O. Nigel, 17, 22, 201 (n. 2)

Book, the, 61, 144, 155, 183

Borome, Joseph, 22, 69, 85, 135, 136

Boule de suif, 50

Bowen, Stella, 57

Brathwaite, Kamau, 34, 35, 36, 37, 38, 46, 70, 72, 87

British Colonial Theories (Knorr), 10

British Historians and the West Indies (Williams), 14, 15

Bromley, Clara, 123

Brontë, Charlotte. See *Jane Eyre*

Brontë, Emily, 168

Brouard, Carl, 29

Brown, Laura, 124

Brown Privilege Bill, 22

Burton, Peter, 3

Byron, Lord, 63, 101

Calypso, 34, 40

Campbell, Elaine, 174, 204 (n. 1)

Campbell, George, 30

Camps in the Caribbees (Ober), 189

Cantwell, Mary, 42

Capitalism and Slavery (Williams), 110

Carew, Jan, 30, 76

Caribbean Artists Movement, 33, 202 (n. 7)

Caribbean peasantry, 13; and West Indian writing, 31

Carib Quarter, 190

Caribs, 188, 189, 190, 191

Carlyle, Thomas, 9, 10, 11, 12, 14, 15, 69

Carmichael, A. C., 123

Carter, Martin, 30

Castries fire (St. Lucia), 70

Cather, Willa, 79

Césaire, Aimé, 32, 162

Chace, Russell E., Jr., 19, 20, 25

Chambers, Ross, 87, 89, 205 (n. 2)

Christie, Agatha, 146

Cixous, Hélène, 60

Class, 45, 50, 60, 78, 89, 116, 119, 120, 143, 147, 152, 155, 172. See also Planter class; West Indian plantocracy

Cliff, Michelle, 73, 206 (n. 5)

Colette, 2

Collymore, Frank, 30

Colonial, 35, 167; and Jean Rhys's identity, 1, 2, 7, 144. See also Creole

Colonialism, 15, 30, 33, 37, 140, 197

Colonialist discourse, 16, 37, 38, 39, 42, 88, 174

Colonist, 23, 135, 136, 139

Confessions of an Opium Eater (Scott), 101

Conrad, Joseph, 6, 57, 59

Contradictory Omens (Brathwaite), 36, 93

Control of the Tropics, The, (Kidd), 162

Cooper, James Fenimore, 79

Corelli, Marie, 63

Coward, Noel, 41

Cowper, William, 63

Crabbe, George, 63,

Creole (language), 39, 40, 171; and white West Indian women, 127

Creole (person): definition of, ix; and the English, 1, 43–46, 125–29, 177, 179; and History, 5–25; and writing the history of the Creole, 8, 58–72 passim; perspective of, 21–24, 37, 40, 43; and West Indian literature,

33–43; mode of subjectivity, 36–39, 42, 46, 66–70, 135, 145, 191; and black people, 37–40, 192–95; and return to the West Indies, 40, 99, 196, 198–99; and writing, 48–51; and self-writing, 55–58; and coloured people, 67, 137, 138, 179, 183–84, 193; and the reading of History, 72–80; and *Jane Eyre*, 80–84; in *Wide Sargasso Sea*, 87–100 passim; in *Voyage in the Dark*, 115, 123–135; in Europe, 144–45, 151, in short stories, 162–79; and Native Caribbean people, 188–92. *See also* Colonial

Creole woman. *See* Gender

Creolization, 35

Crown Colony government, 69, 137

Cultural pluralism, 35

Damas, Léon, 29

Dance, Daryl, 16

Darwin, Charles, 15

Dash, J. Michael, 29

D'Costa, Jean, 3, 33, 80, 108

Death, 131, 135; in writing, 149–50, 196–98

De Certeau, Michel, 150

Dédoublement, 50

Deleuze, Gilles, and Guattari, Félix, 115, 173, 178,

DeLisser, H. G., 17

Demolins, Edmond, 162

De Nève, Edouard, 6

De Rochefort, Charles, 75

Dialogic Imagination, The, (Bakhtin), 140, 149

Dickens, Charles, 15

Difficult Women, 49, 53, 54, 59, 65, 71

Domestic Manners and Social Condition of the White, Coloured, and Negro Population of the West Indies (Carmichael), 123

Dominica, 2, 19, 21, 22, 23, 59, 65, 68, 69, 74, 135

Dominica National Archives, 25

Dominican, 23, 135

Dominican Guardian, 137

Dominicans, 180, 190

Doppelgänger, 98, 116, 132, 197

Double, 50, 197

Dress, 90

Dunham, Katherine, 41

Du Tertre, Jean-Baptiste, 73, 75

Eagleton, Terry, 95

Emancipation, 18, 19, 21, 25

Emancipation compensation, 22, 85

English and Englishness, 1, 45, 162–79

English in the West Indies: The Bow of Ulysses, The, (Froude), 12

English Review (Ford), 57

Erwin, Lee

Expansion of England, The, (Seeley), 162

Eyre, Governor John, 14–15

Eyre Defence Committee, 15

Falconer, Charles Gordon (George Charles), 23, 24, 136, 137, 138

Fall of the Planter Class, The, (Ragatz), 110

Fanon, Frantz, 89, 100

Fascism, 32, 167

February Revolution in Trinidad, 34

Fielding, Henry, 59

"Fishy Waters," 23, 140–44

Flaubert, Gustave, 6

Focus, 29, 30

and original ending, 115, 123, 131, 134; and Anna Morgan, 115–134 passim; and *Nana*, 116, 117, 118; and Maillotte Boyd, 118; and the Hottentot, 118, 129; and class, 119, 120; race and sexuality in, 119, 122, 127; sex and gender in, 120, 121, 122, 125, 126, 127, 129; and travel writing, 123; and England, 123, 129; and imperialist exploitation, 124; and Edward Long, 126, 127; and Maria Nugent, 126, 127; and reverse discourse, 128

Walcott, Derek, 2, 17, 76
Waugh, Alec, 6, 75
West, Rebecca, 46
West Indian Creole (language), 171
West Indian history: imperial versions of, 9–16, 74–75; and West Indian literature, 16, 75–76; cultural nationalist perspectives of, 17–21, 38, 39; Creole account of, 21–23, 48, 67, 69–70, 72, 73, 75–80, 116; and *Wide Sargasso Sea*, 86, 91, 96, 100, 111; and *Voyage in the Dark*, 124, 125–26, 130, 131, 134; and "Again the Antilles," 135–37; and "Fishy Waters," 140–43
West Indian literature: and history, 17, 24; and its emergence, 27; and the English tradition, 28; and anticolonial movements, 29, 30, 34; and West Indian peasantry, 31; and Jean Rhys, 35, 39; practitioners of, 76; and "The Daffodils," 184, 205–6 (n. 5)
West Indian Novel and Its Background, The, (Ramchand), 34

West Indian plantocracy (planter class), 8, 12, 13, 14, 15, 43, 141
West India regiment, 69
West India Royal Commission Report (Moyne Commission Report), 26
West Indies, 2, 4, 72; discursive construction of, 43
West Indies and the Spanish Main, The, (Trollope), 11
White, Hayden, 8
Whiteness: as an ideology, 165. *See also* "Bible is Modern, The"
Wide Sargasso Sea, 23, 24, 35, 36, 37, 55, 79, 83–115, 183, 187; and West Indian literature, 35, 36; and Christophine, 41, 42, 90, 105; and *Jane Eyre*, 42, 80, 82–84; and slavery and postslavery conditions, 85, 86, 90, 91; and *Two Years in the French West Indies* (Hearn), 85, 104; and history, 86, 87, 91, 96, 107, 114; and Antoinette, 87, 90, 91, 97, 98, 99, 101, 102, 103, 106; and Antoinette-Tia relationship, 89–91, 95–96, 100; labor disputes in, 90, 91, 95; and West Indian plantocracy, 90, 93, 95; and Annette, 91, 92, 93; and Mr. Mason, 91, 92, 93, 97; and Myra, 92, 93; and Asian indentureship, 95; and mirror imagery, 96–97, 98, 99; and Amélie, 97, 98; and critics, 98, 201 (n. 5); and Bertha Mason, 99; and the nameless husband, 100, 101, 102, 105, 106, 107; and Daniel, 103, 108, 109, 111, 112, 113; and narrative voices, 108; and illegitimacy, 109, 110; and the West Indies of the 1960s, 114
Williams, Eric, 11, 14, 15, 109

Williams, William, 101

Woman's Wandering in the Western World,
  A, (Bromley), 123

Women: and writing, 46–48, 166;
  and moral behavior, 78, 125; and
  sex, 97, 98, 109; as commodified
  objects, 121–22, 155; and imperialism, 123–24; and English society,
  164, 165, 171, 175; and war, 168

Woolf, Leonard, 29

Woolf, Virginia, 29, 79, 106, 168

Wordsworth, William, 66, 184

Wretched of the Earth (Fanon), 89

Writing: and the Creole, 5, 48, 50, 53,
  55, 58, 62, 80, 87; and women, 46,
  168, 175; as rewriting, 51, 79, 80, 83,
  84, 167, 174, 187; and the self, 53, 61,
  71, 196; and the West Indies, 56;
  and history, 58; as death, 135, 149,
  173, 196, 197, 198; and otherness,
  151, 169, 173; and alienation, 161; in
  West Indian literature, 184

Wyndham, Francis, 3, 7, 8, 16, 34, 85,
  100, 108, 177, 180

Wynter, Sylvia, 17, 34

Zola, Emile, 116